Drunkard's Progress

THE DRUNKARD'S PROGRESS.

Drunkard's Progress;

NARRATIVES OF ADDICTION, DESPAIR, AND RECOVERY,

Edited by John W. Crowley

The Johns Hopkins University Press

Baltimore and London

© 1999 The Johns Hopkins University Press
All rights reserved. Published 1999
Printed in the United States of America on acid-free paper
9 8 7 6 5 4 3 2 1

The Johns Hopkins University Press
2715 North Charles Street
Baltimore, Maryland 21218-4363
www.press.jhu.edu

Library of Congress Cataloging-in-Publication Data
will be found at the end of this book.
A catalog record for this book is available from the British Library.

FRONTISPIECE: *The Drunkard's Progress* (1846),
lithograph by Kelloggs and Thayer, from an original print
at the Fruitlands Museums, Harvard, Massachusetts.

ISBN 0-8018-6008-3
ISBN 0-8018-6007-5 (pbk.)

For the Out to Lunch Bunch
of Skaneateles, New York

Contents

Preface

It is fitting indeed that *Drunkard's Progress* be published in Baltimore; for in 1840 the Washington Temperance Society put Baltimore on the map of antidrink reform—in a way that counterweights the city's notorious association with Edgar Allan Poe, who died drunk there in 1849, having recently taken the pledge with the Richmond branch of the Sons of Temperance, one of several groups to carry on the Washingtonian mission.

Poe's imaginative engagement with his own inebriety once inspired a parody of the genre I am defining here as the *temperance narrative:* a first-person account of a drunkard's damnation and salvation. In "The Black Cat" (1843), Poe created a character so crazed by demon rum that he insouciantly confesses to the axe murder of his wife and the brutal execution of a pet cat. At the end of this "wild, yet homely" story, as the narrator calls it, the unearthly cry of a second cat, inadvertently walled up with the wife's body in the basement, leads to the drunkard's downfall. The lurid melodrama of "The Black Cat" was sometimes the stuff of temperance literature. Several of the following Washingtonian tales attest to the grotesque and potentially lethal effects of drinking, although without Poe's satirically graphic excesses; and it would be easy to read them as ridiculous evocations of a strange Victorian past, when people seemed to believe in the tyranny of King Alcohol.

In choosing excerpts for this anthology, however, I have been guided by a desire *not* to adopt the customary modern condescension toward temperance literature; rather I have sought to take it seriously on its own terms. *Drunkard's Progress* comprises what I think are the best parts of the temperance narratives written during the 1840s, the heyday of the Washington Society. Excerpts are taken from half of the fifteen specimens of the genre I have located so far. I tried to find anything in book form that might imaginably be classified as Washingtonian, and I am confident that my sample was nearly complete. Walt Whitman's *Franklin Evans*, the best known temperance narrative (but rarely studied in its proper generic context), is available elsewhere, so I have not included it here. The most important temperance narrative is John B. Gough's *Autobiography*, and my long excerpt from it dominates *Drunkard's Progress*, just as Gough himself commanded the Washingtonian lecture circuit.

Temperance narratives tend to show "before" in much greater detail than "after"; drunkenness is simply more dramatic than sobriety. This bias is faithfully reflected in my selections. For instance, I have included the first two parts of Gough's *Autobiography*, the story of his alcoholic degradation and conversion by the Washingtonians, but omitted the third part, a rambling account of his public career. I have arranged things, however, so that the trajectory of this book—its collective narrative, so to speak—is from inebriety to sobriety, and also from the rise to the demise of the Washington Society.

Each excerpt highlights one or more themes of the Washingtonian movement: its compassionate attitude, which contrasted the harsh moralism of the temperance mainstream; its critique of American drinking customs and of public facilities for inebriates; the superiority of good fellowship to religious conversion in effecting sobriety; the idea of inebriety as "disease" or at least as "insanity"; class tensions between common drunkards and upper-class reformers; the strategic conflict between moral suasion of drunkards and legislative coercion of tavern owners and other drunkard-makers.

My purpose in assembling *Drunkard's Progress* is, not merely to draw attention to the Washingtonians and possibly to save from obscurity a lost genre of American writing, but also to suggest that such stories by and about nineteenth-century drunkards, despite their distance from our time, can still speak volumes to present-day alcoholics. In reading these narratives now, one might reasonably conclude that, for drunks at least, nothing much has changed since 1840: the course of nineteenth-century "inebriety" turns out to be essentially no different from the course of "alcoholism" today.

In the preparation of *Drunkard's Progress*, I have profited from the erudition of two earlier scholars of Washingtonianism: Charles Bishop Jr.

and Leonard U. Blumberg. Jon Miller offered useful advice about the bibliographies. I am also grateful to Roger Forseth, founding editor of *Dionysos*, for so strongly advocating this book, and to Margie May, steadfast secretary of the Humanities Doctoral Program at Syracuse University, for helping to prepare the copy, much of it taken originally from grainy microfilm. Special credit is due to the Interlibrary Loan department at Syracuse's E. S. Bird Library, for getting me the rare and indispensable texts, on microfilm or otherwise. Finally, I wish to thank Douglas Armato, formerly of the Johns Hopkins University Press, for his abiding faith in this project.

Note on the Texts

The distribution and popularity of Washingtonian temperance narratives varied widely: from the broad dissemination of John Gough's *Autobiography* (32,000 copies sold by 1853) and T. S. Arthur's *Six Nights with the Washingtonians* (175,000 copies sold by 1850) to the very limited circulation of such self-published texts as D. G. Robinson's *Life and Adventures* and Jacob Carter's *My Drunken Life*. There exists a modern (but, unfortunately, defective) reprint of Arthur's book; and Gough's is easy enough to find. (I bought a first edition for two dollars in Vermont, and I've seen later issues at several antiquarian bookshops.) But the others are exceedingly scarce. *Franklin Evans*, in its original form as a newspaper supplement, sells in the $5,000 to $7,000 range. A copy of the third printing of Joseph Gatchell's *Disenthralled* was recently offered in a bookdealer's catalogue for $1,600. Those few research libraries that possess any of these books are understandably reluctant to lend them out—although the Brown University Library generously provided me with photocopies of *Narrative of Charles T. Woodman* and of *Incidents in the Life of George Haydock*—and I have therefore had to rely in most cases on the (seemingly reliable) texts in microfilmed compendia of early American imprints. When I had no access to the first edition, copy was taken from a later printing.

In the interests of clarity, punctuation has been minimally modernized. Antique spelling and vagrant syntax have been preserved, however. Brief omissions within the narratives are marked by an ellipsis; more substantial deletions, particularly in the texts by Woodman and Green, are indicated by an ellipsis as well as a line space with an ornament.

The bibliography includes a full description of the temperance narratives I have recovered so far. There are doubtless others, especially of the local variety; and I have made no attempt—for lack of ready access to files of the Washingtonian press—to include temperance narratives that appeared only in newspapers (these are akin to the brief personal stories in the A.A. *Grapevine*). Though the list is incomplete, it will serve to introduce readers to Washingtonianism. I have provided a supplemental bibliography of later temperance narratives. This list is far from comprehensive, but I hope it will arouse enough curiosity to inspire the discovery of additional titles.

Drunkard's Progress

Introduction

Throughout this century, American public opinion has denounced Prohibition as a ludicrously bad idea whose time should never have come: the triumph of a moralistic minority over the popular will, of Puritanism over *joie de vivre*; the breeder of public cynicism, political corruption, and organized criminality. Although there are recent signs of prohibitionist revival, so far only in regard to demon tobacco, the debacle of the "noble experiment" has stifled serious discussion of the merits of staying wet or going dry.

The taint of Prohibition has also sullied the reputation of the nineteenth-century temperance movement that preceded it. Writing in 1930 of *The Drunkards Progress* (1846), the popular lithograph by Nathaniel Currier from which my title derives, Russel Crouse mordantly recalled "a period in the nation's history when it took years, instead of just one night, for a man to drink himself to death." That day is gone under the Eighteenth Amendment: "The Demon Rum has been abolished. In its stead Americans now drink hair tonic, sheep dip, coffin varnish, and other inoffensive beverages."[1] If not sneering of this sort, then urbane hilarity has served to banish the idea of temperance as a Victorian hangover: out of sight and therefore out of mind; historically encapsulated, as if this part of America's past could not possibly impinge on its present or future.

The Drunkards Progress, from "the first glass to the grave," plays out the melodrama of "inebriety" (known in our time as "alcoholism"). Like Benjamin Rush's temperance thermometer in the eighteenth century, and also like E. M. Jellinek's profile of the stages of alcoholism in the twentieth century, Currier's nineteenth-century lithograph maps the "steps" of alcoholic degeneration.[2] There are nine such steps depicted, up, across, and down a stone arch. In the first, a well-dressed young man takes "a glass with a friend" (a woman of evidently questionable virtue), and then another "to keep the cold out." By the third step he is drooping from "a glass too much"; in the fourth he has become "drunk and riotous," raising his cane against another man. The "summit" is attained in step five when our hero joins his "jolly companions" as a "confirmed drunkard." It's all downhill from there: from ragged "poverty and disease" to being "forsaken by friends" to "desperation and crime" and ultimately "death by suicide." In the eighth step we see the drunkard, pistol in hand, robbing a prosperous gentleman; in the ninth, he turns the gun on himself. Beneath the arch of *The Drunkards Progress,* the print shows how the wages of his sin are visited upon his innocent family. As their homely cottage burns in the background, a grieving woman, with child in hand, averts her gaze from the ruination of her once happy household.[3]

This was, of course, the masterplot for hundreds of temperance tales, in which the hope of domestic bliss is cruelly dashed by chronic inebriety. The locus classicus, told and retold during the mid nineteenth century, was the story of John H. W. Hawkins and his daughter Hannah. Young Hawkins, apprenticed to a hatter, had easily succumbed to drink. The hatting trade, he recalled, was "as perfect a grog-shop as ever existed"; drunkenness was nearly universal.[4] But for many years, in fits of sobriety, Hawkins desperately sought release from the bondage of alcohol:

> I then drank nothing for a while; but it was so hard to do without, that at length I took a glass of ale, and all was over with me again: my appetite rushed on like a flood and carried all before it. And for fifteen years, time after time, I rose and fell; was up and down; would quit all, and then take a little glass. I would earn $15 a week, be happy and well, and with my money in hand start for home, and in some unaccountable way, imperceptibly and irresistibly fall into a tavern and think one glass only would do me good. But I found a single glass of ale would conquer all my resolutions. (P. 16)

By June 1840, swilling whiskey by the gallon in a suicidal binge, Hawkins became too weak to climb out of bed and thus became dependent on faithful Hannah to replenish his supply:

I lay in bed long after my wife and daughter were up, and my conscience drove me to madness. I hated the darkness of the night; and
when light came, I hated the light. I hated myself—my existence. I
asked myself, "Can I refrain; is it possible?" Not a being to take me by
the hand, and lead or help me along, and say *you can*. I was friendless;
without help or light; an outcast. My wife came up stairs, and knew I
was suffering, and asked me to go down to breakfast. I had a pint of
whiskey, and thought I would drink; and yet I knew it was life or
death with me as I decided. Well, I told my wife I would come down
presently. Then my daughter came up and asked me down. I always
loved her—more because she was the drunkard's friend—my only
friend.

She said, "Father, don't send me after whiskey to-day." I was tor-
mented before, but this was an unexpected torture. I told her to leave
the chamber, and she went down crying, and said to her mother, Father is angry with me. Wife came up again, and asked me to take
some coffee; I told her I did not want anything of her, and covered
myself in the bed. I soon heard some one enter the room, and I peeped
out and saw it was my daughter. I then thought of my past life; my
degradation; misery of my friends; and felt bad enough. So I called
her and said, "Hannah, I am not angry with you, and I shall not drink
any more." She cried, and so did I. I got up and went to the cupboard,
and looked on the enemy, and thought, "Is it possible I can be restored?" and then turned my back upon it. Several times, while dressing, I looked at the bottle, but thought I should be lost if I yielded.
Poor drunkard! there is hope for you. You cannot be worse off than I
was, not more degraded, or more of a slave to appetite. You can return
if you will. *Try it—Try it.* (Pp. 24–26)

In Hawkins's plea, a drunkard's destiny is not inevitably to sink into
degradation and death; he may also pivot on a turning point and move
upward to hope and redemption. In this affirmative form, Drunkard's
Progress retraces, not the hellish descent depicted by Currier, but rather
the Pilgrim's Progress of John Bunyan's archetypal journey to the Ce-
lestial City.

Hawkins's narrative and other such accounts constitute one major
type of temperance literature, on the generic cusp between the novel
and autobiography, in which inebriates recounted their enslavement to,
and subsequent emancipation from, King Alcohol. Such first-person al-

coholic confessions—or *temperance narratives*, as I call them—appeared during the 1840s as an outgrowth of the Washington Temperance Society, of which Hawkins was an early member. Some examples of the genre, such as Walt Whitman's relatively well-known *Franklin Evans; or, The Inebriate* (1842), were obviously fictional; others, such as *Narrative of Charles T. Woodman, A Reformed Inebriate* (1843), were probably factual. But all of them had something in common with sentimental and sensational novels, and also with spiritual autobiographies: especially the themes of religious awakening and conversion.

The temperance narrative also resembled another genre that was flourishing during the 1840s, the slave narrative. Although temperance narratives did not commonly invoke the rhetoric of abolition, they did portray slaves to the bottle whose bondage seemed comparable to that of plantation chattel. It so happens that the most important temperance narrative, John Bartholomew Gough's *Autobiography*, appeared exactly the same year, 1845, as the most important slave narrative, *Narrative of the Life of Frederick Douglass*.[5]

The genre of the temperance narrative sprang from the Washington Temperance Society's revolutionizing of antidrink reform. From its start at the turn of the nineteenth century, the temperance movement had been dominated by its respectable elements: the Protestant clergy, the legal and medical establishments, the rising mercantile classes. At first the movement was a means for a declining social elite to retain its diminishing power—by making over Americans "into a clean, sober, godly, and decorous people whose aspirations and style of living would reflect the moral leadership of New England Federalism." While the movement became more national during the 1820s and 1830s, it underwent bourgeoisification: "freed of the symbols of aristocratic dominance and converted into a popular movement to achieve self-perfection among the middle and lower classes," temperance became "a sign of middle-class respectability and a symbol of egalitarianism."[6]

The middle-class improvers took a harder line against the consumption of *any* alcoholic beverages—including wine, the preferred drink of the upper classes, which had previously been exempted from the temperance pledge in its early form and thus distinguished invidiously from "ardent spirits" (i.e., distilled liquor). The new pledge of teetotalism gained so many adherents that *temperance* was redefined in practice as *abstinence*;[7] and the ultraists pursued the logic of their position to a new emphasis on prohibition, to be accomplished by political agitation at the state and local levels.

Early temperance reformers were *disinterested*, in the sense that they did not ordinarily belong to the group targeted for reform. They laid stress on prevention rather than rehabilitation, on smashing the myth of "moderate" drinking and snatching incipient drunkards from the brink of self-destruction. Habitual drunkards, held to be irredeemable, were expected to drink themselves to death and thus to spare society the trouble of dealing with them, except as temporary denizens of the almshouses and jails. In an 1825 letter, the Reverend Mr. Justin Edwards, a founder of the American Temperance Society, envisioned the movement in terms that joined its utopian and macabre elements: "We are at present fast hold of a project for making all people in this country, and in all other countries, temperate; or rather, a plan to induce those who are now temperate to continue so. Then, as all who are intemperate will soon be dead, the earth will be eased of an amazing evil."[8]

When the Washington Temperance Society was founded in 1840 by half-a-dozen Baltimore artisans who pledged total abstinence, vowed mutual assistance, and enticed other topers to attend their meetings, the focus shifted suddenly to the drunkards themselves. What the Washingtonians demonstrated so dramatically was that even those mired in an alcoholic Slough of Despond need not die of drink; they could achieve sobriety through the compassionate aid of fellow inebriates.

It is ironic that the Washington Society originated in a drunken prank. On the Thursday evening of 2 April 1840, six jolly good fellows gathered, as they did most every night, at Chase's Tavern on Liberty Street in Baltimore. This informal drinking club included David Anderson (blacksmith), Archibald Campbell (silversmith), John F. Hoss (carpenter), James McCurley (coachmaker), William K. Mitchell (tailor), and George Steers (wheelwright). The men, who considered themselves tipplers rather than drunkards,[9] were jeering a temperance speaker who had recently come to town. As a lark some of them decided to attend a lecture that very evening and report to the others, waiting in the tavern, about the foolishness they expected to hear.

The evangelist made so deep an impression on the scoffers, however, that they fell into ardently spirited debate among themselves on the merits of temperance.[10] At their meeting the following Sunday, the six boozily proposed to quit drinking together. Mitchell agreed to draft a teetotaler's pledge if all the others would sign it—which they did, hung over, the next day. That Monday evening, having declared themselves "desirous of forming a society for our mutual benefit, and to guard against a pernicious practice, which is injurious to our health, standing, and families," the founders pledged themselves "not to drink any spirituous or malt liquors, wine or cider."[11] The initiation fee was set at twenty-five cents, with monthly dues of twelve-and-a-half cents. They considered naming their fellowship after Thomas Jefferson but decided instead on George Washington, whose mettle in routing King George would inspire them in the mighty battle ahead against King Alcohol.

Mitchell, elected president, exemplified the egalitarian, working-class ethos of the early Washingtonians.[12] Suspicious of the temperance movement's upper-class leadership, especially the Protestant clergy, Mitchell rejected the premise that religious conversion was a precondition to sobriety. "The original Washingtonians had needed no such help, and relied solely on comradely support from the others, and that was the way Mitchell wanted it to stay."[13] Washingtonianism was "a secularized revival."[14] As one early member put it, "Now anyone who knows anything of drunkenness, knows that most drunkards are strongly averse to religion, if not infidel at heart. They want to hear nothing about '*moral reform*' and '*church societies.*'"[15] Mitchell went so far as to ban prayers, hymns, and sermons at meetings, a practice that was not always enforced but that nonetheless evoked outrage from the temperance establishment and earned the Washingtonians a reputation for godlessness. This reputation persisted even after a majority of members had joined with traditionalists in reasserting the indispensability of religion. Mitchell believed that the Washingtonians could best strengthen their commitment to the pledge by combining individual reform with collective acts; in particular, by persuading other inebriates to attend their meetings.

The Baltimore meetings were weekly and private, with each man fishing the taverns and workshops to reel in fellow drunkards. At first, they assembled as usual in Chase's Tavern—until the landlord's wife evicted them for stealing her trade. So they moved to a carpenter's shop and later to a rented hall. It was only when some meetings became public—in November 1840, after the group had swelled to nearly a hundred members—that the movement took off. By February 1841 the Washingtonians had enrolled twelve hundred men, with another fifteen hundred in auxiliary groups for women and children; and, having outgrown its meeting space, the Society sprouted branches all over the city. A year later there was talk of building a hall large enough to accommodate twenty-five hundred for "experience meetings."[16]

The heart's blood of Washingtonianism was the confessional narrative. Instead of cerebral clergymen talking down to the inebriated unwashed, drunkards gave hope and inspiration to each other through the unadorned telling of their own life stories. While the Society continued to resist the churches, its "citings of personal experience were like the 'testimony' that those 'getting religion' at camp meeting were supposed to give at subsequent 'experience meetings.'"[17]

During this period, as the fires of evangelical revivals scorched the national conscience, such camp meetings abounded. But revivalism, as Jed Dannenbaum points out, was only one of several reasons for the amazing grace of the Washingtonians:

> The movement derived its striking intensity and enormous popularity from the economic impact of changes in occupational patterns; from the millenarian mindset created by the Second Great Awakening; from the increased problems generated by alcoholic beverages in the wake of the massive political campaigns of 1840 [when liquor had been liberally dispensed in exchange for votes]; and from the accentuation of all these factors by the severe economic depression that followed the Panic of 1837.[18]

At a time when intemperance was becoming an obstacle to employment, because employers increasingly demanded workers who embodied the Protestant ethic of "industry, thrift, discipline, punctuality, and *sobriety*,"[19] the Washingtonians spoke to economic instability (newly sober men were helped to find jobs and lodging) as well as to mental and moral perturbation. Its members found security in numbers, taking heart from a mutual determination to rid their lives of what was "injurious to our health, standing, and families."

7

Here again, Hawkins's story was exemplary, especially in his faith in the power of Washingtonian comradery to bind up domestic wounds. This is Hawkins's account of his first Washingtonian meeting, attended some ten weeks after the Society had formed:

> Well, Monday night I went to the Society of Drunkards, and there I found all my old bottle companions. I did not tell anybody I was going, not even my wife. I had got out of difficulty, but did not know how long I would keep out. The six-pounders of the Society were there. We had fished together; got drunk together. You could not break us up when drunk. We stuck like brothers, and so we do now we are sober. One said, here is Hawkins, the "regulator," the old *bruiser*; and they clapped me and laughed, as you do now. But there was no laugh or clap in me. I was too sober and solemn for that. The pledge was read for my accommodation. They did not say so, and yet I knew they all looked over my shoulder to see me write my name. I never had such feelings before. It was a great battle. I once fought the battle at North Point, and helped to run away too, but now there was no running away.[20] I found the Society had a large pitcher of water; drank toasts and told experiences. There I laid my plan; I did not intend to be a drone. Alcohol promised me everything, but I found him a great deceiver, and now I meant to do him all the harm I could.

Braced by his commitment to the Washingtonians, Hawkins was ready now to face his family.

> At eleven I went home. When I stayed out late, I always went home drunk. Wife had given me up again, and thought I would be home drunk again, and she began to think about breaking up and going home to mother's. My yard is covered with brick, and as I went over the brick, wife listened, as she told me, to determine whether the gate-door opened drunk or sober, for she could tell, and it opened sober and shut sober; and when I entered, my wife was standing in the middle of the room to see me as I came in. She was astonished, but I smiled and she smiled, as I caught her keen black eye. I told her quick; I could not keep it back. "I have put my name to the temperance pledge, never to drink as long as I live." It was a happy time. I cried and she cried; we could not help it, and crying waked up our daughter, and she cried too. I tell you this, that you may know how happy the reformation of a drunkard makes his family. I slept none that night, my thoughts were better than sleep. Next morning I went to see my

mother, old as she was. I must go to see her and tell her of our joy. She had been praying twenty years for her drunken son. Now, she said, "It is enough, I am ready to die." (Pp. 26–28)

As word spread about the new temperance society in Baltimore, the Washingtonians took to the road. Hawkins spoke in Annapolis, Maryland; and in March 1841, Hawkins, Mitchell, and three others traveled to New York to proselytize. At an outdoor meeting in City Hall Park, the *delegates* (the term they preferred to *missionaries,* with its churchly connotations) rehearsed their tales to a crowd of four thousand people, nearly half of whom subsequently signed the Washingtonian pledge. Comparably marvelous results were achieved on a subsequent tour of Boston and New England by Hawkins and William E. Wright (the Washingtonians preferred to travel in pairs) and a campaign in New Jersey and upstate New York by Wright and J. F. Pollard. The movement reached Cincinnati in July 1841 and took the city by storm; a year later Charles Dickens, on the western leg of his American lecture tour, witnessed a huge and colorful Washingtonian parade. As the reform message spread from town to town, autonomous Washingtonian societies sprang up overnight, sometimes from the seedbed of earlier temperance organizations. By 1843, throngs of pledge-signers had boosted national membership to half a million intemperate drinkers and another hundred thousand confirmed drunkards.[21] Such figures were likely inflated; but even if allowance is made for exaggeration, Washingtonianism still must be counted among the most remarkable social phenomena of the American nineteenth century.

Early on, Hawkins became "the most widely known and most successful" Washingtonian delegate, a workhorse who for eight consecutive months spoke at least once every day, making twenty-five hundred appearances and covering a hundred thousand miles by the close of the 1840s.[22] Although Hawkins undoubtedly had a gift for platform oratory, his method was essentially no different from that of other Washingtonian speakers bearing witness to their suffering and deliverance. Audiences were galvanized, as Abraham Lincoln, then a rising politician in Illinois, observed in 1842.

The *preacher,* it is said, advocates temperance because he is a fanatic, and desires a union of Church and State; the *lawyer,* from his pride

9

and vanity of hearing himself speak; and the *hired agent* for his salary. But when one, who has long been known as a victim of intemperance, bursts open the fetters that bound him and appears before his neighbors "clothed, and in his right mind," a redeemed specimen of long lost humanity, and stands up with tears of joy trembling in his eyes, to tell of the miseries *once* endured, *now* to be endured no more forever; of his once naked and starving children, now clad and fed comfortably; of a wife, long weighed down with woe, weeping, and a broken heart, now restored to health, happiness and a renewed affection; and how easily all is done, once it is resolved to be done; how simple his language, there is a logic, and an eloquence in it, that few with human feelings, can resist.[23]

This, as Lincoln suggested, was a populist movement, infused by a radically democratic spirit.

The temperance movement as a whole was more democratic during the 1840s than in any decade before or after. It was during the 1840s that anxiety over rising immigration spawned Nativism and other forms of xenophobia, and the temperance movement was gradually to align itself with discriminatory politics. At first, however, its leaders generally took an assimilationist line toward the immigrant, "as an object of benevolence; someone they would help to achieve the morally sanctified habits of the native American, of which abstinence had become so cardinal a virtue."[24] Within this assimilationist mode, the Washington Society was exceptionally inclusive. Both Irish and German immigrants were welcome to join; and whereas nearly every mainstream temperance organization shunned blacks, Mitchell himself sought out Negro members in Virginia. Although only men were permitted to speak at meetings, female inebriates could sign the pledge; and in 1841 the Martha Washington Society was formed as a means to greater participation by women.

It has often been observed that the temperance movement envisaged intemperance along strict gender lines, as something men inflicted on women (and children).[25] Such gender differentiation conformed to the emergent separation of the public sphere (male) from the private sphere (female)—the latter governed by the ideology of "true womanhood," the force of which "may well have reduced both the number of women who drank and the amounts consumed by those who continued to drink, thereby widening existing differences between the drinking patterns of men and women." Although, as Jack S. Blocker adds, women did not stop drinking altogether—"indeed, through consumption of some patent medicines many women drank unknowingly, while otherwise abstemious families continued to use liquor in cooking"—most native-born women likely had become "either cautious drinkers or abstainers" by the end of the 1840s, thanks in large part to the Washingtonian influence.[26]

The formation of the Martha Washington Society provided a socially acceptable means for women to participate in the antidrink crusade. The Martha Washingtonians raised money in support of benevolent activities: "food, clothing, loans, and other assistance to reformed drunkards and their families."[27] They also counseled mothers on how to protect their children from intemperance and provided moral support to newly sober youths. Those in charge came from the same artisanal class as the male Washingtonian leadership; it was "the first time that American women of relatively low rank joined and played a prominent role in reform."[28] It was also the first time that women commonly mounted the temperance platform, as they did in the New York societies. Women writers often contributed to Washingtonian publications; the *New York Olive Plant* and the *New York Pearl*, moreover, became "the first papers designed for and edited by women in the history of the temperance agitation."[29]

Although the cult of "true womanhood" drove many female drunkards underground, the Martha Washingtonians, who included significant numbers of reformed women in their groups, put stress, at least at first, on "reclaiming inebriates of their own sex." Getting wives and mothers sober laid "the foundation for the 'moral resurrection' of homes 'previously given to vice and cruelty.'"[30] Female experience narratives "told of violence, abuse of children, and poverty attendant upon male drinking, not only in working class families but also on occasions among the middle classes." But like their male colleagues, women in the mainstream temperance movement "increasingly dissociated themselves from the Washingtonians."[31]

Middle-class temperance leaders soon recognized that the Washingtonian revival reflected, not merely an incursion of "lower" elements into the movement, but also the displacement of intellectual by affective means to sobriety. Instead of rational arguments against drinking, the Washingtonians offered powerfully emotional appeals. John Marsh, leader of the American Temperance Union, was initially sympathetic to the Washingtonians, and he put the best face on what rankled more hidebound observers. Since intemperance "will not be reasoned with," Marsh proposed, it must "be met by a different weapon, and masses of men must throw off the monster evil, either in a spirit of indignation, or in a jovial hurrah."[32]

The Washingtonians favored homespun eloquence over refined erudition in their speakers, the most successful of whom—John Hawkins and John Gough—had little education. "In their evangelical techniques, indifference to theology, and vulgar identification with the manners and language of the masses," Gough and Hawkins were, in fact, "anathema to the more conservative and sedate leaders of the earlier movement."[33] The flamboyant Gough, who has been dubbed the "poet of the d.t.'s" and the "Demosthenes of total abstinence,"[34] signed the pledge in October 1842 and soon surpassed the milder Hawkins as "the cause's champion pitchman and pledge seller," "the foremost platform performer of the century," "unquestionably the most popular orator in America."[35]

As these and other apostles of cold water tramped the lecture trail, harvesting pledges by the thousands, the meetings they led were not only perfervidly serious affairs, at which gallons of righteous tears were shed, but also raucous revels, with plenty of shouting and singing (from either a hymnal or one of the Washingtonian songbooks, in which anti-drink lyrics were fitted alike to sacred and secular tunes). The jovial hurrah supplanted the bar-room brawl. Through their "provision of alternative leisure activities," the Society "both recognized and attempted to deal with drinking's role as the 'centerpiece' of the working-man's culture."[36]

Just as oral slave narratives came to be written down, with or without editorial assistance,[37] and published in support of the abolitionist cause, so temperance narratives, many of which were explicitly identified with Washingtonianism, began to appear as books. Gough's *Autobiography* (1845) was easily the most popular, but several other ex-drunkards published their life stories during the 1840s: James Gale, *A Long Voyage in a Leaky Ship; or A Forty Years' Cruise on the Sea of Intemperance* (1842);

Joseph Gatchell, *The Disenthralled* (1843); *Narrative of Charles T. Woodman, A Reformed Inebriate* (1843); *The Life and Adventures of the Reformed Inebriate, D. G. Robinson, M.D.* (1846); *Incidents in the Life of George Haydock, Ex-Professional Wood-Sawyer* (1847); Jacob Carter, *My Drunken Life* (1847); *The Life and Experience of A. V. Green, The Celebrated Ohio Temperance Sledge Hammer* (1848); *The Life and Sketches of James Campbell, Paper Maker* (1850).

The pseudonymous *Autobiography of a Reformed Drunkard* (1845), authored by "John Cotton Mather," supposed scion of a distinguished New England family, reads like fiction, but it also seems to incorporate personal experience. T. S. Arthur's *Six Nights with the Washingtonians* (1842) was a series of tales based closely on his 1840 reports for the *Baltimore Merchant* about actual Washingtonian experience meetings. Like *Franklin Evans*, which Whitman allegedly wrote on commission from the Washingtonians,[38] other temperance narratives that purported to be autobiographies were really novels cast in the form of anonymous alcoholic confessions. These included *Confessions of a Female Inebriate* (1842), likely written by a male temperance advocate (Isaac F. Shepard), as well as *Confessions of a Reformed Inebriate* (1844) and *The Confession of a Rum-Seller* (1845).

The proliferation of such texts suggests that a responsive readership existed for tales of reformed drunkards, whether fictive or not. This audience was divided between those attracted to uplifting didacticism and those allured by gothic titillation. As David S. Reynolds suggests, the literature inspired by nineteenth-century reform movements sometimes transformed a "culture of morality" into a "culture of ambiguity." The work of "dark" or "immoral" reformers, which was subversive of dominant cultural values, "deemphasized the remedies for vice while probing the grisly, sometimes perverse results of vice, such as shattered homes, sadomasochistic violence, eroticism, nightmare visions, and the disillusioning collapse of romantic ideals."[39]

Many of the same "dark" images can be found in Gough's *Autobiography* and other texts by reformed drunkards; but none, including the obviously fictional ones, matches the luridness of *Franklin Evans*. Like Gough's *Autobiography*, the typical Washingtonian story traced a Dantean transit from Inferno (drunken damnation) to Purgatorio (redemption by the Washingtonians) to Paradiso (apotheosis as a temperance speaker).[40] And like Dante (and Milton), Washingtonian writers had to contend with the aesthetic problem of imbalance between the appeal of Divine light and that of Satanic darkness. Drunkenness, it seems, is inherently more compelling than sobriety; and the depiction of alcoholic extremity often predominated temperance narratives.

As the novelty of experience meetings wore off, audiences soon tired of familiar and formulaic testimony. The descriptions of drunken vice and miraculous reform had hardened into stereotypes. The initial transformative excitement was waning; and like other evangelical revivals during the Second Great Awakening, Washingtonianism was burning itself out. The exponential growth of membership peaked in 1842 and then declined steeply; and although a few scattered chapters, mainly in and around Boston, managed to persist through the 1850s,[41] the Society as a national entity was largely defunct by 1845, vanishing as suddenly as it had materialized.

There were several reasons for the Washingtonians' disappearance. The gradual return of economic prosperity after the Panic of 1837 relieved the anxiety that had driven some working-class drunkards to seek shelter and practical assistance from the Society. As Washingtonianism expanded into a national movement, it was increasingly crippled by organizational weaknesses. In Cincinnati, where a strong local chapter was already in disarray by the winter of 1842–1843, a mainstream temperance leader shrewdly observed: "All seemed to act from one benevolent impulse, without system, without concert, without, in short, any of the elements of permanence or stability. The *pledge was all*; there were no regular meetings, no discipline, no systematic way of securing contributions to sustain the reformed, or keep up the interest."[42]

Another problem was wholesale backsliding among the Washingtonian rank and file as well as among the movement's leaders.[43] As Robert L. Hampel points out, preachers of temperance "sinned with embarrassing frequency." In Lynn, Massachusetts, the Society "secured a pardon for a drunkard, sent him on a lecture tour, and was soon rewarded when the man robbed the store of his pacifist benefactor." The editor of a Washingtonian newspaper supposedly seduced a young factory girl.[44] The most spectacular fall involved John Gough, who, after disappearing for a week in September 1845, was discovered in a New York City brothel, recovering from a binge (with tender female assistance). Gough swore up and down that his enemies had drugged him and then tricked him into taking the fatal first drink. He had unknowingly fallen among prostitutes, he explained, in an alcoholic daze. Although Gough was officially exonerated by his church and defended by prominent temperance leaders, his account was widely disbelieved, and he was pilloried in the temperance press.[45]

Backsliding also took the form of deviation from the sedulously non-political principles the founders had laid down under Mitchell's leadership. In its emphasis on individual reform, the Society regarded intemperance as "a problem of the isolated drinker, not part of a broader social malaise or a matter of ideological neorepublicanism";[46] and it refused to countenance any measures stronger than moral suasion. The Washingtonians eschewed all manner of legal and political intervention, including coercive legislation and prohibition, which had become the main objectives of the establishment reformers. As the Washingtonians slipped politically out of phase with the mainstream temperance movement, leaders such as Gough and Hawkins yielded to the intense pressure to join the prohibitionist crusade. To the diminishing Washingtonian faithful, these and other apostates were traitors to the cause; but the public at large embraced them all the more warmly for their shedding unpopular beliefs.

Even more offensive to the temperance establishment than their political neutrality was the Washingtonians' inveterately secular outlook. Clerical leaders, whom the Baltimore upheaval had taken by surprise, deplored the Society's "atheism," insisting "that the exclusion of religion from Washingtonian meetings was tantamount to a denial of the miraculous intervention of God."[47] Quarrels over religion devolved into a bitter war of words waged in temperance newspapers. Once they had regrouped, the churches advanced toward winning back the souls temporarily lost to the secularists, vying with the weakened Washingtonians for moral ascendancy and control of the movement. The most prominent Washingtonian defector was Hawkins himself, who was ordained a Methodist minister and became a staunch religionist as well as prohibitionist. "Moral suasion for the unfortunate drunkard," he preached, "and legal suasion for the drunkard-MAKER."[48]

Although turncoats and backsliders decimated the Washingtonian rolls, the greatest loss of membership was to rival temperance organizations, especially the fraternal societies that borrowed many of the Society's ideas but adapted them to a more thoroughly bourgeois ethos. The earliest such competitor was the Order of Sons of Temperance, which began as a Washingtonian splinter group in New York City during 1842, the same year that a major British organization, the Independent Order of Rechabites, secured a foothold.[49] The Sons aspired to tighter organization and more rigorously sober membership than the Washingtonians had ever realized. Just as the Washingtonians once had shoved aside the leaders of the temperance establishment, so they in turn were rudely displaced by the Sons, who "attacked the Washingtonian movement as lazy, listless, and unimaginative."[50] Relations between the groups soured, in part because the younger reformers, who had not shared in the glory days of the early 1840s, did not identify themselves with their elders.

Imitating such nontemperance fraternal groups as the Independent Order of Odd Fellows, the Sons also provided insurance policies against financial adversity. Although religion and politics were officially excluded from meetings, the Sons drifted steadily into the orbit of Protestantism and prohibition; and although the founders were all artisans, the society evolved toward "the alliance of improved economic security with grips, passwords, signs of distress, door guards, elaborate 'regalia' and adjective-studded officers."[51] This apparatus of opulent uniforms, bombastic titles, arcane rituals, and secret handshakes served to underscore the Sons' respectability and exclusivity. "Membership was both a sign of commitment to middle-class values and a step in the process of changing a life style." Within six years, the Sons had spawned six thousand units, with a dues-paying membership of two hundred thousand.[52]

A profusion of similar groups soon followed, differing on fine points of doctrine with a strenuosity later characteristic of Marxist sects during the 1930s. There were: the Templars of Honor and Temperance, "an advanced degree of the Sons of Temperance composed of exemplary members who wished to form a knightly inner circle to which all might aspire"; the Knights of Jericho, consisting of those too young for the Sons of Temperance but too old for the Cadets of Temperance, its juvenile branch; the Independent Order of Good Templars, organized in 1851 by Knights who upon reaching maturity disdained the paternal group and formed their own instead (the Good Templars grew into an international organization with six hundred thousand members); the Order of Good Samaritans, which started as an all-white-male society in 1857 but then opened its doors to women and blacks; the Dashaways, founded in 1859 in San Francisco, who soon expanded throughout California; the Temperance Flying Artillery, a similar group in Chicago; the Royal Templars of Buffalo, "whose chief object was to enforce the city's Sunday blue laws"; the Sons of Jonadab, who scorned the laxity of all other temperance societies; the Unitarian Temperance Society, purveyors of scientific materials about drinking; and so on and on into the late nineteenth century.[53]

Unlike the expansive early Washingtonians, the fraternal societies tended to consolidate their success by turning complacently inward. The Sons and the others were not drawn to the "outdoor work" of "seeking converts through street meetings, public speeches by well-known temperance orators, or pamphleteering"; rather "to the quiet and comfort of the weekly division meeting, and to the picnics, celebrations, and holiday festivities where teetotalers could enjoy recreation and social contact without the presence of alcohol."[54] The Washingtonians alone had put such emphasis on personal and public confession, and with them the temperance narrative largely disappeared. Although scattered examples of the genre continued to appear until World War I,[55] the sobering synergy of speech and writing, as briefly attained during the early 1840s, was lost.

Lost, that is, until the embers of the Washingtonian spirit were rekindled in Alcoholics Anonymous. A century after the publication of Gough's *Autobiography*, Bill W. (a.k.a. William Griffith Wilson) was "startled, then sobered" to learn of the astonishing parallels between A.A., the organization he had cofounded in 1935, and the Washingtonian movement. The similarities had been brought to his attention by a fellow alcoholic in a letter to the *Grapevine*, A.A.'s magazine. "It was hard for us to believe," Wilson confessed in his *Grapevine* column for August 1945, "that a hundred years ago the newspapers of this country were carrying enthusiastic accounts about a hundred thousand alcoholics who were helping each other stay sober; that today the influence of this good work has so completely disappeared that few of us had ever heard of it." Thereafter the Washingtonians were kept at least dimly in view by Wilson and other leaders, if only to provide a valuable object lesson for A.A.'s future. "We are sure," Wilson continued, "that if the original Washingtonians could return to this planet they would be glad to see us learning from their mistakes."[56]

Wilson, who had a proprietary interest in stressing the errors of the Washington Society as well as its differences from Alcoholics Anonymous, moralized that the movement had been destroyed by individual ambition ("Overdone self-advertising—exhibitionism?"); institutional arrogance ("Too cocksure, maybe. Couldn't learn from others and became competitive, instead of cooperative, with other organizations in their field"); and political wrangling over issues (abolition, prohibition) irrelevant to the primary purpose of keeping drunks sober. "The original strong and simple group purpose was thus dissipated in fruitless controversy and divergent aims."[57] Although Wilson's analysis may have lacked historical sophistication, it served A.A. well in the articulation of the Twelve Traditions, the rules of governance that were developed to bind together, however loosely, the rapidly multiplying local groups. In his review of A.A.'s first twenty years, Wilson reflected: "The lesson to be learned from the Washingtonians was not overlooked by Alcoholics Anonymous. As we surveyed the wreck of that movement, early A.A. members resolved to keep our society out of public controversy."[58]

Leonard U. Blumberg and William L. Pittman note many features in common between Alcoholics Anonymous and the Washington Temperance Society. These include a focus on inebriates themselves, moral suasion, total abstinence, experience meetings, mutual help, traveling speakers, charismatic leadership, political neutrality, non-sectarian spirituality, and loose organization above the local level. Both groups, moreover, share an institutional culture deriving from their "common ancestry in Anglo-American Protestant religious belief and practice." The authors nonetheless conclude that because Washingtonian principles were "rediscovered and reapplied in a new sociopolitical context" by Wilson and his A.A. associates, it follows that "only in an attenuated fashion do the two social movements have historical ties."[59]

The strongest ties between A.A. and the Washingtonians, however, may not be historical, tactical, organizational, or ideological, so much as *textual*. Beginning with the first edition in 1939, *Alcoholics Anonymous*—the quasi-scriptural "Big Book," now in its third edition, with a fourth being compiled—has always included, not only "Bill's Story" and "The

Doctor's Nightmare" (by A.A.'s other cofounder, Doctor Bob, a.k.a. Robert Holbrook Smith), but also a sheaf of personal stories by other A.A. members. In these modern tales of drunkenness and sobriety the *temperance narrative* has effectively been revived and refashioned into the *recovery narrative*, a genre as essential to Alcoholics Anonymous as its predecessor once had been to the Washington Temperance Society.

In order to achieve sobriety, according to A.A., an alcoholic must first reach a turning point at which resistance yields to surrender and denial gives way to acceptance of powerlessness over alcohol. This moment of truth often comes when prospective A.A. members are astounded to hear their own life histories from the mouths of those already in recovery: "he was telling my story!" The salutary effect of such narrative identification is to belie the "terminal uniqueness," the false sense of difference by which alcoholics "in denial" keep a potentially fatal distance from sober alcoholics in order to rationalize a desire to keep drinking. In A.A. parlance, such persons have self-deceptively chosen to compare stories rather than relate to them. They do not get the message of hope because they fail to find themselves in others' narratives of recovery.

"Listening to stories about alcoholism," as Edmund B. O'Reilly suggests, "may be the best means we have of comprehending and delineating the disorder, because stories alone can begin to contain its bewildering, protean, contradictory nature." No less than modern recovery narratives, I would add, Washingtonian temperance narratives can "lay hold of the lived experience of alcoholism, and sometimes transform seemingly ineffable states of mind into patterns of enacted response that are available to interpretation."[60] With all due allowance for their historical remoteness and their old-fashioned prose, the following tales still speak with surprising force to the miseries of drunkenness and the joys of deliverance. Indeed, a reader familiar with Alcoholics Anonymous will likely feel a shock of recognition in relating to the experience, strength, and hope of Washingtonian forebears who, in their narratives of addiction, despair, and recovery, were uncannily "telling my story."

Notes

1. Russel Crouse, *Mr. Currier and Mr. Ives: A Note on Their Lives and Times* (Garden City, N.Y.: Doubleday, Doran, 1930), p. 21.

2. The conceptual continuity from Rush to Currier to Jellinek is noted by Mark Edward Lender and Karen R. Karnchanapee: "The illustrations from both eras explained alcoholism as a progressive and cumulative process, through which alcoholics passed in a generally predictable sequence of steps. In all these illustrations, clearly defined stages of problem drinking had corresponding social and physical consequences." See "'Temperance Tales': Anti-liquor Fiction and American Attitudes toward Alcoholics in the Late Nineteenth and Early Twentieth Centuries," *Journal of Studies on Alcohol* 38 (July 1977): 1360.

3. In an apparently plagiarized version of the popular Currier print, as issued by Kelloggs and Thayer in 1846, what appears beneath the arch is a distillery, from which a man (perhaps the owner) is carrying away two sacks that look to be money bags; he is observed (perhaps incredulously) by a gentleman astride a sleek horse drinking water at the town pump. In the context of the "nine steps," the point seems to be that if demon rum can make poor fools of rich men, it can also make rich men of "fools" wise enough to exploit the gentlemen's folly.

4. Hawkins asserted that of a dozen apprentices who entered the hatter's trade together, "eight of the twelve have died drunkards; one is now in the almshouse in Cincinnati, one in the almshouse of Baltimore, one is keeping a tavern in Baltimore, and here am I." Hawkins's narrative, transcribed from his public addresses, is quoted in John Marsh, *Hannah Hawkins, The Reformed Drunkard's Daughter* (New York: American Temperance Union, 1844), p. 15. Other quotations are identified in the text. Hawkins's (minimally variant) version of his own story appears in a filiopious biography by his son: William George Hawkins, *Life of John H. W. Hawkins* (Boston: John P. Jewett, 1859), pp. 91–94.

5. On the conjunction of temperance and abolition, see my essay, "Slaves to the Bottle: Gough's *Autobiography* and Douglass's *Narrative*," in *The Serpent in the Cup: Temperance in American Literature*, ed. David S. Reynolds and Debra J. Rosenthal (Amherst: U of Massachusetts P, 1997), pp. 115–35.

6. Joseph R. Gusfield, *Symbolic Crusade: Status Politics and the American Temperance Movement* (Urbana: U of Illinois P, 1963), pp. 5, 44. Gusfield's long-standard account of the origins of temperance reform has lately been disputed. James R. Rohrer detects a radical, evangelical strain from the very start of the movement: "The creation of the American Temperance Society in 1826 did not initiate the evangelical temperance crusade, as students of the reform typically

20

argue. The late 1820s witnessed the dramatic popularization of a movement that had been initiated by reformers in the early 1810s." If Rohrer is correct, then the Washingtonians may be seen as heir to those earlier temperance groups that were less concerned with social control than with "the ruinous impact of ardent spirits upon their families and upon individual conscience." See "The Origins of the Temperance Movement: A Reinterpretation," *Journal of American Studies* 24 (August 1990): 234, 232.

7. As Stuart Berg Flexner points out, the meaning of "temperance," which had denoted "moderation, self-restraint" since the fourteenth century, was radically revised: "by 1830 the American Temperance Society defined *temperance* as 'the moderate . . . use of things beneficial and abstinence from things harmful,' going on to call hard liquor 'poison.' Thus, in regard to liquor, the American Temperance Society changed the meaning of *temperance* to *abstinence*." *I Hear America Talking: An Illustrated Treasury of American Words and Phrases* (New York: Van Nostrand Reinhold, 1976), p. 355.

8. Quoted in Jed Dannenbaum, *Drink and Disorder: Temperance Reform in Cincinnati from the Washingtonian Revival to the WCTU* (Urbana: U of Illinois P, 1984), p. 38.

9. Sources differ slightly about how "moderate" the drinking of the founding six had been. Marsh, for instance, describes them as "devoted in no small degree to their cups, and usually known as intemperate men." *Hannah Hawkins*, p. 23. John Zug, an early historian of the Washingtonian movement, reports that they "drank moderately, and freely too." Alcohol had "made its ravages on their characters, their minds, and their hearts," but the men still possessed "the energy of manhood," and they all supported their families. *The Foundation, Progress and Principles of the Washington Temperance Society of Baltimore* (Baltimore: John D. Toy, 1842), pp. 8–9. One recent history suggests that Mitchell, a self-described "periodical drunkard," was distressed by his loss of control: "In a speech delivered before the society at a later date, Mitchell said that he had been trying for 15 years to regulate his drinking on his own and had been unable to do so. Indeed, he argued, 'whenever I hear a man say he can regulate *himself*, I say to him I know *that* man will be a drunkard.'" Leonard U. Blumberg (with William L. Pittman), *Beware the First Drink! The Washington Temperance Movement and Alcoholics Anonymous* (Seattle: Glen Abbey Books, 1991), pp. 61–62.

10. The identity of this speaker remains in dispute, the two contenders being Matthew Hale Smith, a Congregational minister, and Jacob Knapp, an

itinerant Baptist preacher. Weighing the inconclusive evidence, Blumberg argues that it was more likely Knapp than Smith who inspired the Baltimoreans, but speculates that the six "really did not tell their story as completely as we would like. It is probable that Knapp did, in fact, raise the temperance issue when he *was* in Baltimore [some time before April 1840] . . . and that it had been a topic of occasional discussion among these drinking companions at Chase's Tavern from that time onward." Blumberg, *Beware the First Drink!*, pp. 60–61.

11. Zug, *The Foundation . . . of the Washington Temperance Society*, p. 6.

12. Mitchell's own class status was evidently different from that of his drinking companions: "he was more than a mere journeyman tailor. Apparently he had his own shop and may have had other tailors working for him." Blumberg, *Beware the First Drink!*, pp. 59–60. Mitchell thus had ties both to the artisanal working class and to the entrepreneurial middle class.

13. J. C. Furnas, *The Life and Times of The Late Demon Rum* (London: W. H. Allen, 1965), p. 93.

14. Dannenbaum, *Drink and Disorder*, p. 36.

15. Zug, *The Foundation . . . of the Washington Temperance Society*, p. 62.

16. According to Blumberg, the first public meeting, held on 19 November 1840 in the Masonic Hall on St. Paul Street, "was when the transformation took place from a society of reformed drunkards (although even then there were a few non-drunkards in the membership) to a therapeutic social movement." *Beware the First Drink!*, p. 64. Washingtonian membership was never restricted solely to inebriates. On the contrary, the Society's goal was to create "a support network that would link drunkards and moderate drinkers with long-standing abstainers, drawing those who wished to give up alcohol into a social milieu that would reinforce rather than denigrate those intentions." Typically, the proportion of actual drunkards in Washingtonian groups "appears to have been about 10 percent or less of the total membership." Dannenbaum, *Drink and Disorder*, pp. 38–39.

17. Furnas, *Demon Rum*, p. 89. Mitchell is usually credited with the idea of having the Washingtonians tell their stories to each other during meetings. In his early history of the movement, Zug commended the efficacy of "experience" narratives: "How much more influence then has the man, who stands before an audience to persuade them to abandon the use of strong drink, when he can himself tell them of its ruinous and blasting effects on his own life and character—trace the progress of his own habits of intemperance—and warn others to

avoid the rock on which he split. A reformed man has the best access to a drunkard's mind and heart, because he best knows, and can enter into all a drunkard's feelings. And such appeals from such sources, properly directed, can rarely fail of entire success." *The Foundation . . . of the Washington Temperance Society*, pp. 42–43.

18. Dannenbaum, *Drink and Disorder*, p. 35.

19. Gusfield, *Symbolic Crusade*, p. 33. Gusfield and other scholars of temperance have shown that the movement fostered a shift toward more abstemious values as the industrial revolution created a demand for workers more ascetic than those of the eighteenth century—whose wages had often included a steady supply of alcohol, in part because it was thought to improve their health and productivity.

20. On 11 and 12 September 1814, Hawkins, then a seventeen-year-old apprentice, had taken up arms to repel the landing of British troops at North Point, fifteen miles southeast of Baltimore. Two days later, as the Americans retreated and the British fleet neared the city, the bombardment of Fort McHenry inspired Francis Scott Key to write "The Star-Spangled Banner."

21. As Milton A. Maxwell points out, the "often repeated" figure of six hundred thousand derives from the 1843 annual report of the American Temperance Union, which states: "A half million hard drinkers often drunken, and a hundred thousand sots . . . may safely be considered as having been brought to sign the total abstinence pledge within the last two years." "The Washingtonian Movement," *Quarterly Journal of Studies on Alcohol* 11 (September 1950): 427.

22. John Allen Krout, *The Origins of Prohibition* (New York: Knopf, 1925), p. 92.

23. Abraham Lincoln, "An Address, Delivered before the Springfield Washington Temperance Society, on the 22nd February, 1842," rpt. in Blumberg, *Beware the First Drink!*, p. 105. Blumberg explains that although Lincoln probably took the Washingtonian pledge at the height of the movement's success, it is doubtful that he was ever "a constitutional member" of the Society (p. 103). Lincoln once described himself as a lifetime teetotaler: "I am not a temperance man, but I am temperate to this extent—I don't drink." Quoted in John Kobler, *Ardent Spirits: The Rise and Fall of Prohibition* (New York: Putnam's, 1973), p. 63.

24. Gusfield, *Symbolic Crusade*, p. 55.

25. From a reading of three hundred temperance novels, Karen Sánchez-

Eppler deduces that, aside from the story, akin to *The Drunkards Progress,* that chronicles "degeneration from first misguided sip to destitution and death," the second most common plot, present in fully a quarter of the sample, is the "story of a drunken father creeping into bed with his young child." In the case of *Hannah Hawkins,* "The redemptive power of 'daughter-tenderness' serves as a mark of the daughter's obedience. Her submissiveness protects the father from the 'fierce' need to combat the threat of being disciplined by his child. Her submissiveness enables him to submit." "Temperance in the Bed of a Child: Incest and Social Order in Nineteenth-Century America," in Reynolds and Rosenthal, eds., *The Serpent in the Cup,* pp. 60, 78. On the gendering of drinking, see also Mary Ann Clawson, *Constructing Brotherhood: Class, Gender, and Fraternalism* (Princeton: Princeton UP, 1989).

26. Jack S. Blocker Jr., *American Temperance Movements: Cycles of Reform* (Boston: Twayne, 1989), pp. 10–11, 37. Practice differed among immigrant groups: some German wives accompanied their husbands on Sunday outings to the beer garden; some Irish women drank out of desperation at "the domestic violence and desertion that marked their marriages," thereby contributing "more than their share of female drunkards" (p. 37).

27. Ibid., p. 44.

28. Ruth M. Alexander, "'We Are Engaged as a Band of Sisters': Class and Domesticity in the Washingtonian Temperance Movement, 1840–1850," *Journal of American History* 75:3 (1988): 764.

29. Ian R. Tyrrell, "Women and Temperance in Antebellum America, 1830–1860," *Civil War History* 28:2 (1982): 138.

30. Alexander, "'We Are Engaged as a Band of Sisters,'" p. 771. Alexander remarks that by the mid-1840s, "female Washingtonians may have lost much of their former sympathy for female alcoholics, viewing them as women who lived in defiance of the parameters of acceptable womanhood. While they still treated male inebriates as victims reclaimable by womanly persuasion, they may have come to see female inebriates as lacking the moral will essential to 'true women'" (p. 780).

31. Tyrrell, "Women and Temperance," pp. 139, 145.

32. Quoted in Ian R. Tyrrell, *Sobering Up: From Temperance to Prohibition in Antebellum America, 1800–1860* (Westport, Conn.: Greenwood Press, 1979), p. 163. Marsh, a minister, was eventually alienated by the vehement anticlericalism expressed by some Washingtonians.

33. Gusfield, *Symbolic Crusade,* p. 49.

34. David S. Reynolds, *Beneath the American Renaissance: The Subversive Imagination in the Age of Emerson and Melville* (New York: Knopf, 1988), p. 67; Furnas, *Demon Rum*, p. 150.

35. John Lardner, "Drinking in America: An Unfinished History," in *The World of John Lardner*, ed. Roger Kahn (New York: Simon & Schuster, 1961), p. 217; Kobler, *Ardent Spirits*, p. 66; Lyman Abbott, "Introduction" to John B. Gough, *Platform Echoes; or, Leaves from My Note-Book of Four Years* (Hartford, Conn.: Worthington, 1885), p. 65. Gough, who kept meticulous records throughout his career, boasted that he had delivered 6,064 lectures and traveled 272,235 miles between 14 May 1843 and 1 June 1869. *Autobiography and Personal Recollections of John B. Gough* (Springfield, Mass.: Bill, Nichols, 1869), p. 544. Gough was no less active during the remaining seventeen years of his life.

36. Clawson, *Constructing Brotherhood*, p. 163. Blumberg also recognizes that "Washingtonian speakers were a part of the popular entertainment of the period, moralistic though it might be." *Beware the First Drink!*, p. 154.

37. Charges of forgery were routinely leveled against slave narratives, the authorship of which was, in fact, complexly collaborative in some cases. As Robin W. Winks observes, many of the texts were "ghost written, or taken from dictation, or were almost wholly the work of another person, and thus more nearly biography than autobiography." "The Making of a Fugitive Slave Narrative: Josiah Henson and Uncle Tom—A Case Study," in *The Slave's Narrative*, ed. Charles T. Davis and Henry Louis Gates Jr. (New York: Oxford UP, 1985), p. 113. Even Douglass's *Narrative* was assailed as inauthentic. In this regard, it is notable that the foremost temperance narrative was likewise suspected of fraudulence. Under assault by his enemies, Gough was forced to admit that he had, indeed, received help in writing his 1845 *Autobiography*. He insisted that the book was nonetheless his own: "John Ross Dix, then calling himself John Dix Ross, was an inmate of my family, and I, pacing the room, dictated to him, he being a good short-hand writer. When he had copied it out, we read it together and made alterations, and I wish to say that, excepting only three, or, at most, four instances, *my* language, not his, was used." *Autobiography and Personal Recollections*, p. 545.

38. In later days Whitman disparaged *Franklin Evans*, his first book (issued as a newspaper supplement). It was, he said in 1888, the worst kind of hack work: conceived in cynicism and carried to term in three days for a quick $75— the composition fueled by intermittent trips to the "Pewter Mug," a Bohemian bar, where the temperance author stoked his imagination with port wine and

gin. The slapdash incoherence and outrageous melodrama of the plot lend some plausibility to this account! But the earnestness of Whitman's other early temperance tales suggests that he was more caught up in the Washingtonian movement than he later chose to remember. Even as he denounced *Franklin Evans* as "damned rot," Whitman conceded that the novel was "not insincere perhaps." It is difficult to detect any irony in the panegyric to the Society in the final chapter: "They called themselves WASHINGTONIANS. Long may the name be honored—and long may it continue to number among those who are proud to style themselves by the title—upright and noble spirits, determined never to turn back from the work, or to discredit the name they bear, and the Society to which they belong!" *Franklin Evans; or The Inebriate: A Tale of the Times*, ed. Jean Downey (New Haven: College & University Press, 1967), pp. 19, 186.

39. Reynolds, *Beneath the American Renaissance*, pp. 59, 106. See also Reynolds, "Black Cats and Delirium Tremens: Temperance and the American Renaissance," in Reynolds and Rosenthal, eds., *The Serpent in the Cup*.

40. Gough made this Dantean parallel explicit. In describing the nadir of his drunkenness, he recalls the gateway of the Inferno: "Over every door of admission into the society of my fellow-men, the words, 'No Hope,' seemed to be inscribed. Despair was my companion, and perpetual degradation appeared to be my allotted doom." When Gough recalls the horrors of delirium tremens, he claims that he "endured more agony than pen could describe, even were it guided by the mind of a Dante." *An Autobiography by John B. Gough* (Boston: By the Author, 1845), pp. 61–62, 45.

41. In 1858 the Bostonians established a Home for the Fallen, in which Washingtonian principles were used to rehabilitate inebriate inmates. Under various names, this institution continued to exist until 1980, when the Washingtonian Center for Addictions was finally closed down. See also Grace Clifford Howard, "Alcoholism: Its Treatment at the Washingtonian Hospital," *Scientific Temperance Journal* 49 (Autumn & Winter 1941–42): 57–68, 91–95.

42. Samuel Cary, quoted in Dannenbaum, *Drink and Disorder*, p. 41.

43. Mark Edward Lender and James Kirby Martin accept the traditional estimate that by the late 1840s perhaps six hundred thousand drunkards had quit drinking under Washingtonian guidance. Of these, they claim, "about 150,000 ultimately remained abstinent. This meant, of course, that 450,000 relapsed at least to some degree; as one temperance historian put it, however, to save so many of a class generally thought hopeless was in any case 'a glorious fact of

moral triumph.'" *Drinking in America: A History* (New York: Free Press, 1982), p. 75.

44. Robert L. Hampel, *Temperance and Prohibition in Massachusetts 1813–1853* (Ann Arbor, Mich.: UMI Research P, 1982), p. 121.

45. For details of the scandal, see Gough's own statement, added as a "Supplement" to later editions of his 1845 *Autobiography*. The anti-Gough view appeared in an anonymous tract: *Goffiana: A Review of the Life and Writings of John B. Gough* (Boston: Ruggles, 1846). Reynolds points out that Gough was satirized in George Thompson's novel, *City Crimes; or, Life in New York and Boston* (New York: William Berry, 1849), where a hypocritical temperance lecturer named Samuel Cough concocts an alibi for his recent trouble: "I got infernally drunk, and slept in a brothel, which was all very well, you know, and nothing unusual—but people *found it out!* Well, I got up a cock-and-bull story about drinking drugged soda." Since "temperance spouting is a great business," the wily Cough vows to protect his credibility: "Now when I get *corned*, I keep out of sight." Quoted in Reynolds, "Black Cats and Delirium Tremens," p. 30.

46. Lender and Kirby, *Drinking in America*, p. 75.

47. Blumberg, *Beware the First Drink!*, p. 170.

48. John Hawkins, quoted in Furnas, *Demon Rum*, p. 94.

49. The Rechabites took their name and mission from Jeremiah 35:5–6: "And I set before the sons of the house of the Rechabites pots full of wine, and cups, and I said unto them, Drink ye wine. / But they said, We will drink no wine: for Jonadab the son of Rechab our father commanded us, saying, Ye shall drink no wine; *neither* ye, nor your sons for ever."

50. Dannenbaum, *Drink and Disorder*, p. 58.

51. Furnas, *Demon Rum*, p. 96.

52. Gusfield, *Symbolic Crusade*, p. 47.

53. Kobler, *Ardent Spirits*, pp. 73–74. On the later proliferation of fraternal societies, many of which promoted temperance, see Mark C. Carnes, *Secret Ritual and Manhood in Victorian America* (New Haven, Conn.: Yale UP, 1989).

54. Dannenbaum, *Drink and Disorder*, p. 53.

55. Texts I have read include: *Autobiography of Festus G. Rand; A Tale of Intemperance*, with a preface by John Gough (1868); George M. Dutcher, *Disinthralled: A Story of My Life* (1872); Luther Benson, *Fifteen Years in Hell: An Autobiography* (1877); Joseph H. Francis, *My Last Drink: A Tragic Human Story; The Greatest Story Ever Written* (1915). The most famous and accomplished later ex-

ample is undoubtedly Jack London's *John Barleycorn* (1913). But nothing quite compares to *Eleven Years a Drunkard; or, The Evils of Intemperance, as Evidenced in the Thrilling Experience of Thomas Doner. Having Lost Both Arms Through Intemperance, He Wrote This Book with His Teeth, as a Warning to Others* (1878). Such mishaps were apparently not uncommon. Festus Rand too suffered the loss of his hands from passing out in a snowbank as he staggered home from a tavern; he learned to grip a pencil between his stumps in order to write his temperance narrative.

56. "Modesty One Plank for Good Public Relations," in *The Language of the Heart: Bill W.'s Grapevine Writings* (New York: A.A. Grapevine, 1988), pp. 4–5.

57. Wilson, *Language of the Heart*, pp. 4–5.

58. *Alcoholics Anonymous Comes of Age: A Brief History of A.A.* (New York: Alcoholics Anonymous Publishing, 1957), p. 125. Here, as on other occasions, Wilson reiterated his view that the Washingtonians had been destroyed by the rancorous politics of abolition and prohibition. Such "outside issues" (as external social causes are termed by A.A.) divided the Washingtonians and distracted them from their organizing singleness of purpose: helping alcoholics to get and stay sober.

59. Blumberg, *Beware the First Drink!*, pp. 205, 220.

60. Edmund B. O'Reilly, *Sobering Tales: Narratives of Alcoholism and Recovery* (Amherst: U of Massachusetts P, 1997), p. 1.

I

T. S. ARTHUR

"The Experience Meeting," from *Six Nights with the Washingtonians* (1842)

Timothy Shay Arthur (1809–85) was an incredibly prolific writer of stories in the sentimental vein. It has been estimated that he was himself responsible for 5 percent of all the fiction sold in the United States during the 1840s. *Six Nights with the Washingtonians* was Arthur's first book-length foray into the temperance field, but by no means his last. After *The Ruined Family and Other Tales* (1843), an oft-reprinted collection of temperance stories, Arthur produced *Ten Nights in a Bar-Room, And What I Saw There* (1854), his best novel and the best-selling temperance novel of the nineteenth century. (It also flourished in a stage adaptation.) *Ten Nights* was followed by *Three Years in a Man-Trap* (1872), a companion volume set in a city rather than a country town; *Woman to the Rescue: A Story of the New Crusade* (1874), a tale of the anti-saloon demonstrations that led to the formation of the Women's Christian Temperance Union; *Danger; or, Wounded in the House of a Friend* (1875), an exposé of "moderate" drinking; *The Bar-Rooms at Brantly* (1877), another assault on the saloons; and *Grappling with the Monster; or, The Curse and the Cure of Strong Drink* (1877), a miscellany of temperance lore.

Arthur enlisted other writers to help him fill the numerous—and strictly temperance—periodicals he edited, some of them designed for a working-class readership. While he was working for the *Visiter* in Baltimore, he became friendly with Edgar Allan Poe, whose disastrous career of inebriety may have aroused Arthur's sympathy for hopeless drunkards. He was certainly inspired by the early Washingtonian experience meetings he covered for the *Baltimore Merchant*. In 1842 these newspaper reports were retailed as fiction in a series of pamphlets—*The Broken Merchant, The Experience Meeting, The Tavern Keeper, The Drunkard's Wife, The Widow's Son, The Moderate Drinker*—and then collected the same year into *Six Nights with the Washingtonians*. In "The Experience Meeting," Arthur captures the initial excitement of the movement: the days when the first public meetings were held in Baltimore and the city was abuzz about the new temperance society; when, as Arthur writes, "the eyes of the whole community were fixed upon them, with an expression of a strange surprise and wonder."

PREFACE

*W*hen these Temperance Tales were commenced, the writer did not anticipate so favorable a reception as they have obtained in all directions. He believed that, if he were to enter a field so full of rich materials as the one opened by the great Temperance Reformation, he might present scenes that would not only deeply interest, but act as powerful auxiliaries in the promotion of that noble cause. His success has been far beyond his expectations. But this success has resulted entirely from the fact that, in nearly every one of the stories presented, there has been, as its groundwork, a basis of real incidents; and these have been detailed without any aim at artificial effect, but simply with a view to let truth and nature speak forth in their legitimate power and pathos.

At every step of his progress in these tales, the writer has felt with the actors—sympathizing with them in their heart-aching sorrows, and rejoicing with them when the morning has broken after a long night of affliction. This is because they were not mere fictions of his own imagination: and it is because they are not mere fictions that they have any power to awaken a corresponding interest in the mind of the reader.

Their title, "Six Nights with the Washingtonians," was suggested, naturally, from the fact of the writer's having been present at some of the first experience meetings in Baltimore, only a few months after the formation of the original Washington Temperance Society. The impression then made upon his mind by the simple but eloquent details of its members, as they related their sad experiences, can never be effaced. Many of the very experiences to which the writer alludes have since been related by these pioneers, in almost every city in the Union, and the whole country can now attest their power to move the heart.

THE EXPERIENCE MEETING

A few weeks after my first visit to the Washingtonians, I again attended one of their meetings. Even in that brief period their influence had become more largely extended. Hundreds had signed the total abstinence pledge, and coming in among them greatly increased their strength and importance. The eyes of the whole community were fixed upon them, with an expression of strange surprise and wonder. They were in the thoughts of all, and their doings were upon every tongue. If you met a friend in the street, the first words, after the greetings had passed, would almost certainly be—

"Have you been to any of these temperance meetings?" Or—

"They are wonderful doings really, of our temperance men." Or—

"Would you believe it? Mr. —— has joined the teetotallers!"

As might well be supposed, the tavern-keepers were greatly alarmed, and used the weapons of ridicule, and sometimes of oppression, to counteract the movement. But their efforts were altogether vain. Every opposition but gave renewed power to the impulse.

How many a poor wife ejaculated, with freshly kindling hopes, "O that my husband would join!"

And perhaps the next man to sign the pledge would be he for whom the ardent wish was breathed. Into many an abode over which for years had hung thick clouds, the warm sunshine suddenly penetrated. Smiles lit up many an eye, too familiar with tears, and joy trembled in many a heart long the dwelling place of sad despondency.

On the night of my second visit to the society, I found the large hall in which their meetings were held crowded to excess. As before, the interest I felt prompted me to push my way up as near to the speaker's stand as possible, and my position there enabled me to look almost the entire audience in the face. Really it was a sight that moved my feelings, in spite of myself! There sat an old man, whom I had seen staggering in the street, many and many a time—an old man with sons and daughters, and grandchildren, moving in respectable stations. How many tears had been shed for that old man; vain, hopeless tears! How like an almost insupportable weight had his name and image rested upon the hearts of his children! Now his face was calm and full of hope and confidence. Though marks of the destroyer were still upon him, there was yet a moral dignity in the expression of his countenance which I could not have believed that it would ever have worn.

Near by was another, scarcely past the prime of life, whom I had known for ten years as a common drunkard. To have met him on a race course, gambling at a faro table, or brawling at the polls on an election day, or talking politics in a grog-shop, I should not have been surprised; but here, in a temperance meeting, he seemed, at first glance, to be out of his place. But the more narrowly I observed him, the more palpably apparent was the change that had taken place. He, too, whom all had considered past the hope of reformation, had renounced the cup of confusion!

"Really this is wonderful!" I said. "Surely I must be in a dream!"

But no; it was a blessed reality!

"There is Mr. ——, as I live!" whispered a person sitting near me.

I turned towards the door with renewed surprise, and there, sure enough, came steadily up the aisle an individual, well known as not only a drinking man, but a very bad man. His wife, an amiable woman, and three sweet children had been for years utterly neglected; and this fact was notorious. And his conduct in other respects was too vile to admit of record here. His step was firm, and there was an expression of sad determination in his face, as he came up towards the head of the room, and sought a place amid the crowd.

"And young Mr. —— also!" the same person said, surprise and pleasure in his tone.

Young Mr. —— was there, sure enough. He was a young man, scarcely twenty-five, who had only been married two years, and in that time had been repeatedly intoxicated, and from neglect and abuse had well-nigh broken the heart of his young wife, who had been compelled to leave him and seek refuge in her father's house. I looked him steadily in the face for a few moments—it was calm and serious.

"There is yet hope, young wife and mother!" I murmured with a thrill of emotion as I gazed upon Mr. ——: "there are yet bright days in store for you!"

Subsequent events have proved the truth of that impression.

More than twenty others did I notice there, whom I had known for years as moral plague spots on the community. How changed they seemed!

After the preliminaries of the meeting were over, the President announced that an hour or so would be spent in the recital of their experiences by such members of the society as felt inclined to speak. The first who arose was a middle-aged man, with a thoughtful intelligent countenance. As he straightened himself up, all eyes were turned towards him, and there was a breathless interest manifested throughout the room.

THE RECLAIMED

"Mr. President," he began, in a clear, distinct, and emphatic tone, "a man said to me, yesterday, that, for his part, he would be ashamed to tell of his miserable misconduct, if he had been a drunkard. Now, for my part, I am deeply grieved at and heartily ashamed of the life I have led for the past ten years—that grief and that shame I know to be sincere, and I wish them to be permanent, and one use in telling my history to others is to confirm these feelings in myself, and another use is to encourage others to lift themselves out of the pit from which I have been elevated. I will not, therefore, keep silence—it seems to me that if I were to do so, the very stones would cry out against me.

"Twelve years ago, Mr. President, I married a young woman, to whom I was deeply attached—(here the voice of the speaker trembled, and fell to a lower tone). How purely and fondly she loved one so unworthy of that love as myself, her unwavering devotion, her patient suffering, her uncomplaining endurance through many weary years, too abundantly testified! Ah, sir! it is a sad thing for a woman to be a drunkard's wife! (And the speaker dashed aside, hastily, a tear.)

"I am a mechanic. When I married, I was in business for myself, and doing very well. I furnished my house comfortably, and provided everything that persons in our circumstances could properly desire. And we were happy—at least so far as such a condition of affairs, united with a true regard for each other, could make us happy.

"I had not been to a place of worship for many years before our marriage, and had a strong disinclination to going. My wife was a religious woman, and at first I went to church with her, but so irksome did the task become, that I made first one excuse for staying at home, and then another, and finally declined going altogether.

"This I could see pained her exceedingly, more especially as I gener-

33

ally met some friends in a neighboring tavern, and either sat and talked politics in the bar-room, or strolled out to some drinking gardens in the suburbs of the city. But I thought it very foolish in her to be thus pained, and, indeed, her evident disquietude of mind, at my conduct, irritated me, in spite of my better judgment and feelings, especially after I had been drinking, and caused me to think unkindly of her. It is very hard for us to cherish unkind thoughts, without their some time or other showing themselves in unkind words. I remember, as distinctly as I remember any occurrence of my life, the first time I spoke a harsh word to Mary. It was about a year after our marriage. She had been to church, the first time in many weeks, and I had been at the tavern as usual, and had drank rather freely. When I came in, I found her sitting with her babe, only a few weeks old, on her lap. The dinner table was on the floor, and Mary had evidently been waiting for me for some time. She looked up, her face still pale from her recent sickness, and said, half smiling, half in earnest—

" 'Oh, James, how can you spend your time on Sundays, as you do?'

"My wife, as I have just said, had been to church for the first time in many weeks. She was religious in her feelings, and conscientious in the discharge of all her duties, and, besides, felt deeply concerned for me. Absence from worship for many weeks had caused the services of the church to make a stronger impression on her mind than usual, and the natural consequence was that she felt a more anxious concern for me, which prompted her to speak as she did. But I was not in a condition to appreciate fully her feelings. Had I not been drinking, I should have felt little, if at all, annoyed at her gentle reproof. But blinded and excited by liquor, I became instantly aroused into anger, and replied sharply:

" 'Mary, I won't submit to be catechised by you; and so, let this be the last time that you interfere in what does not concern you! If you relish going to church, go—I shall not hinder you—but don't, as you value your peace of mind, attempt again to dictate to me!'

"As I said, I felt angry with Mary, and spoke sharply. Poor creature! I shall never forget how pale and frightened she looked; nor how long after the shadow that then fell upon her countenance rested on her gentle face. Indeed, from that hour, I believe she was never again happy. She had suddenly awakened from a delusive dream, to a perception of painful realities; and the impression then made, time could not efface from her memory. I was instantly conscious of the wrong I had done, but alas! had not the manliness to confess it. My pride, the weak, stubborn pride of a man under the influence of liquor, was offended, and shrunk from any thing like an acknowledgment. The dinner hour passed in oppressive, embarrassed silence. After it was over, instead of spending the afternoon with my wife, as I had heretofore done, I took my hat and went out. Of course, I joined my cronies at the tavern, where I passed several hours in drinking and talking politics.

"I came home towards nightfall, more under the influence of liquor than I had been since our marriage. The first glance at Mary's face told too plainly that the arrow had entered her soul. This indication, instead of softening my feelings, naturally kind, irritated and angered me.

" 'It's all put on,' I said to myself, indignantly. 'But she needn't think to play off such tricks upon me!'

"As I seated myself near the window, moody and reserved, I was conscious that her eyes were upon me, but I avoided meeting their earnest glances. I felt, in spite of my effort to throw her into the wrong, that her heart was yearning towards me. But such a consciousness did not soften me in the least. I was, in a degree, insane from the influence of the liquor I had taken—insane, as every man is, who indulges in strong drink—and saw all things through a false and perverted medium. O, it is dreadful how men will give up the pure, generous freedom of calm and rational thought for a gratification so low and sensual, and become slaves to evil thoughts and evil affections! As I glance through a period of some ten years, occupying the position that I now do, and seeing things in such clear light, I can scarcely believe that I am the same being that I was. I seem like a man who has been partially deranged for a long series of years, while his memory has remained active. What I once was, and what I now am, a man of kind feelings to all, I see to be my real character; but that dreadful period between, during which every good point in my nature was changed to an opposite, was the period of my insanity. O, sir, it is indeed dreadful to think of that wild and strange delusion! But to proceed:

"That moody silence, the silence as of the grave to Mary's gentlest affections, continued even while we sat at the tea-table. Once or twice she made a remark, but I did not reply. I was possessed of an evil spirit, and, conscious all the while of the wrong I had done, cherished a feeling of blame against her. After supper, I repaired again to the tavern, and drank to a state of partial intoxication. When I came home, about ten o'clock, Mary had gone to bed with her babe. I felt glad of this, for, but half conscious as I was, I was yet willing to avoid that distressed, appealing look, which had, in the evening, irritated instead of softening me. She seemed to be asleep as I entered the chamber, and perceiving this, I undressed myself very silently, and, half intoxicated as I was, had sense enough remaining to get quietly into bed. I was soon lost to consciousness in profound slumber.

"It was daylight when I awoke, and Mary lay by my side as hushed as a sleeping infant. But I felt that she was not asleep—her breathing was too still. O, how wretched I felt! How painfully conscious of the deep wrong I had done! I would have given worlds, it seemed, if I had possessed them, could the events of the previous day have been utterly obliterated from the memory of both Mary and myself. But this was impossible. The arrow had sped, and the wound been made, and, even if healed, a scar, I felt, would ever remain.

"From these painful feelings, my mind naturally turned to thoughts of reconciliation. And I pondered long over what I should do, and what I should say, to restore the light and smile to Mary's face. But alas! some evil spirit was near to suggest thoughts of pride. It seemed as if it would be too humiliating for me, a man, to make confession of wrong to a woman. The moment this idea was presented, I turned myself away from the half formed resolution to tell my fault openly, and thus relieve the heart upon which I had laid so heavy a burden.

"Then I got up and dressed myself, without uttering a word, and went down stairs. It was about half an hour after that Mary entered our little breakfast room where I was sitting. I lifted my eyes as she came in, and she looked me in the face with a calm, sad expression that touched my heart. Then the impulse came upon me strong, to spring to her side, and folding her in my arms, confess the wrong I had done her—for I loved her tenderly. But I seemed held back by a powerful hand; and then pride came with its mean suggestions. Few and brief were the words that passed between us at the morning meal. When I left the house for my shop, I proceeded, as was my custom, to a neighboring tavern, and drank a glass of brandy and water. Then I repaired to my business, still thinking of Mary, but less kindly. It occurred to me, during the morning, that she was only putting on a show of great distress of mind, merely to punish me. I felt irritated at the thought. Another glass of liquor confirmed more and more this impression, until I began, really, to believe it true.

"So much did this false idea irritate me that it was with difficulty that I could restrain myself from rebuking her angrily, at dinner time, and more especially in the evening. Gradually, however, this little breach, instead of widening by another opening rupture, grew less and less. But the unclouded sunshine of Mary's face never returned. Still, she was cheerful, and seemed to have forgotten the circumstance—but not cheerful as she once had been. No one can tell how deeply the change pained me at times; especially as, from the fact that she never afterwards expressed surprise or disappointment at any act or omission of mine, it was evident that an impression had been made that time could not efface.

"But she was ever even-tempered, mild, gentle, and affectionate. And though, through a long series of years, I neglected her, and debased myself, she never uttered a reproach, or neglected a duty. If I blamed her, or spoke in my drunken moments, unkind and cutting words, she did not reply. But I am going ahead of my story.

"From drinking two or three glasses a day, my appetite for liquor increased, and soon demanded double that number. Still, I thought not of danger, until I was carried home from the tavern, one night, in a state of drunken insensibility. When I awoke in the morning, I endeavored to recall the events of the proceeding evening, but could recollect nothing beyond my sitting and drinking in the tavern. One glance at the face of my wife confirmed the sudden thought that I had been drunk. How pale and distressed was the expression of that face, yet how full of anxious yearning affection, as she turned her eyes upon me!

"I asked her no questions, and she made no allusion to the condition I had been in. But I resolved to drink less.

"How feeble is such a resolution, when tempted by a single draught of liquor! Instead of six or eight glasses, I only drank four during that day; but on the next I drank nine, and when I came home at night, could just make out to find my way to bed. For two weeks from that evening I did not draw a sober breath! One night about the end of that period, I came home in a feverish state of mind. My nerves had become excited to a

37

high degree, from their long-continued, excessive stimulation; I felt wild, restless, and irritable. It was three years after our marriage, and our only child, a little girl, was about two years of age. She was not well, and, in consequence, was very fretful. Her crying annoyed me exceedingly.

"'Hush!' I said in an angry tone to her, a few minutes after I came in. But she cried on.

"'Ain't you going to hush?' I said, louder and more angrily. Still her crying did not cease. I now felt very much excited, and my whole body seemed to burn with anger against her.

"'If you don't hush this moment I will half kill you!' I exclaimed, advancing towards the little girl I loved so tenderly when sober, but against whom I now felt a bitter indignation. But little Mary did not hush. Then I caught her up madly by one arm, and commenced beating her with all my strength—the strength of a nervous man inspired by intoxication and anger, exercised on a delicate child but two years old! One blow, such as I gave her, were enough, it would seem, to have killed her. The poor child ceased crying on the instant; but I was in a rage and ceased not my blows until her mother, terrified at the scene, sprung forward, and snatched the little creature from my hand that held her high above the floor. To this I responded with a powerful blow on the side of my poor wife's head, and she fell senseless to the floor, and at the same moment, I kicked my child, who was clinging to her mother's garments, half across the room.

"For a moment after, I seemed in the centre of a whirling and confused mass—then I became suddenly sober, and as perfectly conscious and rational as ever I was in my life. O, the agony of that terrible moment! I shudder and grow sick at heart, even now, when I think of it. There lay both wife and child, pale and insensible, and for all I knew dead, before me; and my hand had done the deed! My wife and child that I loved so tenderly! My gentle, uncomplaining wife, and sweet innocent child!

"But I cannot dwell longer here; I must pass on, or I shall not be able to finish my narrative—(and the voice of the speaker trembled, and his tones were husky). From that hour, my wife never smiled; and my little one seemed to me to have a sad expression in her dear young face: and I doubt not that the appearance was real. These changes always irritated me when I had been indulging to any considerable extent in drinking, and caused me to speak many an angry word to both. O sir!—well may strong drink be called a *devil,* for when it has once entered into us, we are possessed as of an evil spirit. For about a week after I had struck that blow, I was a sober man; but my reflections, while sober, were too terrible, and at last, to drown these, I drank to intoxication.

"Under circumstances like these, my business could not, of course, long remain prosperous. It gradually became involved, and the consequent perplexity caused me to drink still deeper. Six years from the day that I was married, I was sold out by the sheriff, and with two children and my wife, turned out upon the world without a dollar in my pocket. This, instead of sobering, only caused me to drink the harder.

"From the master workman in a large business, I sunk to the condition of a journeyman; and from a commodious house, neatly furnished, my family retired to two small rooms, with but a few necessary household articles. I cannot tell you how this change really affected my poor wife, for I was too ill-natured to feel for and sympathize with her, and too much and too constantly bewildered by intoxication to be able to make any correct observations on her appearance. But that her sufferings must have been intense—beyond the power of human language to describe—may be inferred from the fact that in one year she sunk into her grave. Not from any sudden illness—not from that slow but sure destroyer consumption—but from the agonies of a wounded spirit, gradually wearing away the vital energies of her system. Ah! sir—How many a woman has sunk thus, into an early grave, during the last twenty years!

"When she was borne away from the comfortless tenement in which we lived, I was, would you believe it, sir, too drunk to attend her funeral! Three days after, I got one of our orphan asylums to take my two children—both girls, one six years of age, and the other four. I was then free to sink as low as I pleased, without the dread of encountering a pale, sad, suffering face, or meeting daily with two neglected children, to reprove me. I was freed, also, from the necessity of providing for them, and this left me a larger sum to spend for liquor, or rather relieved me from the necessity of working so many hours in the day. Gradually I sunk lower and lower, until I became really unfit to work at my trade, and then no one would employ me. This was two years after the death of my wife, and during this time, I had not once seen my children, nor did I care to see them. All natural affection seemed gone from my bosom. I loved only myself, and sought only the lowest sensual gratifications. How like a picture drawn by a sickly imagination does all this appear! It does not seem possible that a human being can become so utterly degraded. But alas! it is too true. Thousands of heartbroken wives, neglected children, and debased drunkards, covering by thousands the length and breadth of this land, attest the awful truth. I say awful—for it is awful to contemplate the wide-spread ruin of soul and body that has been caused among the people of this country by drunkenness.

"Unable to get work at my trade, I resorted to any expedient that presented itself to earn a penny with which to buy liquor; for liquor I would have. Sometimes I broke stone on the turnpikes near the city; sometimes I scraped the streets as a common scavenger. But I usually soon lost even such employment from drunkenness; I was too worthless for even that! Then I would seek little jobs about—such as piling wood, holding horses, or carrying home market baskets. As for lodgings— Howard's woods or some lumber yard sufficed during the summer months; and in winter, I was an almost nightly tenant of the watch-house. Thus I continued, sinking lower and lower, if it were possible to descend lower than the point I had reached, for three or four years.

"It was in the month of June last—on a warm, sultry evening, that I repaired, about nine o'clock, to Howard's woods, there to pass the night. Although the night was clear, there was no moon, and it was quite dark in the woods. I entered from the Falls Road, and pursued my way to the fence that encloses the garden of the old Howard mansion. I made out to climb over this, and then lay down just within it, and was soon sleeping as soundly as if I had been reposing on the softest bed.

"I suppose that I must have been sleeping about two hours, perhaps three, when I seemed to be suddenly awakened by some one laying a hand upon my shoulder, and calling my name aloud. Instantly, I was surrounded by a light, which appeared to emanate from three figures, all in white, that stood before me. One glance was sufficient to tell me who they were. I could not mistake the face of Mary, nor the forms of my two children. But how changed they were. Each was dressed in garments white and shining, and upon each face reposed a peaceful smile. Instantly, however, as their eyes rested upon me, when it seemed they became suddenly conscious of my presence, did that quiet, happy smile pass away, and a sad expression rested upon each lovely countenance. Then they fixed their eyes upon me reprovingly, and slowly faded from my sight. All around was now thick darkness.

"My next perception was that of the rain falling heavily upon my face, as I lay upon the ground. I was perfectly sobered—more so than I had been for years. For some moment, after rising to my feet, I mused upon the strange apparition I have mentioned, and the more I mused upon it, the more it troubled me. I could not, of course, lie again upon the wet ground. Nor could I find my way out of the wood. Suddenly, however, a broad flash of lightning blazed around, and in the instant that it lighted up the air, I saw the direction that it was necessary for me to take, in order to return to the city.

"The storm now began to rage violently. The rain fell in a heavy incessant shower; the lightning was frequent and flashed out with a fierce glare, running it seemed along the ground, now about my feet, and now circling some tree like a blazing serpent. How deep and solemn was the darkness that followed each flash—quickly succeeded by terrific peals of thunder that jarred the earth upon which I stood as if shook by an earthquake! And the war of the tempest in that old wood was loud and wild.

"As I groped my way along, guided by the frequent glare of the lightning, drenched with the rain, and shrinking at each tremendous crash that broke over my head, my heart sank within me, filled with an awful fear. At last I was clear of the woods, and turned my steps towards the city. As I reached Franklin Street, the storm began to subside, and, in the course of half and hour, the sky was cloudless, and the stars shone with a clearer brightness than before. I was standing at the corner of Howard and Lexington Streets, irresolute as to which way I should go, when the town clock rang out the hour of two. There were yet two hours before daylight, and I was wet to the skin, shivering with cold, yet raging with a most intolerable thirst for liquor. To abate, in some degree, the latter, I drank ladle-full after ladle-full of pure cold water from the pump near which I had paused. Then, laying down upon a neighboring cellar door, I tried again to sleep. But I was so chilled from the dampness of my clothes, and so much unnerved, that I sought in vain to sink into unconsciousness, until near day-dawn. Then my sleep was brief and troubled, and I was awakened from it by finding myself shaken by a firm hand. I had been awaked thus, a hundred times before, and had ever met rude and irritating language. For this I was again prepared, and rose up with an angry scowl upon my face. But the first words disarmed me.

"'What a dreadful life this must be for a man to lead!' the person who had aroused me said, in a kind sympathizing tone.

"This melted me right down. For years a kind word had never been spoken to me.

"'O, it is dreadful!' I replied, earnestly, looking up into his face.

"'Then, my friend, why do you lead such a life?' he asked, encouragingly.

"'I wish I could lead a different one, for there is no pleasure in this—' I replied in a desponding tone.

"'You may, if you will,' he said, and he spoke earnestly.

"But I shook my head, and answered—

"'No—no. My case is hopeless. I cannot resist the intense desire for liquor. I must have it.'

"'But you can resist it,' he said. 'I know many who were as much enslaved as you are, who are now sober men.'

"'That cannot be,' was my positive, half indignant reply, for I thought he was trifling with me. 'Who has heard of any one so far gone as I am, ever being reformed? No—no!—I shall fill a drunkard's grave'—and I shook my head in the bitterness of despair.

"'I have heard—I have seen very many who were as little likely to be reclaimed as you are, who are now sober, industrious men, with their families again around them, and again happy. This is a new era, my friend, a new power is at work; and what was once considered hopeless is now an every day occurrence. Hundreds of men, who have been in the constant habit of drinking, have renounced liquor altogether, and are now banded together for mutual assistance. Come! Will you not join in with them?'

"Thus the stranger urged me, and I listened as if in a dream. After he had ceased, I said eagerly, as I rose to my feet:

"'O sir, do not trifle with me! Is what you say, indeed, true? Can a drunken wretch, debased as I am, be reclaimed?'

"'He can, my friend!' was the emphatic answer. 'For ten years *I* was a drunkard. It is now six months since I tasted liquor, and I have no desire for it!'

"How strange all this sounded to me! And as he spoke, a new hope sprung up in my bosom. But this hope quickly faded, and I said in a sad tone:

"'Others may reform, but I cannot. If I were to quit drinking what could I do? I have no home, no friends, no clothes that are even decent—all men would continue to shun me as a loathsome wretch, who had lost all claims to human consideration.

"'Do you really wish to reform?' the stranger now asked me in a decided, serious voice.

"'I do most sincerely.'

"'Then you *can* reform. Come with me,' he added, taking hold my arm. 'Wherever there is a will, there is a way.'

"I followed him mechanically. We soon came to a small two-story house in a narrow street or alley, running down south from the Lexington market. Into this we entered, when I was taken up into one of the chambers. Here I was supplied with plenty of clean water, a clean, coarse shirt, and a pair of coarse linen pantaloons. As the latter were produced, the man said to me:

"'Are you willing to sign a pledge never again to drink any kind of intoxicating liquor? In a word—will you join the temperance society?'

"'Will it be of any use?' I asked.

"'Yes, if you wish to reform,' he replied.

"'Then I will join, and try my best,' I said.

"'Do so, and you are safe,' was the cheerful and encouraging answer.

"After I had washed myself, and put on the clean, dry clothes with which I had been furnished, I went down stairs. There I was invited to partake, with the family, of a warm, plentiful breakfast. The man had a wife and three children, and each seemed cheerful, and even happy. To me, they were all kindness and attention. After breakfast, I was invited to go up stairs and lie down, until my coat, which had been drenched with rain, could be dried. This offer I accepted, for, now that I had taken no liquor since the day before, I felt quite weak. I soon fell asleep, and was conscious of nothing further, until my unknown friend came up and asked me to take some dinner with the family. Now I was in a calmer and more rational frame of mind than I had been in for years, and as I descended with him, and met his cheerful family at the table, I thought of my own children, sheltered in a charitable institution, and of

my poor wife, long since laid in the peaceful grave. It was a bitter reflection.

"At the dinner table, the conversation turned upon the wonderful reformation that was going on among the drunkards—a reformation, the
most distant whisper of which had never, before that morning, reached
my ears. My unknown friend spoke of his own history, of how he had
been enslaved to the love of strong drink—how he had neglected his
business and abused his family—how he had despaired of ever becoming reformed; and how, at last, he had been sought out by some of the
Washingtonians, and persuaded to sign the total abstinence pledge. The
result of this pledge he pointed out in the changed and happy condition
of his family.

" 'I was found by a Washingtonian,' said he, 'sleeping one morning on
a cellar-door, as I found you; and I was persuaded by him to go and sign
the pledge. His kindness and evident concern moved me, and I resolved
that I would take his advice. And I did so. That night I went to one of
their meetings and signed the pledge. Since then, every thing has gone
well with me. And now, I get up early every morning, and look out for
the drunkards on the cellar-doors and in the market houses. I have already induced nineteen, whom I found thus, to sign the pledge; and if
you go with me to-night to the meeting, as you have promised, you will
make the twentieth.'

"I went, of course, and signed. After I had put my name down, I felt
a new power within me. I felt that I could keep the pledge. And I *have*
kept it, and mean to keep it as long as I live.

" 'You must go home with me to night,' said this kind individual,
touching me on the shoulder after the meeting was over, 'and to-morrow
we will see if we can get you something to do.'

"I accepted his kind offer, gladly, and slept, for the first time in three
years, on a comfortable bed. On the next day, sure enough, he went with
me to three or four places where my business was carried on, and at last
obtained work for me. From that time I have had as much as I can do,
and am now earning twelve dollars every week.

"Soon after I was reformed, I went to see my children. I had not
looked upon them for five long years. How changed they were! When
told that I was their father, they seemed scarcely to credit it, and evinced
no affection for me. This touched my heart. I staid but a few minutes the

44

first time, for the interview was too painful to me, and, I saw, too embarrassing to them, to admit of being prolonged.

"In a week I called again, and then the distance and reserve of my children were in some degree broken down. Another week passed, and I paid them another visit—a smile lit up each face as I entered. O sir, words cannot express my delight, as I saw that smile! It was a ray of sunshine to my heart. Thus I continued to visit them regularly, until I could not let a day pass without looking upon their faces, and listening to their sweet voices. And they even greeted my coming with expressions of gladness.

"I now made application to the directors of the institution to have my children restored to me, but was positively refused. I represented that I was reformed—that I was earning ten and twelve dollars a week, and had already money enough to buy the few articles of furniture that we should want. But they would not trust me with my children. How wretched I felt, as I turned away from those to whom my earnest petition had been addressed! But I determined never to rest until I could get my children. Every three or four weeks I renewed my petition, and every time the reluctance of the directors seemed in some degree to yield. Finally I prevailed, and this day, thank Heaven!—I received my children back again!"

Here the speaker's voice gave way, and he sat down and sobbed like a child.

There was a deep silence for nearly a minute after he had taken his seat, a silence of profound emotion. Every heart was moved, and almost every eye was wet.

•　　•　　•

[Omitted here are The Drunkard's Bible, *concerning a rumseller's conversion, and* The Man with the Poker, *a tale of delirium tremens.]*

•　　•　　•

AFTER TO-DAY; OR,
TREATING RESOLUTION

He was past the prime of life, and his whole appearance was that of a man with an original good constitution, broken down by dissipation. There was not that cheerful air about him, that had been exhibited by the last two speakers. When he spoke, there was something subdued and melancholy in his tone.

"I have never, before this moment," he began, "attempted to address an audience, and were it not that I feel constrained to do so, under the belief that what I have to say will be useful to some here, who may not yet have fully made up their minds to sign the pledge, I should most certainly hold my peace.

"Twenty years ago, Mr. President, three men sat drinking in the Theatre tavern, Holliday Street. For five or six years previous, they had met there, regularly, every evening, to drink, smoke, and talk politics. Of course, their love of liquor, from being thus regularly indulged, increased, until all three were usually two-thirds intoxicated every night. When I say two-thirds, I mean that near to perfect insensibility. One of these men, Mr. President, now addresses you. The other two are dead. But, I must not anticipate.

"On the night to which I allude, being somewhat at a loss for a subject, we commenced talking about our mutual capacity for imbibing liquor, and, finally, resolved to enter upon a regular contest.

"'What kind of liquor shall we drink?' asked one, whose name was Joseph—or Joe, as we familiarly called him.

"'I go in for pure brandy,' I replied—

"'No—gin,' responded the third, whose name was Henry.

"'Good old Irish whiskey is my favorite,' said Joe, 'and at good old Irish whiskey I can put you both under the table.'

"'I doubt it,' the other remarked. 'But I'm for a better test than either brandy, gin, or whiskey.'

"'What is that, Harry?' I asked.

"'Why, all these, one after the other, and ale, wine, and cider. That's the true test. First brandy, then wine, then whiskey, ale, gin, and cider, a glass every five minutes. What do you say to that?'

"'I would rather not,' I said—for I had once been drunk on brandy and ale together, and knew what it was.

"'I'm agreed,' Joe said—

"'Well, what do you say?' Harry asked of me. 'Not afraid, I hope? I thought you more of a man.'

"I was just drunk enough to do almost anything if told that I was afraid, and so I agreed to the proposition. We then retired into a small room, in the centre of which stood a table, and arranging ourselves around it, called for three glasses of brandy. These were at once turned off, to begin with. Five minutes were allowed to pass, and then each drank half a pint of wine—at the end of five minutes, more, a strong draught of whisky was taken, and so on until we had drank, besides these, ale, gin, and cider. This occupied just half an hour. By this time I began to feel a little light about the head. But I resolved not to be beaten, and so commenced and went through another course. By the time this was completed, the room seemed to be moving around; but brandy was again called for, and again the trial renewed. Four times did we drink, or at least, did I drink through this villainous series. The last thing I remember was the vain effort to get a glass of cider to my mouth in the fourth round. I do not know whether I succeeded or not. When next conscious, I was lying on a bed, at home, with a physician by my side. My feelings were awful. It seemed as if my head would burst with the rending pain that throbbed through my temples; and my whole body felt as if swollen and benumbed by the heat of a large fire before which I seemed to be roasting alive. As soon as my recollection returned fully I became dreadfully alarmed, for it seemed impossible that I could live after what I had done. But a good constitution carried me safely through.

"On the third day I was able to go out. The first man I met was my friend Joe. He looked pale and feeble.

" 'I am really glad to see you, George!' he said, grasping my hand. 'I was afraid, from what I have myself suffered, that it was a gone case with you and Harry. How is he? Have you heard from him?'

" 'No, I have not,' I replied.

" 'Suppose, then, we go around and see him?'

"I assented, and we called at his house. His wife, for he was married, met us at the door. She was the picture of woe. Her eyes were red with weeping, and her face was pale, and wore an expression of deep heart-aching distress.

" 'How is Mr. ——?' we asked, anxiously.

" 'Come in and see,' she said, and gave way for us to enter. We followed, as she led on and in a moment or two entered a chamber where our friend lay, without life or motion, upon a bed. His eyes were half

47

closed, and his face had a ghastly expression. As I paused, and bent over him, I placed my hand upon his forehead. Instantly I started back. That forehead was rigid and cold like marble.

"'Dead!' I exclaimed, striking my hands together, while my head reeled, and I became sick and faint.

"'Dead!' ejaculated Joe, staggering back, and sinking into a chair.

"Ah, sir! That was a terrible moment! When I had so far recovered my senses as to look about me again, I saw his poor wife seated by the bed-side, silent and tearless. One little girl, his eldest child, was sobbing in a corner of the room, and a little boy, not over two years of age, had crept to his mother's side, and crouching there, hid his face in her lap. As for her, the heart-stricken wife and mother, her grief seemed too deep for utterance. There was something cold and frozen in the expression of her eye and face—something that I could not comprehend—something that I do not like to think of even now.

"We lingered in the chamber of death but a short time, and then went away. In the afternoon, we returned, by agreement, to make such ar-rangements for the funeral as were required under the circumstances. We knew that Mrs. —— had no one to perform these sad offices for her, and therefore, poorly as we both were, and much as we desired to shun so painful a scene as that which the house of our dead companion pre-sented, we attended during that afternoon, and at the funeral, on the next day, to all the required arrangements.

"As the company that attended the remains of Mr. —— to the grave turned away from the little hillock of fresh earth that marked the place where he was laid, Joe and I lingered behind.

"'I really feel awful about this,' I said, as we still remained standing near the spot where we had laid our friend.

"'Not worse than I do, George.'

"'If you'll agree,' I said, 'we will pledge ourselves here over Harry's grave, never, after this day, to drink a drop of any kind of liquor. We can do without it Joe, for neither of us, I believe, has tasted anything stronger than tea or coffee since that night. It doesn't do us any good—and has done us great harm.'

"'Agreed,' was Joe's prompt response. And arm in arm we took our way, with slow steps, towards the city. Our temperance resolution dispelled, in some degree, the depression of our spirits, and by the time we came to the edge of town we were conversing quite cheerfully. As we were passing the Vauxhall Gardens, in Light Street, Joe paused, and said:

" 'Come, George, let's have a drink!'

" 'Didn't we promise each other not to take any more liquor after to-day?' I replied.

" 'True! so we did.'

"Then, after a pause, he added:

" 'But it's *to-day* yet. *After* to-day, we will not drink. So come along, *let us treat resolution!* This is sad business that we have been on, and a little spirits will cheer us up.'

"The sight of the tavern in which I had drank so often, the idea of the liquor, suddenly conjured up in my mind, wrought so powerfully upon me, that it seemed almost impossible to resist the strong desire I felt for another drink.

" 'You are right, I believe,' I said, after a single moment's hesitation. And then we went in and called for brandy and water.

"After drinking this, we sat down to look over the newspapers. I felt very comfortable, and quite happy in mind, as the pleasant excitement of the liquor began to pervade my whole body. Presently the appetite for another glass was felt, and I was just going to ask Joe to drink again, when he anticipated me, with—

" 'As this is our last day, George, we must make good use of it; so come, let us have another drink.'

"I was ready to join him, of course. A third, a fourth, and a fifth drink followed in quick succession. And then we began to feel quite merry, and could even allude to our dead companion in a light and trifling way—

" 'Harry thought to use us up, all to pieces,' Joe said, laughing. 'But he wasn't half a man. I could kill a dozen like him.'

"To this, I remember, I responded with a loud laugh. It seemed exceedingly smart. And then both of us jested, gaily, about our recent drinking duel, as we called it.

"It was after ten o'clock when we left the Vauxhall, and then we staggered off home, arm in arm.

49

"On the next morning I felt wretched, and blamed myself for having violated the spirit and meaning of the pledge I had taken over Harry's grave. But during the morning I met Joe.

"'Well, George,' he said, laying his hand familiarly upon my shoulder. 'Are you going to drink any more after to-day?'

"'No I am not,' I replied positively.

"'Then come, let us treat resolution, and have a glorious spree while to-day lasts.'

"'Joe! you are trifling in a serious matter!'

"'Not a bit. You ain't going to drink any more *after to-day*, neither am I; and surely we ought to have one good time before we bid our old friend brandy good-bye. So come along, George, for I'm awful dry.'

"And he caught me by the collar, and almost dragged me into a tavern near which we were standing. Once within the charmed precincts of a bar-room, all power of resistance was gone, and I drank eagerly and freely.

"I made no further effort to keep my twice broken pledge. Whenever Joe and I met, after that, the question usually was,

"'Well Joe!' or 'Well George, when are you going to reform?'

"'After to-day,' was, of course, the witty answer, and then came the response:

"'Well, come along, and let us treat resolution.'

"Since that time, until within a few weeks, Mr. President, I have been a regular drinker, becoming more and more enslaved every year to the debasing vice. But I will not detain this company by relating to them the particulars of an ill-spent, useless life; a life of wretchedness and painful degradation. I sunk very low, sir, and I suffered much more than tongue can tell.

"It was about five years ago that Joe entered the United States army, as a private soldier. He had become so worthless that no one would give him work, and to prevent starving, or going to the poor-house, he enlisted.

"From the day I parted with him at the fort, a few weeks after his enlistment, until six weeks ago, I neither saw nor heard of Joseph ———. I knew not whether he were living or dead.

"It is between one and two months since that, as I was staggering up McLellan's alley, one night after having filled myself with liquor at Mrs.

H——'s oyster house, I heard some one groan. I was near Fayette Street, and the sound came from the entrance of the narrow alley that runs in the rear of the Fountain stables. I paused to listen, and the groaning was repeated. There was something in the sound that half sobered me, and produced an involuntary desire to go back a few steps and see who was suffering in such a deserted spot, at such an hour. As I obeyed this impulse, I became still further sobered.

" 'Who's there?' I cried, as I paused at the entrance of the alley.

"My question was answered by a deep groan, almost at my feet. I started, and looking more narrowly around, saw a dark mass near where I stood. A closer observation revealed the figure of a man. To my repeated questions, the only answer I could get was groan after groan that seemed of mortal agony. I took hold of him, and attempted to lift him up. But he had only one leg! In endeavoring to support him on this, I grasped at his right arm, and found in my hand but a small protruding stump!

"I then laid him down gently, and went over to a house opposite, to get assistance. It happened to be the house of a temperance man.

" 'What do you want,' he asked, 'at this late hour?'

" 'I want help for a poor creature in the alley here, who is dying, I fear,' I replied.

" 'A drunkard, I suppose,' he said, as he reached for his hat.

" 'I should think so,' was my reply.

"He accompanied me at once, and we succeeded, in a few minutes, in getting the poor wretch into his house. He presented, indeed, a pitiable spectacle. He had but one arm and one leg; appeared to be drunk to unconsciousness; was sick, and perhaps dying. His face was shockingly distorted and disfigured by exposure and the effects of habitual drunkenness. Really I felt appalled as I looked at him, and thought that all this was rum's doings.

" 'What ails you?' asked the kind individual who had taken him in, as he laid him down before a good warm fire.

"But the drunkard murmured something incoherent.

" 'Are you sick?' he inquired.

" 'Yes,' was half articulated, showing that he was in some degree conscious.

" 'What ails you? what can we do for you?' continued the man.

"'Give me, ah—give me, ah—drink,' he replied, in a thick, muttering, drunken tone.

"A glass of water was held to his lips, as I raised him, myself scarcely able to stand from intoxication.

"'Ugh!' he ejaculated, as the water entered his mouth, starting back, and discharging what he had taken, with the strongest indications of disappointment and disgust.

"'Gin, whiskey, rum, anything!' he now said with an earnest, rapid articulation, endeavoring to support himself with his hand. 'Give me liquor or I shall die.'

"'I cannot give you liquor. But you shall have coffee, tea, anything you want, but liquor,' his stranger-friend replied, soothingly and kindly.

"'No—no—no! Give me liquor,' was the earnest response.

"'Liquor will do you no good, my friend,' he replied 'and therefore I cannot give it to you. You must stop drinking, or it will kill you.'

"'So I will stop, *after to-day!* Ha! ha! ha! Wasn't that a good joke!' And the poor wretch swung his single arm around his head in momentary excitement; but, alas! like the flashing up of the dying taper, it was the last feeble glimmer of life. He fell back, as his arm returned nerveless to his side, and, in a minute after, was a ghastly corpse.

"Once again, in many years, I was perfectly sober. And I stood, horror-stricken, by the side of the mutilated, disfigured, and lifeless body of my old friend Joe ——. But the sight was too painful, and I turned away and left the house, sick at heart. I still had a home left; thanks to a neglected, abused, and sorrow-stricken creature, who clung, despite the remonstrances, advice, and anger of her friends, to the debased, unfeeling wretch she still called by the name of husband. But for her tender care, her unswerving affection, I should long ago have been dead. To my house I returned, my poor, comfortless home, and entered, just as the clock struck twelve. I found my patient wife still sitting up, and sewing by the light of a small dimly burning lamp. As I entered, she lifted her pale, thin face, and looked into my own with something so sad, so tender, so heart-touching in its expression, that I was affected almost to tears. How many and many a time, no doubt, has she looked at me thus, and I too drunk to perceive or feel its import.

"'Sarah,' I said, walking steadily towards her, for I was never more perfectly sober in my life: 'Sarah, I've quit drinking; from this moment I will never touch liquor again!'

"O sir, if you could have seen that poor creature, as I did, start to her feet, and stand looking at me, for a moment or two, her face agitated with doubt and hope, fear and joy, you would have been moved to tears! But she saw that I was in earnest; she felt that I was in earnest; and springing to my side, she laid her head upon my shoulder, as I drew my arm tightly around her, and wept and sobbed passionately. But her tears were tears of joy and hope.

"On the next day, I signed the pledge; and though still a sad, yet I trust that I am a better and wiser man. As for my home, there has been sunlight there ever since. O, sir! This pledge":

But the man's voice trembled—tears sprung to his eyes—and, overcome by emotion, he was forced to take his seat.

SIGNING THE PLEDGE

The time had gone on until nearly ten o'clock, and, as the last speaker took his seat, Mr. Mitchell, the President, rose, and in a brief but pertinent address, invited and urged those who had not yet done so to come forward and sign the pledge. The Secretary was then directed to read the pledge, which was done. After this followed a scene hard to be described.

"Come along," cried the President, as the Secretary resumed his seat. "Who will sign first to-night? Ah! there he comes! The very man for whom I have been waiting these two months. That's right, friend L——. I thought we should get hold of the same end of the rope again. Many a drinking frolic and fishing frolic have we been on, together! And now we strike hands again"; grasping the hand of the individual he was addressing, who had, by this time, reached the secretary's table— "and shoulder to shoulder, hand to hand, and heart to heart, will we wage together a war of extermination against old KING ALCOHOL and all his emissaries!"

The man who had gone forward was one well known in the community. He was an old drinker, and, although he had, from a strong resolution, been able thus far to keep from sinking into a low and abandoned

state, yet his example and encouragement had been exceedingly pernicious, and very many who had commenced drinking with him had already become sots. For a time, he had sneered at the temperance movement. But he had now yielded to its imposing claims.

"You never did a better deed than that in your life, friend L——!" the
President said in a lively, exulting tone, as the man rose from the secretary's table. "And now who will come next?"

"Come along!" I heard a man say, in an under tone, near me, and I
turned to observe him. He had a miserable looking creature—bloated,
disfigured, ragged, and filthy—by the arm, and was endeavoring to urge
him to go up and sign. But the drunkard hesitated and held back.

"Come! Come! Go up, now! You will never repent it!" urged the temperance man.

"I don't think it's any use," the poor creature said. "I'm sure I can't
keep it."

"O yes you can! I know you can! There's old B——, who drank harder
than you ever did. He signed last night."

"He did?" in tones of surprise.

"Certainly he did! And so did Mr. ——, who hadn't drawn a sober
breath in fifteen years."

"But they can't keep it, I know they can't."

"You don't know any such thing! I know that they can keep it, and
will keep it. And there's Mr. F——, there, you know what a sot he was?
He signed two months ago. Look at him now. He's well dressed, looks
cheerful, and hasn't a carbuncle on his nose, that used to be as rough as
the Liberty Road, and as red as scarlet. Now do come along and sign
to-night!"

"If I thought!——"

"Don't think any thing about it. Go right up and sign, and you are
safe."

And as he said this, he gave the drunkard's arm a slight pull, and he
yielded, and suffered himself to be led up to the secretary's table, where
he sat down and signed.

"Now don't you feel better?" asked his persevering friend, as the two
returned to their seats near me.

"Yes, I do—a great deal better."

"Of course; and you are not sorry that you have signed, I know."

"O no. I'm glad now. And I feel that I can keep it."

The smile that lit up his disfigured face, and the air of confidence that he assumed, were indeed pleasant to look upon.

"Ten names already!" the President now cried out, loud and cheerfully, "and the table crowded. Come along! we have room for hundreds and thousands; we'll stay here all night if you'll keep coming."

For about a quarter of an hour the table was crowded with men of all conditions in life, and of all grades of drunkenness; from the moderate drinker of two and three glasses a day, to the wretched inebriate whose intolerable thirst forty or fifty "drinks" a day could not satiate.

"Sixty names!" said the President, as the space in front of the secretary's table became once more vacant. "We must have more than that number to-night. Yes, come along my friend!" he continued, his voice changing, to one of encouragement and sympathy, as he looked steadily towards the door. "Come along my friend, and we will do thee good!"

I glanced, as did many others, in the direction his eye indicated, and there, just within the door, stood a man, who seemed half intoxicated. A woman, evidently his wife, was holding on to his arm, and apparently urging him to go forward and sign the pledge. Still he hesitated, and she urged with an earnestness that seemed all unconscious of the presence of a crowd. There was an immediate, profound silence throughout the room.

"Do go, John!" I could now hear the woman urging. "Do go! and we shall be so happy!"

"Yes, John, come along!" the President said, taking up the earnest persuasion of his wife, "and we shall all be so happy. Come along, my good man!"

The poor wife, thus suddenly conscious that all eyes were upon her, seemed painfully confused, and shrunk into the shadow of the entrance to the room. Her husband felt the general impulse, and started forward towards the secretary's table. All was again hushed into profound silence. As he took the pen into his hand, and commenced writing his name, a sudden burst of weeping, half suppressed, was heard, distinctly, at the door. I am sure that there was not a dry eye in the house. My own were running over with blinding tears. But they were tears of joy. Who can tell—who can imagine—the gladness of that poor wife's heart? After the man had signed, he returned to the door, and went out.

"O John, how happy I feel!" I could hear the wife say; then both disappeared together.

"I can't stand that!" a man muttered in a low but earnest voice, near me, rising to his feet as he spoke. "I must make my poor wife happy, too."

And he walked resolutely up to the table and signed.

"Come along, we are waiting!" again urged the President. "Don't put it off a single day. Come along, and make your wives happy, as John did just now. None of you like to see their faces clouded, and yet how can sunshine rest there while you are neglecting and abusing them? Come along! Why, eighty signed at the last meeting, and here we have only sixty-two. Surely we haven't got all the drunkards yet! O no. I see three or four down there that ought to sign. So come along my boys! If you want excitement, come and get a little of this teetotal excitement. It makes one feel a thousand times better than rum-excitement, and produces no after consequences but good ones. Ah! there comes another!—and another!—and another! That's the way. One helps another. You don't know how much good you may do by coming forward. You influence one, and he another, and he another, and they others, until from the impulse given by a single individual, hundreds are brought in. There were only six at first, and now we have hundreds upon hundreds. Suppose these six had held back, where would we all have been? Come along then, and do your duty to yourselves and society."

To this about ten more responded.

The last but one who signed was, like many who had inscribed their names before him, poorly clad, and miserable in appearance. He came up reluctantly, urged and argued with at almost every step of the way by a person who seemed to take a deep interest in him.

"You must sign, Thomas! I shall never give you a moment's rest until you sign," I heard him say to the reluctant drunkard, who paused near where I was sitting, "I have helped to ruin you, and I shall have no peace until you are reclaimed."

"Let me have another week to think about it, Mr. W——."

"Another week, Thomas! Surely your poor wife and children have suffered enough already! Think of them and be a man."

This had the effect to cause the drunkard to move onward. But he paused again and again. At last, however, the table was reached, the pen placed in his hand, and his name inscribed.

How light was his step! How cheerful and resolute his air as he came down the aisle! I could hardly realize that it was the same individual.

"Ain't you glad that you have done it, Thomas?" his friend said, as they passed me.

"Indeed I am! But it was a hard struggle. I wanted to do it, and yet it was not easy to give up the liquor. But it's done now, and I am glad enough!"

"Any more?" the President asked.

"Yes, one more at least," said a man near the door, rising to his feet. "You've just got my last customer, and now you might as well have me. I've sold liquor for fifteen years. But you temperance folks have broken me up. And now I am forced to try some better and honester means of getting a living."

And so saying, he walked resolutely up to the table, and signed the pledge.

"And now, friend P——," the President said to him, "what are you going to do with the liquid fire you have on hand?"

"What am I going to do with it?" in a tone of surprise.

"Yes, what are you going to do with it?"

"As to that," the man replied, "I never gave the subject a thought."

"You won't sell it, I hope?"

"And why not?"

"Sell poison!"

"What shall I do? Give it away?"

"O no. That would be as bad."

"Well, sir, what would you do, if you were in my place?"

"Why I would throw every drop of it in the gutter. It will hurt no one there. You needn't be afraid of the hogs getting drunk, for a hog won't touch it."

"My liquors cost a good deal."

"No doubt of it. How much do you think?"

"Two hundred dollars, I should suppose."

"No more?"

"I think not."

"There must be some mistake in your calculation," the President said. "You have forgotten the sighs and tears of abused and neglected wives and children. The money that bought your liquor cost all these, and more."

The man paused a moment, and then said, emphatically:

"I'll do it! I've made enough men drunk in my time!"

And thus saying, he turned away and mingled with the crowd.

The books were then closed, seventy-five having signed the pledge that night. A few remarks were added by the President, and then the meeting broke up, and I returned home.

"How many a heart has been made glad to-night!" I said as I threw myself upon my bed, and lay, for hours, musing over the wonderful things I had seen, before my senses were locked in slumber.

2

from *A Long Voyage in a Leaky Ship* (1842)

James Gale, a self-described "plain, unlettered man," was born in Templeton, Massachusetts, on 21 May 1795. He later moved to upstate New York and then returned to eastern Massachusetts. A butcher by trade, Gale also worked on farms. His erratic employment shows the increasing emphasis, under the influence of the temperance movement, on sobriety among laborers who had previously been encouraged to drink and had often been supplied with spirits on the job.

A Long Voyage recounts Gale's downward spiral into inebriety. At one point he attempts to steady his lurching craft by switching from rum, the common drink of the working class, to cider and beer, perceived to be more refined and less harmful, and therefore not subject to the temperance pledge in its loose construction. (Even Benjamin Rush, in his temperance thermometer, had associated beer, wine, and cider with "cheerfulness, strength, and nourishment, if taken in small quantities, and at meal.") That Gale's experiment fails—he gets just as drunk on cider as on rum—argues implicitly for the stricter pledge of total abstinence.

The following selection depicts the nadir of Gale's drinking, when alcoholic despair led him to attempt suicide, and his subsequent salvation, probably in 1841, by the Washington Total Abstinence Society of Brighton (Massachusetts), to whom the book was dedicated. Gale's self-destructive urges seem to come over him so suddenly that the reader may wonder if some clarifying details have been omitted. But, in fact, there *is* no motivation given other than the drinking itself. Gale's matter-of-fact treatment suggests that within the depressive logic of inebriety, shooting or hanging oneself requires no explanation.

In the Conclusion to his temperance narrative (not reprinted here), Gale blesses the Washingtonians even as he remonstrates with "moderate" drinkers and with purveyors of "the destructive poison": "Give up your dreadful trade, and instead of rendering your fellows wretched, strive to make them comfortable and happy. I would I had the power to strike some chord that should vibrate through your hearts. But I am a plain man, and can use only simple expostulation. O! let the voice of one who has long suffered under the cursed influences of rum reach your hearts. Listen to the voice of entreaty, and, if compassion have a place within your breasts, O! be induced to renounce your traffic in your brother's bane." Such moral suasion of drunkard-makers as well as drunkards exemplifies the original Washingtonian stress on individual reform rather than political agitation.

CHAPTER X

Still deeper into woe,
The hapless victim sinks. Sorrow,
Disease, and death are thick around,
And deep remorse within.

*I*t would seem that there must be a bottom somewhere and that after an individual has fallen to a certain depth he would find it impossible to fall lower. But this is far from being the case with the hapless victim of rum. He falls, and falls, and unless snatched by some potent and mighty power, he will continue to fall till he sinks into eternal night. The lower he sinks, the fewer obstacles to his fall he encounters, until the way becomes perfectly easy, and his utter fall almost necessary and absolutely certain.

So it was with myself. I found there was no stopping place where I might rest, but at each stage in the descent, the way became easier, and each successive obstacle gave me less trouble than the preceding. My prospects were becoming more and more dark, and all hopes of their brightening again were becoming farther removed. My health, moreover, was fast failing, tho' I continued to work, whenever I could get anything to do. Sometimes a little hope would rise, but it would soon be extinguished, and all be dark again.

In the fall I worked considerably for Mr. Brackett, killing cattle, for so much a head, in company with another man who was as fond of drink as myself. Mr. B. used every means to induce us to leave our cups, but in vain. He bore with us until we had finished killing for barreling, and then we were discharged. I managed to get along until spring when I commenced stone work again. I did some small jobs through the first of the season, and the mean while kept myself pretty steady. I then undertook considerable work for the Messrs. Winships, which occupied me upwards of two months. I hired help all the season, and did considerable work.

In the fall I found I had some money left after paying all my help, and still continued work thro' the winter, mostly at butchering, both in Brighton and other places. I continued to drink freely, but seldom got drunk, and my poor wife really began to think I might yet reform. But it would seem that I was a great way from it, at this time at least, since I could hardly get along unless I drank a quart a day, but with that I made out tolerably well, working steadily, and being able to provide for the maintenance of my family.

Soon after this, however, I was taken sick with the pleurisy fever, which I think was entirely owing to my long continued habits of intemperance, which were fast increasing upon me, and seemed to threaten ere long my final destruction. I was confined for over a month, and my sickness was pretty severe, which the reader may well believe kept me pretty nigh sober for a month at least. When I got able to work again, the momentary restraint was speedily thrown off, and "old King Alcohol" and myself met again, like old and hearty friends, who have long been separated by distance.

We shook hands right heartily, and if we had lost any friendship by separation, it was all made up, and we were soon as well acquainted as ever. To me, fatal acquaintance! Alas what evil has it brought upon me, into what difficulties thrown me, and how fatally deceived me! "Evil communications corrupt good manners," is an old saying and a true one. And so I believe it has always proved with an acquaintance with the destroyer rum. No one is benefited by it, thousands have been destroyed, every one who has ventured upon it, has been corrupted and depraved.

I soon went to work where my feet were wet nearly all the time, and, the weather being very cold, notwithstanding all the warming assistance I could get from my old friend, the bottle, I nevertheless found this a very uncomfortable situation. I took a severe cold, and the rheumatism, or something else, set in with dreadful force, and I found myself confined to the house for six weeks, being able scarcely to stir. I have never wholly recovered from it, perhaps never shall. I receive it greatly as a reward for my friendship for the fiend, as I do also various other bodily troubles, sicknesses of various kinds, pains in my flesh and limbs, and last of all delirium tremens. They are all the work of rum, the gifts of long-continued, hard-followed intemperance.

In the spring of 1835 I began to work again on small jobs, as I could get them; but my work was very scarce, as but few people were desirous of employing me if other help could be had. Nor for this had I any one to blame but myself. I had unfitted myself for work, and was really unable to do a day's work in a day. So much for the assistance of my friend, Alcohol. I became exceedingly down-hearted, and but for the kindness of my wife and daughter, I know not what I should have done. They endeavored to sustain my sinking spirits, and though undeserving of their sympathy or kindness, I really found it, at this period, of very important benefit.

I now began to think of getting employment elsewhere, as I could get so little in Brighton, and accordingly started off for some of the neighboring towns, that I might obtain amongst strangers, what I could not where I was known. But I found that it was not my name that people were opposed to, for even amongst those who did not know that, I fared but little better than amongst those who did know it. It was my sign at which they looked, and this I always carried in my face, and at this time, I doubt not, it was a sight so dreadful that every one must have been effectually frightened from ever having any thing to do with me. "Drunkard!" was written on my face, and who would employ a drunkard?

I returned home thoroughly dejected, but resolving to reform. I did so partially, but not entirely, and still cherished as warm an attachment as ever for the fiend. A return to my old habits, therefore, I found exceedingly easy, and with that return I had a severe attack of the rheumatism, which laid me by for some time. By fall, however, I had so far recovered as to be able to work at butchering, which enabled me to get through the winter in a tolerably comfortable manner.

In 1836, I became somewhat more steady, and continued so through the year, although I still drank, and sometimes to excess. I did several jobs in company with a man named Powers, and might have done very well, had it not been for rum. As it was, however, I made out to get through the summer very well, and through the fall and winter I was engaged in butchering, which enabled me fairly to keep my head above water. The spring following, I did considerable work for Mr. David Cooledge, of Brookline, at building wall. I was engaged for him about three months, and might have worked longer, had I not loved the bottle so well. I then worked for Mr. N. A. Griggs a while, building wall, and doing other work.

My practice of drinking at this time brought on another attack of the rheumatism, which disabled me for work for a long time. Here was more of the reward of the friendship of the fiend, and as I obstinately refused to harken to the advice of those true friends, who were desirous to induce me to leave off drinking, I was under the necessity of suffering the rewards of my folly. Had I listened to the voice of friendship, instead of the voice of the fiend, how much evil, and pain, and sorrow should I have been saved! But as though under the influence of some invincible charm, I closed my ears to the kind voice of love, shut my eyes upon the dangers of my situation, and blindly rushed forward apparently to destruction.

I continued thus through the fall and winter, doing but little work, and getting along as I could with the assistance of my wife and daughter. Their kindness has at times affected me exceedingly, and then I would resolve to do better, to quiet the voice of conscience which at such times would be awakened within me. But such repentance was generally short-lived, and my resolves were seldom persevered in. In 1838, my course was still downwards. I did but little work, for I could now get less than ever to do. My health and spirits too were fast failing me, and I began sometimes to feel that it was all over with me. Without a friend in the wide world, as I sometimes felt myself to be, and but few even who would employ me in any work, my spirits sunk so low that I sometimes even meditated the taking of my life.

This I once attempted, though not while in a moment of insanity caused by rum alone. The circumstances were something like the following: I had been at work in the field without my hat, the weather being warm, and the heat of the sun in the middle of the day excessive. I had drank but very little spirit through the forenoon. There was another man in company with me, and at twelve o'clock, he left the field. I did not see him leave, and when after a while I looked around, I found my-self about a mile in a contrary direction from my house, which was about a quarter of a mile from the field.

I was somewhat alarmed, and hastened home as fast as I could. When I arrived at home I attempted to take my life with a pistol, which I had previously loaded. It was snatched from my hands by a friend, and not long afterwards when I again attempted to take my life by hanging, I was prevented by my daughter. This, as I have said, was not purely the effects of rum; but then rum was in it, and lay at the bottom of it all. It had nearly destroyed my mind, as well as my body, and was fast sinking me in the dark abyss of woe. My moral feelings had become weakened and almost extinct under the palsying influence of intemperance, and the little power that my mind ever possessed was now nearly annihilated and utterly destroyed.

I imagined to myself enemies, where I doubtless never had any, and after all was my own, I had almost said, my only, enemy. Had I been a true friend to myself, I never should have allowed my worst foes—the foes to my reason, my prosperity, and my health—to have obtained such complete triumph and victory over me. It was my enmity to myself which caused me to make friendship with that which was really my en-emy, and instead of endeavoring to defend myself against his insidious shafts, to surrender myself entirely to his control and direction. And greater evidence of insanity is not needed.

But I must hasten this mournful part of my history to a close. My friends now endeavored to keep the poison from me, but it was like an endeavor to separate long and sworn friends. It was almost a hopeless case. If I could not get the poison myself, I had friends, as I supposed them, who would get it for me. And this they no doubt supposed they did purely from kindness, but, alas, how mistaken were they, and how dreadful was the result. Instead of friendship, it was the opposite, and what they thought was love, was hate. It was the fiend, who had "put the garb of friendship on," in order to make more sure the victory which he must have supposed was already complete.

I was now bloated in a shocking degree, and afflicted with sores of the most painful and loathsome kind. In the fall I drank less, and acted bet-ter than I had for some time previous, got employment in a slaughter-house, and made some money, which enabled me to get through the winter very well. In the spring, the temptation was strong upon me to indulge myself more in drink, yet I knew that my employment must fail in that case, and now [that] I had a prospect of considerable work, I was enabled for a while to resist, and found considerable to do. But the task was too severe—the monster had too strong [a] hold upon me.

Again I returned to my cups with more eagerness, if possible, than ever, and spent nearly all the money I could get in drinking and gambling. I was now almost reduced to my very last penny, when, as fortune would have it, I made what the gamblers call "a rise" of some little amount, a good portion of which I laid out for provision for my family, which enabled us to get through the winter very well. In the spring of 1840 I began to think of going out of town to get work, as I could get but little at home, and consequently set out. In Newton I found some work, which employed me for a while, as well as an individual whom I hired to assist me. When I had finished it, I returned to Brighton, and engaged for some time in haying, &c., and then went back to Newton, and engaged in stone work again.

Through the summer, while engaged in haying, I drank pretty freely, which induced fits, greatly to the injury of my nerves, and what little of health and strength I had remaining. I, however, became more *sober* before I began to work in Newton, and was enabled to complete my jobs there to the apparent satisfaction of my employers, at the time agreed upon, received my pay, paid off my help, and then had some change remaining. But it did not last me long, as I eagerly renewed my acquaintance with the bottle, which I had never broken off entirely, and for this acquaintance I have always found that I had to pay, as Franklin did for his whistle—"too dear."

CHAPTER XI

> The clouds grew darker, and the storm
> Seemed nigh; but sudden thro' the gloom
> There shone the sun of peace. The clouds
> Dispersed, and all was joy again.

My money being well nigh gone, I made out to find some employment in the slaughter-house of Mr. Hudson, though not for any length of time, and I soon found myself entirely destitute of work. Now and then

I would be able to get a small job, but the money I received for it was barely sufficient to furnish me with "grog," for which it was soon spent. My family, however, were not in a suffering condition, as we had plenty of "pork and potatoes," as well as of wood; so we got through the winter tolerably well, so far as "living" was concerned.

But alas for the peace of my family—the happiness and comfort of my wife! What comfort can the family of a drunkard enjoy? Their protector, he who is bound by the most solemn obligations to love and cherish them, is sacrificing at the shrine of the demon Intemperance! His affections are all engrossed by one darling object—his much loved bottle. For aught he would seem to care, his family might suffer—nay, often does suffer, for want of the necessaries of life. But even if this is not the case, what can atone for the deep anxiety, and long-continued watchings, of a loving yet abused wife? But the reflection is too cutting, too severe.

In the spring I was again attacked severely with the rheumatism, which caused me much suffering, and for a long time disabled me for work. But I got over it so as to be able to do some little jobs, laying stone, &c., for various individuals, which kept me pretty busy until the first of June. I then had an offer of employment made me, on condition that I should drink nothing stronger than beer or cider, but as much of those as I pleased. The offer, as I thought, was an advantageous one, and I resolved to accept it. Accordingly I resolved to leave my rum bottle for three months, or, as one writer has expressed it, "to give up the old devil for his children."

In making this arrangement, it was doubtless supposed that my love for rum would be weakened, and that these "harmless drinks" would do me no evil, or at least far less evil than rum. But I have found that this is a poor way to destroy one's love for drink, indeed that it is an entirely mistaken course. Nor can I believe that a pond was ever filled by closing up one outlet and opening several others.

I found moreover that this was a much more expensive course than the one I had formerly pursued. The cider and beer cost me a great deal more than the "New England" I had been drinking, and more than I could well afford. Indeed I could *afford* nothing. My old drink made me poor, but these made me a great deal poorer. Besides their effects were much more injurious and evil for the time, I perhaps may say, more serious in their final consequences. I was not able to work more than half my time, far less than I could have done under the influence of rum.

I kept my pledge, however, the three months, and right glad was I when the time was out. I returned to my old bottle again with a keener relish and a sharper appetite. But I had not yet quite done with the cider and beer; for when the rum met them, seeming to consider them intruders, who had no right or title to its place, it raised such a "hullabaloo" at my expense that my now frail carcass was nigh to being torn in pieces. My body was convulsed throughout, and my limbs refused to do their office. So much for the expediency of the cider and beer plan.

I was at this time, I suppose, a complete sot. My credit was utterly gone, my health was fast going; my prospects were dark as night, and my name became a hissing and a reproach with all. I was shunned by the virtuous and sober, despised by the toper who was not quite as bad as I. The very boys would scoff at me, and every one turned from me in sorrow or disgust. I was now *certain* that I was a confirmed drunkard, and every body supposed it was "a gone case" with "old Jim Gale." And so indeed it was but for the interposition of that power which "causeth light to shine out of darkness."

It is said "the darkest hour is just before the day"; and so it has seemed to me, it was with me at this time. Sunk to the lowest degradation which it would seem was possible this side of the grave, utterly destroyed, as it were, in body and mind, I stood on the brink of destruction. The crazy bark, in which I had so long sailed, had long been approaching the fearful shore, and now she seemed in the midst of the breakers. Another wave and the fearful surge must swallow me forever. Oh how my very brain reels, as I think of that fearful crisis. Yet just as the last wave comes rolling on, I am snatched from my dangerous position, as it were by an Unseen Power—and *I am safe!*

Yes, just at this fearful crisis, the Washingtonian ship appears in sight, and perceiving my dangerous position, comes to my rescue. I was induced to sign the pledge of

> Perpetual hate
> To all that can intoxicate.

The old and leaky ship in which I had sailed so long was now abandoned, and I was received on board the new, the true cold water ship.

How glorious my deliverance! How astonishing the change! He who but a short time before was given up for lost, the scoff and the derision of all the thoughtless and unfeeling—he, whose very friends had almost abandoned, and given up as hopeless—old Jim Gale become a temperance man! Methinks I can now see the astonishment which works in the countenance of all who have ever known me, on first hearing such intelligence.

But notwithstanding the marvellousness, the supposed impossibility of the thing, such is really the case. I have renounced entirely and forever the accursed bowl. I have broken forever all friendship with the fiend. Never again will I listen to the destroyer of my peace, my prosperity, my happiness, and my health. "Taste not, touch not, handle not" is now my motto, and with God's help will I follow it while life shall last.

As the reader may well suppose, my friends were exceedingly rejoiced at this unexpected step which I had taken, and already seemed to look upon me as one risen from the dead. But my wife and family—how shall I be able to describe their ecstacy, their joy, their really inexpressible delight? I cannot, will not do it; it exceeds my power of language. If any can imagine the feelings of one who has long mourned over the utter ruin of the one she loves, whose peace has been destroyed, and her entire life embittered by the desolation of all her hopes—if any one, I say, can imagine the feelings of such a one, when she sees her loved one restored to her embrace, her peace again brought back, and her hopes again revived, he may then know in some measure how to sympathize with the joy of my wife and family.

My appearance and health are of course much improved since my reform, though I still suffer the rewards of the fiend. That friendship I have broken forever, but its consequences follow me still. How long they may I know not, or whether I shall ever entirely regain my health; but this I am certain of, that fatal friendship shall *never* be renewed.

3

[ISAAC F. SHEPARD]

Confessions of a
Female Inebriate (1842)

As mentioned in the Introduction, the Washington Temperance Society gradually incorporated the conception of inebriety as a problem exclusive to men and, perhaps, to women of dubious class and virtue. In this context, it is understandable that *Confessions of a Female Inebriate* is the only temperance narrative to focus on a woman and the only one presented as the work of "a lady"—although it was most likely a novel written by Isaac F. Shepard, to whom the copyright was issued. (In an advertisement appended to the novel, the publisher, William Henshaw, listed a dozen other temperance titles, including Shepard's *Village Pencillings* and *Cold Water Army Tales, No. 1—The Dead Child* by "the author of 'Confessions of a Female Inebriate.'")

In studying a woman drunkard, the author inverts the plot of *The Price of a Glass of Brandy*, a novel by "a Lady of Baltimore," which had appeared in 1841 with a fulsome dedication to William K. Mitchell, cofounder and first president of the Washington Society. The "authoress" of this earlier novel had expounded the consequences of a husband's drunkenness for his wife, driven to misery, penury, and death.

The narrator of *Confessions* is acutely aware of the double standard in regard to alcohol: "She may be forsaken, abused, trampled on, but amid all, the thought of separation does not enter her heart; if the whole world scorn and forsake him, it is the reason why she clings more closely to the wreck, but let the wife be scorned and forsaken of the world, and the husband will not bide the disgrace." The "lady," whose unseemly fraternization with the servants betrays her loss of caste, seems to accept the relatively harsher judgment upon her because of her failure as a mother and wife: as if unsexed by drink. She blames herself for the neglect and death of her first-born child and the exile of her husband, whose ruthless pride demands that he abandon her and their surviving child to their own devices.

INTRODUCTION

*I*t is the common impression that intemperance among females is confined to the very lowest class in society. We wish it were so; but we do know that the fiend dares sometimes set his cloven foot in the lady's carpeted parlor. Wealth has forged no locks to exclude him; but she has woven a broad mantle to cover the disgrace. We believe the following tale exposes the secret cause of the evil, and when this is pointed out, no one can mistake the remedy.

April 15th, 1842.

CONFESSIONS OF A FEMALE INEBRIATE

Earth has had but one paradise; but to my happy, youthful eye, the little village of S—— seemed a counterpart to the Eden of old. To the stranger, there was probably nothing uncommon in the immense old maples and elms that shaded the dwellings, or in the old church with its misshapen belfry, or in the little river that ran along so quietly, unmindful of the cares and anxieties of those who lived and died on its green banks. There was one beautiful dwelling on the hill fronting the church, that attracted the traveller's eye by the singular beauty of its shrubbery and its profusion of elegant flowers. In that house my father lived; there was I born, and there I passed the gayest, though not the happiest, part of my life.

At nineteen I was married. Charles L—— resided in one of the pleasantest cities of New England, about thirty miles distant from my native village. He was the junior partner in a firm of great respectability, the senior member of which had taken up a permanent residence in London, for the transaction of foreign business, while the other two conducted the home department.

Our establishment met all my ideas of taste and gentility, and my husband had every affection of my heart. I loved and prized the bounties of God's providence; but few and short were the moments of gratitude to the Giver. My character peculiarly needed the discipline of adversity; I never knew but one human being who had so much pride as myself, and that was my husband. My pride needed to be humbled, but, "O Lucifer, son of the morning," how was it humbled! Several happy, prosperous years passed by. I loved the world and the things of the world, but I loved my husband better, and possibly my two children better still. But there is no sunshine of earthly happiness without its shadow; no summer sea so gentle but the spirit of the storm may lurk beneath the billow. My health failed, and for four weary months, I was the inmate of a darkened chamber. The distant hum of the city, as it reached my ear through the open casement, seemed like a very mockery; but at length I was partially released from my prison-house, though health did not return, and the succeeding winter we passed under the sunny skies of Florida.

Immediately on our return home, the following summer, my husband called in a physician of much skill and celebrity, and requested his opinion of my case. After a minute examination, he gave it as his opinion that I had no disease whatever, but was suffering, under great debility, the effect of previous disease, and that much exercise, together with the use of some fine old wine, would restore me. Mr. L. was greatly elated, and my own spirits rose much more than I would willingly have confessed. During the long period that I had been an invalid, I had, most of the time, been exceedingly depressed. I had laid the foundation of all my hopes and happiness on the earth; I had yet to learn the wisdom of laying it above the region of darkness and decay.

Reader, do you think I linger long from the purpose of my story? When you have seen the whole sky overcast with clouds, and no spot of brightness but the little arch of blue in the eastern horizon, did not your eye instinctively turn from the darkness, to rest upon it? So, amid the sorrows of later life, memory still loves to linger about the brightness of its morning. Though every hope has been crushed, and all I loved can be remembered only in bitterness and tears, though I have forgotten the world, and hope my sins have been pardoned by His blood who wore the crown of thorns, yet pride still lives. I still shrink from the story of my own disgrace.

My physician prescribed wine. I commenced its use sparingly, intending to increase it, if it proved beneficial. It was decidedly so. The sensations of weariness, languor, and faintness at the stomach, from which I had suffered so much, were immediately relieved by it. My health began to improve gradually, and at the end of three months, I was nearly well. Yet I did not dream of discontinuing my medicine; on the contrary, I was gradually increasing the quantity, from week to week, as its effects were less perceptible.

Six months passed away, and considering my health restored, I thought it would be best to relinquish all restoratives. I did so, but my sickness, as I termed it, began again to show its symptoms. I felt very languid, very weak, very faint at the stomach, and very miserable; and my wine was immediately resumed, and the symptoms vanished.

Once and again I made the same attempt and failed, and then I told Mr. L. that my health was not as firm as I had supposed, for I found it impossible to relinquish my wine; he replied that I ought not to attempt it. Some months elapsed much in this way, but one well-remembered day my own eyes, at least, were opened. The evening previous, my youngest child, little Annette, only two years old, was attacked with symptoms of croup; our family physician was called, and I passed a night of most intense anxiety. In the morning she was entirely relieved from all danger, but I was completely exhausted by watching and weariness. I directed the chamber-maid to bring me a glass of wine. She did so; I then told her to place a bottle of it in the closet of the nursery, where I was sitting. I would sit and soothe the little sufferer, and then again and again, before I was conscious of what I was doing, I found myself at the closet, drinking wine.

At length, things to my eye began to look brighter; I called Lucy, the nursery-maid, to see how fast Annette, who was lying in my lap, improved. She said she did not see any difference for the last ten minutes, but I insisted that she had improved astonishingly. I then felt very sociable, and, as there was no one but Lucy there, I talked to her. I told her of all Annette's little wonderful actions, things, by the way, that Lucy knew much better than I. I now began to grow generous. I told Lucy she had been with me a long while, and had been very kind to the children in all that time (she had been there just six weeks); and I intended soon to make her a handsome present; but in the mean time, as I was so weary and sleepy I must lie down, and she must watch Annette.

I arose, reached the door in safety, and, passing the entry, entered my own room and closed the door after me. To my amazement the chairs were engaged in chasing the tables round the room; to my eye the bed appeared to be stationary and neutral, and I resolved to make it my ally;

I thought it would be safest to run, as by that means I should reach it sooner, but in the attempt I found myself instantly prostrate on the floor! I made several attempts to rise, but to no purpose, and very soon, under the combined effect of wine and weariness, I was asleep.

How long I slept I know not; but when I awoke I was still on the floor, and alone. I awoke to a full consciousness of the whole truth. I have since been through all the heights, and depths, and labyrinths of misery; but never, no never, have I felt again the unutterable agony of that moment. I wept, I groaned, I actually tore my hair; I did every thing but the *one thing* that could have saved me. I resolved, *firmly*, ay firmly, to drink but a very *little* wine at any time. I did not resolve to *drink none at all*. I was not, I presume, at that time suspected by any one; but a sense of guilt, shame, and remorse haunted every waking and sleeping moment. Still the habit was not abandoned; the chains had been riveted in steel, ere I had known them to be on me; and now I struggled in vain! I intended to be very cautious, and this, I thought, was all I could do; and my caution amounted to this, that I drank only wine enough to make me exceedingly fretful and unreasonable, and the whole misery of this fell on the heads of my unoffending children. The little accidents of infancy which require patience, but not punishment, were met by me with unmerited severity. I recollect sitting one day, moody and fretful, in the nursery, when little Annette came running to me in great delight, exclaiming, "See, mama, I have got tick, tick!" at the same time holding my watch to her ear. I extended my hand to take it, and in attempting to give it to me she let it fall to the floor, and the delicate crystal was broken. I instantly gave her a blow which felled her to the floor; and then with the inconsistency of a mind unhinged, I lavished caresses and candy to atone for such barbarity. The little creature had found the beautiful plaything, as she thought it, where I had myself laid it, within her reach, upon my dressing-table, and not dreaming of offence, intended to bring it to me, and her mother met this freak of infancy with—O memory! memory!

Another incident of this period is written on my heart in letters of living fire. My husband was absent for a week, on business in another city. If there was any thought that sent a pang of perfect terror through my whole frame, it was the possibility that he might discover my disgrace. With my strong attachment to him, there had always mingled an element of fear. He was exceedingly proud, lofty in his notions of female dignity, and acutely alive to the possibility of disgrace. Knowing his temperament, I was too well aware that, if a discovery were made, it would be met, if not by a storm, at least by the hush of life that precedes the tornado. He was away, and the second day of his absence, Ellen, my eldest daughter, four years old, was seized with a fever; the physician was called, and for three days she was very ill, and during that period I successfully resisted the temptation to take any stimulant. On the fourth, she appeared somewhat better, and at night the doctor directed me, in the event of great restlessness, to give her thirty drops of paregoric. I had watched over her much of the time for three nights; I was weary and worn out, and my better genius fled. With the first stimulant, my resolutions were gone, one potation followed another, until all other consciousness was lost in the one desire for sleep. Still little Ellen was restless; the time for sleep had not arrived, it was only eight o'clock; but it was midnight with my senses, and remembering the order of an anodyne, I prepared it in my own room, that she might not see it to be medicine, and then prevailed on her to swallow it. I then directed the chamber-maid to sit by her, as Lucy was too much overcome by previous watching. I told her, if she fell asleep, to sit there till I came, as I should sleep but a few moments. She was a kind-hearted daughter of the "Green Isle" [Ireland —ed.], but knew absolutely nothing of sickness. Had not every faculty been blunted by absolute intoxication, I should never have trusted her for one hour. But sleep, sleep was all I wanted, and to sleep I went, almost instantly on reaching my bed.

When I awoke, the sun shone brightly. I sprang up and grasped my watch—it was eleven o'clock—my head whirled. It was the day I expected Mr. L. to return. I was perfectly conscious that I could not walk, but I dared not wait, I actually reeled as I entered the nursery; and there the first object I beheld was my husband, and the second the physician, and the third the pale face of Ellen, apparently in a profound slumber. With some faint foretaste of what the guilty soul will feel when it stands up before the Throne, I stammered out an inquiry as to his return; and then without waiting for a reply, I inquired of the doctor, what he thought of little Ellen. "I should be glad to know precisely what she has taken during the night," was his reply, "for the servant who watched with her informs me she has been asleep since nine o'clock last night, and now I find it impossible to arouse her." What reply I might have made I cannot tell, for at that moment I caught the eye of my husband fixed on me with a look that told me I was betrayed. He was pale as ashes, and there was an expression in his eye absolutely appalling. He instantly rose and left the room.

The doctor repeated his wish to know, if possible, what she had taken. I told him I did not know, for I had slept longer than I intended, and I would inquire of the servant. "O," said he, "that is unnecessary; she told me that she gave her nothing, as you did not direct any thing, and that she had slept soundly all the time." I became exceedingly alarmed, but I tried to collect my thoughts. "I gave her, as you directed, thirty drops of paregoric; that was the last thing I gave her." "Will you let me look at your paregoric?" I recollected after sometime that I had left it in my own room where I had prepared it. I found it standing just where I had used it, with the stopper out. I took it up, looked at the label with a *sober* eye, and it was laudanum! [tincture of opium, a widely used panacea —ed.] I carried it as calmly as I could (and excess of misery made me calm) to the doctor, and pointed to the label. He understood it at a glance, and shook his head; but immediately added, that if I gave her no more it would not do her any eventual injury. I made no reply; for I knew full well that if I had made so great a mistake in the *article*, the *quantity* might be equally uncertain. He said he would remain a while and see the result, and I, wishing for a moment to think, left the room and entered my own, and there sat Mr. L. O that stern look of misery haunts me even now!

It were vain to attempt a description of that terrible interview. It appeared that on his return, Lucy, the nursery-maid, who was then watching over Ellen, had detailed what had happened; and the fact of my leaving the sick child in the manner I did aroused strong suspicions that he said had existed in his mind for a long while, from the strangeness of my conduct at times. He had come to my bed and endeavored to arouse me, but in vain; the stupor of intoxication was too deep, and the fumes of wine were not to be mistaken. He then left me to consult with the physician relative to Ellen. He closed the conversation by saying, with a dreadful emphasis, "There is but one alternative before you, Mary; this disgraceful, fatal habit must be abandoned, or we *part*." The last word sunk in a convulsive whisper, and his stern eye was for a moment dimmed by a tear; but it was only a moment, and he added, "Remember, Mary, I mean all I say; for the future, let us forget this scene, and only remember the time when we were happy."

O how wide the difference with the heart of a woman! She may be forsaken, abused, trampled on, but amid all, the thought of separation does not enter her heart; if the whole world scorn and forsake him, it is the reason why she clings more closely to the wreck, but let the wife be scorned and forsaken of the world, and the husband will not bide the disgrace.

I should have felt utterly stupefied by misery, but the situation of Ellen demanded exertion. And over this part of my story let me hasten, that my fortitude may not fail ere I have done.

She awoke from her long sleep soon after this, and the doctor expressed the opinion that she was not injured by it; but she gradually sunk, and in five days the little spirit had "gone to lie down in the green pastures of the better land."

Reader, in this dark and stormy world, whatever may befall you, never dare to think yourself unhappy if you have a conscience at rest; for surely an accusing conscience *is* the worm that never dies, and the fire upon the heart-strings that cannot be quenched. It is true that our physician assured me, again and again, that my mistake did her no injury, and in no way hastened her death; but the busy fiend still mutters in my ear, "How do you know so *certainly* that it did not injure her?"

We laid our darling in the tomb, and we wrote above the entrance, "God took her in his mercy, a lamb untasked, untried." O how gladly would the wretched mother have laid down beside her!—but for me the storms were not yet over. Still, the lesson which had been taught me at such tremendous cost proved salutary, and for many long months I was not again overcome by temptation; my husband's confidence seemed restored, and the flickering shadow of our former happiness hovered about us. But I felt keenly at my inmost soul that there was a place in his respect and affection that I never could regain. He made an effort to feel that entire and forgiving affection for me that, had the cases been reversed, and he the erring one, I should *really* have felt for him.

For the first time since the death of our daughter, he requested me one day to arrange a small evening party of select friends to meet a friend of his from England. I complied with great cheerfulness, because I felt it a mark of returning confidence. Not because society had now any attractions where it once had so many; for in every scene of gayety or splendor, my ear caught the dirge-notes of my departed happiness. I made my arrangements with great care and some personal trouble, and I extended my invitations somewhat beyond the limits at first proposed; about fifty were invited.

On the morning of the appointed day, one of my servants was taken severely ill; and in the afternoon I was disappointed in the attendance of another head-servant, hired for the occasion. These accidents disturbed me, and far from meeting them with the self-possession I should once have done, I became nervous and excited, for my mind had been jarred out of tune by constant stimulants, and the native tone could not be recovered. I was a little at a loss what to do, as it was getting late. I was fatigued with some preparations I had been making; what did I do to remedy a temporary inconvenience? I drank again. Yes, I write it for a warning; and from that moment I felt like a lost spirit! I was distracted by the apprehension that Mr. L. might suspect it, and to quiet this fearful foreboding I drank again. It was now time to dress. I gave the necessary orders, under existing circumstances, and began to prepare myself. With the delusion that invariably accompanies partial intoxication, I feared no detection except from my husband, and I cared for no other, comparatively.

I finished my preparations; my guests began to arrive. I trembled so excessively from mere agitation that I could not stand. It was absolutely necessary that I should descend without delay. I drank again, to brace my nerves to the scene, and descended. The rooms were brilliantly illuminated and splendidly decorated, but the remembrance of that evening is so fearful, that I never think of the dwelling-place of the lost, but that parlor scene and all its associations are instantly before me. The little I remember distinctly, I cannot detail; the reader may imagine it all. I was far too agreeable, far too happy, to see my friends, far too loudly talkative for a lady hostess. I sedulously shunned the eye of my husband, vainly hoping to escape his notice. Wine was occasionally passing, but I desisted several times, until some of the company had left, and then the thought of the moment when *all* would be gone and I should be left alone with him recurred to mind, and I took a glass and drained it to the very bottom. The company and the lights began to multiply and flit before me—a vague thought crossed my mind that I would feign illness and leave the room. I attempted to cross the floor for this purpose, but ere I reached the door I fell prostrate in the midst of the company! I remember nothing more until the following morning, and then the very sunbeams looked hateful to my eyes. Breakfast passed in entire silence, and Mr. L. left immediately after. Dinner came, but he did not return; evening, but he came not with it. At length, at a late hour, he appeared; he seemed agitated, and traversed the room in silence for some time. I sat perfectly quiet, and I thought there was not another drop of misery for me in the cup of life; but there was yet another. At length the sentence came: "Mary, we must part! I never can or will endure again what I did the last evening. I will not dwell on it for one moment, or it would madden me. I have been employed all day in making an arrangement with Mr. R., who you know is now in this country, to take his place in London; it is finally arranged, and I sail in two weeks; in that time I shall make every possible arrangement for your comfort; and I give you one strong proof of remaining confidence—I shall leave Annette in your care. I could have wished to confide her to my honored mother's care, but the mother shall not be bereft of all. When I am assured that you have resisted temptation for one year, I shall return to you and to my country, but Mary, if that time never comes I will lay my bones in the father-land."

How little of the real misery of this fallen world is known to the dwellers on its bosom! How little is known of the struggles of our onward journey, even by our fellow-pilgrims; the keenest miseries of our life lie below the surface. My husband's absence passed with the world as a mere business transaction; its real cause was never told.

I must conclude my melancholy story. Its recital has wrung my heart anew. But I have written it for a warning, that none of my sex may be innocently lost upon the rock where my bark was wrecked; yes, wrecked, under a calm sky and on a summer sea.

For eight months after the departure of my husband I was inexpressibly wretched, yet there was one star left on my horizon. I kept his promise of return, and laid it to my heart, and it did not break. I heard from him at distant intervals, but I was utterly unprepared when I took up the paper one morning, and this paragraph met my eye:

> Died, in London, Charles L——,
> Esq. of —— city, U.S.A.

He indeed laid his bones in the father-land!

4

CHARLES T. WOODMAN

from *Narrative of Charles T. Woodman, A Reformed Inebriate* (1843)

Born in Newburyport, Massachusetts, on 13 April 1802, Charles Woodman was only fourteen when he left his widowed mother to learn the baker's trade. He soon changed course, becoming instead a clerk in a New Hampshire general store, where he dispensed rum to the neighboring farmers. Many of these topers were heroic veterans of the American Revolution, and Woodman was disgusted "that they who scorned to submit to the tyranny of the mother country, despising their ease and comfort for liberty and independence, should . . . suffer a greater enemy than ever oppressed our sires to hold in the strong chains of habit these otherwise free and independent sons of liberty."

After Woodman moved to Londonderry, New Hampshire, joining his older brother as clerk in another general store, he became privy to the underside of the liquor traffic: the exploitation of the poor and ignorant; the adulteration and fabrication of ostensibly pure spirits. When his brother died of consumption in 1821, the nineteen-year-old Woodman went to Boston to pursue the baking trade again. He also got religion and became the butt of his profane coworkers, who induced him to imbibe with them occasionally.

The habit grew stronger once Woodman had finished his apprenticeship and opened his own business. Drinking bouts and bad debts led him to skip town, and he was irregularly employed in Philadelphia, New York, and New Haven. Woodman married Verilda Jerome on 11 October 1826; his wife proved to be unfaithful and eventually left him. Woodman, now drinking heavily, took to the road, bouncing from job to job throughout New England.

In January 1832, after overdosing with opium, Woodman resolved to seek refuge in Boston police court and have himself committed to the House of Correction. Upon his release two months later, he immediately reverted to public drunkenness; and his life thereafter alternated between binges and incarceration. Much of the *Narrative* is devoted to the horrendous conditions of jail and the cruel indifference of jailers.

Woodman was befriended in prison by a kind-hearted chaplin, who encouraged him to write poetry, several pages of which interlard his *Narrative*. In exchange for rum, he also wrote poems, letters, and articles for patrons he met in bar-rooms. His health in steady decline, he took to aimless wandering again. At Newburyport, Massachusetts, Woodman was admitted to the almshouse, where he finally stopped drinking on 20 November 1841. Soon thereafter, as the following excerpt attests, he was reformed under the influence of Washingtonian delegates.

After quitting the almshouse in April 1842, Woodman himself became a temperance orator, with many engagements in the Boston area. He emphasized the healing compassion of the Washingtonians, especially in contrast to the disdain shown drunkards by the legal system and the traditional temperance movement. In fact, Woodman's abrasive hostility toward the clergy and other upper-class authorities appalled respectable temperance leaders, who denounced him in their newspapers. In October 1842, Woodman was remarried in Boston's Washingtonian Hall, to Margaret L. Davis, reputed to be a former prostitute. Exhausted by his temperance activities, he again sought winter retirement in the almshouse, and wrote his *Narrative* there.

Woodman did not, it seems, live soberly ever after; he went back to jail for six months in 1844, apparently as the consequence of his renewed drinking.

PREFACE

The author's intention in embodying portions of his experience in the form of a book for the public eye was to give "a plain unvarnished" narrative of some of the prominent incidents in his checkered life, divested of all romance but the romance of reality; to show the gradations in the drunkard's career—the steps by which the insidious destroyer leads him on, from the drinking of the first glass of wine in the convivial circle or the fashionable bar-room, to the lowest degradation to which Alcohol subjects his victims. . . .

Whatever other motive might have been reasonably imputed to the author in preparing this work, he must be exempted from all suspicion of having been influenced in the undertaking by an ambition for the celebrity of authorship. This would be absolutely preposterous, since he makes not the least pretension to the erudition of the scholar, having never devoted a day's study to grammar in his life; and this confession will account for the lack of polish in his style, and also commend his unpretending work to the charity of the critic. But deficient as he frankly acknowledges himself to be in the learning of the schools, he may say, he thinks, without subjecting himself to the charge of vanity, that in a practical knowledge of the world, he is surpassed but by few men of his years. He has mingled much with mankind under every aspect—in prosperity and adversity, with the high and the low, the vicious and the virtuous—at the happy fireside, and within the prisons's walls—and he has made it a point to study human nature in whatever condition he has found it. . . .

In apology for his apparent immethodical and often disconnected style of writing, the author would say, it is difficult for him to concentrate his mind for any length of time upon one subject; and that the work was written at different times, as opportunity offered; and this must also be his excuse for any tautology that may be apparent.

The Washingtonian reform, in whose past triumphs the author has been an humble, but he trusts not an altogether inefficient, participator, has much yet to accomplish; and let us who have enlisted to fight under its banner, falter not in its support, nor ask for a discharge, till that banner shall wave triumphant over every land and every sea. . . .

Snatched, as the author has been, from the very verge of ruin by the magic might of the PLEDGE, and raised by its heaven-lent influence from the depths of degradation and misery, to his former respectability and happiness, may his hand be palsied, and his tongue cleave to the roof of his mouth, when he shall deny that PLEDGE as his benefactor, or refuse it his support.

In conclusion, the author would dedicate his humble production to the cause of WASHINGTONIANISM; and he is willing to regard it as the *meanest* tribute that has been offered at its shrine. If, however, it shall be instrumental, in any measure, in benefitting that cause, so near his heart; if it shall be the means of strengthening the faith of a single reformed inebriate in the PLEDGE, or of adding another name to its already countless host, the author will feel that his labor has not been in vain, and that he has contributed *something* in aid of that noblest of human enterprises, to which, under God, he is indebted for all that makes his present life desirable to himself and useful to others, and in support of which he intends to devote whatever remains to him of ability and life.

"Success to the PLEDGE, and God speed it."

CHARLES T. WOODMAN.

Boston, April 1843.

NARRATIVE

My native place is Newburyport, in Essex county, a town in former years considered very remarkable for its religious character.

I was born on the 13th April, 1802; my father was a master mariner, whose name was Joseph H. Woodman; the maiden name of my mother was Hannali Bartlett. My father was lost at sea, as it is supposed, in the memorable snow storm in October 1804, I then being eighteen months old, the youngest of six children left by him. My mother was a woman of limited education, but endowed by nature with a vigorous mind. Myself and three brothers were kept together until we had arrived at a proper age to learn a trade or be put in a store. When a mere boy I was considered quite eccentric, which was attributed to a constitutional infirmity, and this adherent feeling exhibited itself in my temperament. In the midst of enjoyment, a deep gloom would suddenly shroud my sense of delight, and in the midst of apparent health, and when hope shone the brightest, despondency of the most trying character would influence every buoyant feeling, and overcloud the brightest anticipations. The strongest delusions took possession of my mind; in the very hey-day of youth and health, I would sometimes imagine I was breathing my last. I remember distinctly of a peculiar feeling which raised a delusion that a heavy weight was pressing upon me; my limbs I imagined were powerless and incapable of performing their functions, and I sometimes felt a stranger sensation like choking. These delusions were laughed at by my brothers, and whenever they were exercising their influence, they attributed my feelings to a new "fit of the hypo," which it undoubtedly was. [*Hypo* was short for *hypochondria:* depression —ed.]

My mother attended divine worship at the Church of the late Dr. Spring. I remember *now,* how that venerable form of his struck my young mind with awe; that ponderous wig with ringlets hanging over his shoulders, his stately consequential walk, his awe-inspiring look, struck terror to my very soul. Whenever he visited my mother, I was afraid he came to bring the news of some calamity, or to thunder forth reproof. I remember well, when he passed me, the obedience due the minister in taking off my hat, and making a low bow. I always stood in fear, but never loved him; I thought he knew my very thoughts, and this belief operated as a check-rein upon me when out of his presence. Such slavish fear never will, in my humble opinion, excite to willing obedience the heart of man, but on the contrary, [will] lead the mind unconsciously to dissemble, while the heart is at complete antipodes with truth. How irksome were the duties of the sanctuary to me; the slow, lagging hours at Church, I always dreaded, and more especially the duties of Sunday evening, in reading the Westminster catechism—many a Sunday evening have I feigned indisposition, in order to rid myself of the accustomed task.

The task at school I dreaded; how my little heart would bound when the master was so disposed as to be unable to keep school. I remember playing the truant a number of times, and can in imagination now view the stern countenance of the pedagogue, as he interrogated me respecting my absence. I can in memory's mirror see him now, with the instrument of torture, which consisted of a large mahogany rule which the delinquent felt for hours after it had been frequently applied to his hand. This monstrous practice of flagellation was thought to have a salutary effect on the young offender, but like coercion of any kind, it defeats itself in the object which it has in view; forced obedience never instills in the mind those feelings of reverence which the genial influence of love causes to spring spontaneously in the erring hearts of the children of men. From childhood I have felt the withering influence of bigoted and mistaken notions in regard to coercion. And I believe I can, with the fear of God before my eyes, say that the true and only cause of most of the prominent errors of my life sprang from that domineering spirit, that prostrates all before it, that dissents in manner, opinion, and judgment from a preconceived opinion. The expanding mind of the natural genius, cramped by the narrow, stinted views of the cool calculating bigot, becomes misanthropic, or seeks relief in the convivial glass, which sweeps him on to the vortex of ruin.

How many wrecks of men are there now in our midst, who have fallen victims, to cold calculating men, who seek to enforce truth with a scourge. How many now whose rags dance in the winds of winter might have been clothed in fine linen, and fared sumptuously every day, had kindness been extended to them before the storms of adversity had steeled their hearts, and destroyed that laudable ambition which might, under other circumstances, have rendered them ornaments to society and an honor to the world. How many there are, whose expanding minds and towering genius bid fair to rise to an envied distinction in society have been eclipsed to the eyes of all—the star of promise which appeared so conspicuous to all around, overshadowed by the darkness cast over them by the frown of tyranny, or the mistaken idea that harsh measures excite to obedience or drive to duty.

This was the order of the day at the period I am speaking of, but I am digressing from my history. I was indifferent whether I ever learnt any thing at school or not, and every excuse I could make to stay away from school I readily used, to rid myself of what I considered an irksome restraint; consequently the reader must expect I could not make any great proficiency in learning—I did not, although by attention I could easily have outstripped some of the first boys in the school. It was unfortunate for me that a public house was near the spot where I passed my juvenile days. Here my young mind became tainted with the mistaken and once prevailing opinion of former days in regard to alcoholic drink. The public house I refer to was the "Dexter House"—of course there were a number of bowling alleys attached to it, and so little danger was seen in those days, when popularity sanctioned the use of ardent spirit, by frequently seeing it drank. My mother viewed no danger when I visited this tavern to set up the pins on the bowling alley. She was not conscious that by mingling with them, I should sow the seeds of future misery.

How blinded indeed were our fathers and mothers to this great enemy's encroachment. They presented us in childhood with the poisoned chalice, in belief that it contained medicinal virtue. We asked for bread, they gave us a stone, a fish, and unwittingly they gave us a serpent, thus entailing a curse on each succeeding generation [see Luke 11:11 —ed.]. I became therefore early initiated in the practice of tasting the poison, which gradually diffused itself in every vein in my system. The old fashioned convivial party is still fresh in my recollection. I can almost by the power of imagination see the females assembling together in the afternoon, enjoying a pleasant *tête a tête*; nothing was spoken that raised feelings of envy or jealousy toward each other, until after the huge salvor went round, filled with glasses containing Annis, Clove and Snakeroot Cordials, the last being the most appropriate name, for at last it did sting like a serpent and bite like an adder [see Prov. 23:32 —ed.]. After the salvor had passed round and these before-described cordials had been drank by the female part of the company, a low hum of female voices, apparently in the distance, were heard; then came a babel confusion of tongues, then the prices of silks, bobbinett and laces were discussed; the high price of this article and the low price of that; then an occasional hit at some dry goods dealer for exorbitant prices; and increased interest in speaking seemed to pervade the short time since silent assembly, and each tried to drown the shrill voice of their neighbor. I remember how the change seemed to me and considered what made the women's tongues have the speed of the locomotive. Religion and ministers were discussed, the merits and demerits of a sermon were handled, as the Irishman said, by the tongue—their powers were sharpened by the inspiring cordial, while their organ of reverence rose in mock adoration by the steam of Annis and Snakeroot.

Then the men came in the evening to see their better halves; they were moderate in conversation, till an invitation was given and accepted to retire to the next room to refresh themselves with a little of the sophisticated creature, in the form of Brandy and Gin. After having taken the above false-named refreshments they returned into the room where the female part had refreshed themselves. Then additional garrulity broke into the company and the deep bass tones of the men, responding to the treble voices of the women, commenced a jargon that a linguist skilled in all languages could not understand; such a concord of sounds, and such untiring patience in continuing them, would set at defiance the skill of a Paganini and exhaust the perseverance of a Hayden [*sic*].

After their magazines were exhausted, and a motion being made to adjourn, it was thought advisable to have another interview with the above-named salvor, to protect them against the chilly air of the evening, and thus the huge salvor was again presented, loaded with the then universal panacea for every disease the human frame is liable to.

In presenting this picture of the popular custom of our ancestors, I do it to have the reader learn that this hitherto innocent custom was the means of entailing one of the greatest curses on each succeeding generation that ever befel them—a curse which was sown in the early part of my life—

> Bearing the fruits of misery and wo,
> Which increas'd as onward they did flow.

The universal custom in furnishing rum and cordial was not confined to any rank or grade in society; on all occasions, the goblet passed round to enliven every scene. In summer heat it was called in to add to the enfeebling rays of the solar beam. In winter's piercing cold it was summoned to impart heat to the body, and raise the desponding mind. It was brought forward to bind a contract between parties, while it always stood ready to break the tie which it was witness to in the contract; at the birth of infants, to heighten the joys of parents; and in the dread hour of death, even when by its shafts a beloved relative was laid low, the side board glittered with the bright decanter, and surviving friends made bare their own breasts to the same poisoned arrow that had just laid low a valued relative and friend. Thus was laid the foundation of a habit which has robbed man of his fairest prospects and his fondest hopes. These popular habits have been the origin of most crimes which have shaded our fallen world. When a boy I remember my peculiar fondness for military training. Our little mimic band would march to the back yard of one of the officer's dwellings, and the can of cider would be passed round among the little soldiers, and sometimes cordials would be drank. This was only in imitation of "children of an older growth." And when I look back on the custom once so popular, I have no cause to wonder that our land should have been cursed as it indeed has been; but I wonder that millions more have not filled a drunkard's grave. How blinded, indeed, has the past generation been to their best interests, by allowing an enemy to take a part in all their deliberations, and spread a physical and moral mania wherever his polluted touch was known.

The Washingtonian movement began while I was an inmate of the almshouse, and there its invigorating power first cheered my heart, and bid me hope and live. In the spring of 1842, I was taken sick, very suddenly, had been in the almshouse three months at that time, was attacked in the oakum cellar, and had to be carried to a chamber by two men. Three months I suffered all, it appeared to me, a man could suffer. My legs were contracted and an abscess formed on my thigh, which literally drained off all my rum-fed flesh from my bones. I had been partially frozen in the fall, and in the spring when a reaction of the blood took place, my body became a mass of corruption. I could clasp my hand around the calf of my leg easily. For three months I could not help myself—yes, reader, one half of my life in the almshouse has been spent on a bed of sickness, and the cause can be spelt in three letters—RUM.

One day while lying on my bed revolving in my mind the scenes of my past life, Mr. Johnson came into the chamber and informed me that six reformed drunkards of Baltimore were giving lectures on temperance. This to me was a new idea. He read to me from a newspaper an account of their sayings and doings. How novel it appeared to me, yet I had no hope, even if my life was spared, that I could live a sober life.

One day while weeping, Mr. Richard Plummer of Newburyport came to my room with three Washingtonian delegates from Boston (Messrs. Rowan, Bennett, and Moody) and requested me to sign the pledge—a Washingtonian pledge—and they described the Washingtonian platform. I could hardly believe my senses. One of these delegates observed to the other, there is no need of his signing, for he will not live long; and indeed every one around were of the same opinion. But I thought I should live, and I resolved in my mind if God spared my life, that life should be devoted to admonishing the inebriate—that I would be a laborer in the cause of Washingtonian reform. Lying in bed, on my back, a mere wreck of what I once was—*I signed on the New Testament,*

"THE PLEDGE OF TOTAL ABSTINENCE *from all that intoxicates.*" A glorious event to me, and the one from which I date the commencement of my present happiness.

Since I have been a Washingtonian lecturer, I have neglected no opportunity of informing myself where the greatest obstacle lay in this glorious reform; and I conceive it is principally in the want of cooperation generally by the "*higher circles*" of life. Pride seems to be the great obstacle to aiding in the reform, with a certain portion of the community; and by not lending their countenance in a direct manner, they clog the wheels of the locomotive car of temperance. There appears to be a suspicious feeling with some in regard to the Washingtonian movement. This arises from its being an *elevating* movement—the *gutter drunkard*, so called, being restored by it at once to his forfeited station in society. There is a class who, though they acknowledge themselves to be temperance men, look with a different eye on the Washingtonian movement than an eye of faith; they consider it as an insect of a day that flutters by excitement, soon to die and be forgotten. These men belong to no one particular class in society, neither are they of a particular sect in religion, nor of a particular grade in community; but they are from all sects, all grades and denominations, whose faith is bounded by their own narrow conceptions and long-cherished prejudices.

When I had been but a short time from the almshouse, I was invited to lecture in Salem. Two nights I lectured in the Washington Hall, and one night at the Mechanic's Hall, to crowded audiences. A man well known in Salem for his strict religious character, who kept a large hat store in Essex street, heard me lecture, and in speaking of the temperance men of the old school, I perhaps spoke not exactly in accordance with his feelings; and I will honestly confess when I first lectured I was rather severe on the old pioneers in this case; but any man who had the cause near his heart would have overlooked my remarks when he had heard my recital, and would have given me the right hand of fellowship, in consideration that in my hours of degradation, no friendly hand in the old temperance times ever gave to me encouragement to rise and live; but many were not only indifferent to my situation, but actually, in more ways than one, were my oppressors. Never did an individual ever actually act the part of a good Samaritan to me but old Father Cleveland, our Chaplain to the House of Correction. But this Salem gentleman prophesied, after hearing me lecture, that I would fall from my pledge in three weeks. Not content with once mentioning it, he made it a business to promulgate his prophecy to many individuals belonging to different places. This man was a strict professor of religion, and he told me in his store, on my interrogating him on his remarks, that I would not, in his opinion, stand to my pledge but a short time, and in fact he believed *no man* who appeared and expressed himself as sanguine in the power of the pledge as I did would stem the current of appetite but a short time. He appeared very indignant at my remarks, and actually it abated my ardor in the cause after I left the store. I told him plainly that it was such religious bigots as he that had kept the drunkard confined to his cups for years, and that I considered him more in the way of the cause than ten open opposers; and in fact such men are complete icebergs around any reform, chilling the atmosphere wherever they approach.

I turned from that man with disgust, and was half inclined to think that all professors were like him; but I soon found there were the *genuine* Christians in our good cause, who manifested that they possessed that charity which "suffereth long and is kind"; that "believeth all things, hopeth all things" [see 1 Cor. 13:4, 7 —ed.]. I mention this case because some one may see here reflected their own image and by the reflection may open their hearts to receive the light which now shines for all, dispensing the former clouds which hung around such reformers who believed that no man could be reformed from intemperance, but who conformed to the rules which their own narrow, prejudiced mind conceived to be the only ones right.

The many hair-breadth escapes and exposures I have been subjected to through the influence of strong drink, were I to point them out, would seem to the reader a fictitious narrative formed by an over-excited imagination. I remember once of falling down in a butcher's barn in the night, among the hogs, and was very much injured, and had to crawl out through the underpinning. At another time I found myself "lodging" in a hogshead on the city wharf, and hearing somebody snoring very loud in the next hogshead to me, I told him to wake up, or he would attract the attention of the private watch. In the morning I discovered the head of an old House of Correction comrade looking down in my hogshead, and he inquired who I was, and we soon became acquainted with each other, or at least had an opportunity of renewing an old acquaintance. The first inquiry I made was, "have you any money to buy the bitters this morning?" I found he had a spare sixpence, and we trudged on together to a victualling cellar which was formerly kept open most of the night: he spent the money for two glasses of liquor, and another old comrade came in and treated us to our second glass, for one glass was not considered what we used to term *"a settler."* I have frequently drank ten times before I ate any thing in the morning. I observed to my comrade that I had a little writing to do for a man, but as my shoes were minus of soles, I felt ashamed to go and see him. He told me he could procure me a better pair of shoes if I would go with him; and, reader, where do you suppose he guided me? To a shoe store? No, but to the back bay scavenger heap, where the city dirt was carried, and there he picked up a pair of cast away shoes that were better than mine, but poor enough, in all conscience.

I mention this fact to show the destitution ardent spirit will bring a man to. The story of his degradation, as dark as it has fallen from the reformed inebriate's lips, was never equal to the reality. No reformed man from this slavish vice, I believe, is so lost to modesty as to tell *all* the disgusting reality.

This day, March 28, a man has just dunned me for a whole load of fresh fish that I bought of him when I was intoxicated some years since. I have a faint remembrance of the transaction. How it was possible I could have traded with the man, and get his confidence to trust me with the fish, drunk as I was, I am not able to tell; for at that time my wardrobe would have set off a scarecrow in a cornfield with a very good grace. But I have displayed at different times, under the excitement of liquor, a peculiar kind of cunning. It was owing to the concentrative power of the liquor on the brain, which caused it to send forth meteoric flashes of wit, to be succeeded by almost Egyptian darkness.

I was one of that class of inebriates that ardent spirit injures the most, for when I was the most exposed I felt the most secure. Without a cent in the world, I had in imagination an abundance of riches at my command. I thought I was clothed in purple and fine linen, when in fact the dogs barked at me at the sight of my rags. When in liquor I have frequently made offers of pecuniary assistance to others, when I was incapable of rendering myself any assistance, however small. When excited by strong drink, my organ of veneration rose in mock adoration toward the deity, when the whole was the effect of the fumes of alcohol. My friendship was unbounded for all, when I had not a solitary friend on earth. My patriotism assumed a devotion to my country, when I was an incubus on the tree of liberty. The sublime and beautiful rose before me in prismatic beauty, when all the sublime and beautiful was the prism reflected from the flowing decanter. I have often gone into stores, and ordered a hundred weight of sugar, and coffee, tea, &c., to be put up, when I had no credit, nor a farthing to pay for them. I would walk into a gentleman's store and inquire the lowest price, by the quantity, of his goods, and do it (though after I became sobered I was unconscious of it) with such a good grace that all my questions were readily answered. I felt so consequential that I allowed no one to know me than myself, when in fact I had not discernment enough to know whether I was barefooted or not. My cunning always turned against myself at last, and subjected me, when sober, to great mortification; and then I would immediately fly to the bowl, to patch over or drive away these sensations. When in liquor, I was suspicious that people did not think well of me, and this was well founded, for in truth I believe but very few did. I was very particular in discussing some religious tenet, and contending for some trifling article of faith, when my whole practice was irreligious. I felt as powerful as Sampson [*sic*], when I was most enfeebled by alcohol, and imagined I could fly, when I could not walk without taking a serpentine course.

Yes, reader, these are a part of the illusions that rise up before the victim of intoxicating drink, subjecting him to be a laughing-stock wherever he is seen. A man who has not become a drunkard often exposes himself to after-shame by his careless or silly remarks, which he had uttered under the influence of ardent spirits. I remember once of riding in a stage coach from Worcester to Hartford, and having drank enough to inspire my self-esteem, I sat listening to some remarks of the passengers. A lady observed that she was very glad that a Judge (whom I will call Jones) had decided in the Supreme Court of the State that a Universalist was not a competent witness. I observed I thought it was very strange that the judge should make such a decision, for I believed that Judge Jones' character was far from being very moral, if we were to judge from his wife's statements. I had not sooner uttered these words, than a lady in the stage called me by my name, and introduced me to Judge Jones' daughter. Here I was in a very curious position. I remained *mum* for a time, but, the fumes of alcohol having raised my garrulous powers, I recommenced conversation. In the course of the remarks, they spoke of the Greek character, extolling the Greeks. I observed I did not agree with them, for I believed the modern Greeks had lost all that nobleness of soul which distinguished their ancestors in early times; and also observed that when supplies were sent them from this country, they choose rather to steal them than to receive them as gifts. I had no sooner uttered these words, than the same lady introduced me to a gentleman in the stage as a Greek, from Scio, who was studying at Yale College. Chagrined at this unexpected introduction, I then asked, "and who, lady, may you be?" She answered, she was a clergyman's wife, who knew me well when I lived in a certain town in Connecticut.

The reader will see by this how liable a man is to get himself into a disagreeable position, by his unguarded manner, while under the influence of alcohol. In [a] thousand such instances have I been caught by the locomotive speed of my tongue, induced by the power of the reason-robbing enemy, alcohol.

After having arrived at Stafford Springs, I rode with the driver to Hartford. The next morning I put my name on the stage-book for New Haven, being the only person I saw enrolled for a passage; but the first house the stage came to, the driver took in the identical Greek, Judge Jones' daughter, and the clergyman's lady above mentioned. I told the driver I believed I should ride outside, as I was not in a very enviable situation inside. Thus I rendered myself odious, in my own eyes, by my indiscreet manner in conversation, caused by my devotion to the bowl.

I recollect one night sleeping in a crate containing straw, and having on a straw hat; the hogs came in the night and commenced an attack on the straw, and my straw hat fell a victim to their rapacious appetite. This was in the city of New York. I have never for three months in the summer season, during my drinking days, slept in a bed. My lodging was either the cold ground, or in some barn or outhouse. I have been told af-

93

ter a lecture, by some of the officers of different societies, that rum never injured my lungs, as I spoke very loud. In justice to the cause I have espoused, I have told them the reason, for ardent spirit, all reasonable men acknowledge, will injure the man some way, in his corporeal frame, as well as his mental capacity. The reason is obvious to those who have known me, and will no doubt silence all who have drank for years, and have never experienced any harm, being blinded as to the real cause of some defect in their body, occasioned by their free use of ardent spirit, or willfully denying the truth. The reason my lungs and brain have never been more injured was an ulcerous leg (mentioned before), which became a common-sewer, if I may so term it, for the humors of the body. For years has that leg been in such a state that I have frequently thought mortification would ensue. The cords of my leg have been visible, and my suffering in this respect has been beyond the conception of any one who has not experienced the same. This will explain the mystery why my brain has not left greater traces of the effects of this subtle poison. And to those who are suffering under the same affliction, let me prescribe the universal balm and panacea which restored the limb of mine again to soundness. And the secret lies in the use of cold water by an inward and outward application; keeping the diseased limb constantly moist with water will do that which no liniment has been successful in doing. I am not the only reformed man that can testify to this fact. Try it, sufferer, and save expense of the advertised nostrums of the day. But the greater blessing is the tranquility of mind which this cold water remedy brings. The sweet influence of peace will cheer your hours, and the scenery of reviving nature dispelling winter's gloom will afford the same delicious and indescribable sensations that it did in the halcyon days of thy youth, before thy sensitive feelings were blunted by the muddy vapor from the dram-shop.

How my mind revolts when some of the disgusting scenes of my life arise before me. One night, in the fall of the year, I was drinking in a low grog-shop in Boston, where I came across a brother-baker, who, finding I had no place to stay during the night, invited me to his boarding-house. He had, as well as myself, suffered everything by strong drink. I, in accordance with his wishes, went with him, and such a lodging room! it was filled with drunkards. In the course of the night a great cry was made for water to cool their parched tongues. My thirst was indescribable. My comrade got up, and went below to get some water; after a while he returned, and brought up a piggin of the liquid. I drank very freely, and could almost hear it *siss* as it went down. The next morning my shirt had changed its color, and was as blue in front as I had been the night before; but the mystery was soon explained by my looking into the vessel, and seeing some of the water left; and what do you think it was? He had gone into the yard, and not finding a pump, had taken from a wash-tub a liquid which proved to be *bluing water*, and in my haste to drink I had spilled it on my shirt, which gave it the appearance I have described. This is what I call literally, in the strictest sense, *getting blue!*

To entertain the reader with anecdotes was not the design of this work; but for higher and, I trust, nobler purposes. How sad indeed is the recital of misery which is now unfolded by the reformed inebriate; but this course has been the salvation of many a poor wretch who would have filled a drunkard's grave. For the reformed inebriate knows each avenue to his brother's heart; he highly touches the string on which hangs all his sorrow; no rebuke mingles with his invitations of welcome; he presents him with the life boat of safety, the Pledge, and tells him how nobly she stemmed the current of appetite, in his own case, and bounded over the billows of despair to the haven of security; he well knows that one rude breath would contract his expanding hope—and the great key which Washingtonians use to lock up for the present all those excitements which tend to destruction is the soothing voice of kindness. They take their erring brother immediately into the hospital of their affections, and pour in the oil of hope, and fan, with gossamer lightness, the almost expiring embers of self respect, to a steady yet increasing flame, and raise a desire within him to climb the barrier walls which have stood between him and well-regulated society. The reformed man does more than this; he brings his brother shoes for his feet, and for rags presents him with comfortable apparel; he lifts the veil from his own heart and his suffering brother sees reflected every prism of his most ardent desire. Finally, he gains his confidence by kindness, and stirs within him an emulous spirit to rise from his degraded state and become a man among men.

What a contrast is this to the cold, withering look men of the old school cast on the poor victim of appetite. No longer are heard threats in his ears of the curtailment of his liberty by imprisonment in the common jail or house of correction; the bolts and bars of the prison fly not open so readily. Heaven has interposed in behalf of the self-immolated victim of habit and philanthropy claims him as her own, and shields and protects him from the cold charities of a frowning world.

Reader, go then in the spirit of meekness and love to a fallen brother, and feel the reward in thy own bosom that thou hast indeed saved a brother from the error of his ways, and by thus doing, you will learn what constitutes a Washingtonian.

The Drunkards Progress, lithograph by Nathaniel Currier (1846).

In the Monster's Clutches: Body and Brain on Fire, frontispiece to T. S. Arthur's *Grappling with the Monster* (1877).

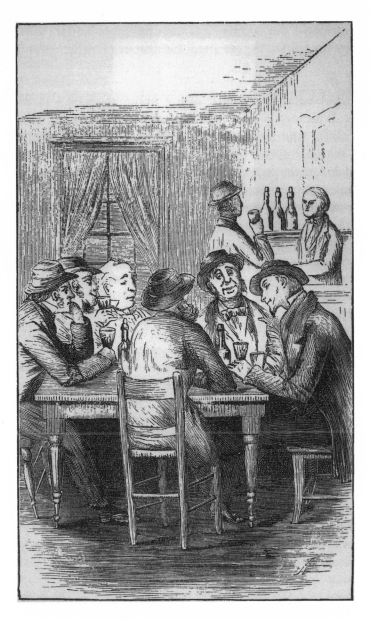

The Original Washingtonians, from an old print.

Portrait of John H. W. Hawkins, frontispiece to *Life of John H. W. Hawkins* (1859).

Portrait of John B. Gough, frontispiece to *An Autobiography by John B. Gough* (1853).

"Father, don't send me after whiskey, to-day!" frontispiece to John Marsh, *Hannah Hawkins* (1844).

Portrait of John B. Gough, frontispiece to Gough's *Platform Echoes* (1887); engraved by J. J. Cade from a painting by Sir Daniel MacNee, presented to Gough by the Scottish Temperance League, 22 May 1855.

Portrait of T. S. Arthur, frontispiece to Arthur's *The Lights and Shadows of Real Life* (1853).

BOYHOOD.
The First Step.

YOUTH.
The Second Step.

MANHOOD.
A Confirmed Drunkard.

OLD AGE.
A Total Wreck.

Four Stages of Inebriety, from T. S. Arthur's *Grappling with the Monster* (1877).

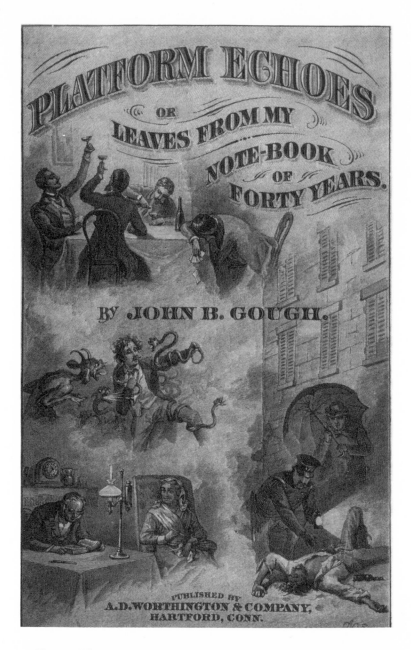

Illustrated Title-Page to Gough's *Platform Echoes* (1887); designed by F. O. C. Darley to present "a powerful contrast between two sides of life, one showing the reward of temperance and virtue, the other the results of intemperance and sin."

5

[JOHN COTTON MATHER,
PSEUDONYM]

from *Autobiography of a Reformed Drunkard* (1845)

The *Autobiography*, originally serialized in a popular periodical, consists of eight "Letters" purportedly written by an inmate of the almshouse in Norwich, Connecticut, and of ten "Recollections," from the inmate's perspective after four years' sobriety. Although the book takes the form of a temperance narrative, it is probably a fiction, whole or in part. Surely the author's alleged name, which invokes two distinguished and staunchly sober Puritan divines (John Cotton, Cotton Mather), is so ironically inapt for a drunkard that it must be considered a comic touch.

The *Autobiography* centers on the colorful characters, including Mather himself, who inhabit the almshouse. The theme throughout is the culpability of drunkard-makers and "moderate" drinkers in debauching their fellow citizens. That is, the "Letters," which first appeared before the Washingtonian revival and were published in a pirated edition in 1841, reflect the mainstream temperance advocacy of established religion and inhibitory legislation. The later "Recollections" take account of the appearance, in the interim, of the Washingtonians, to whom the book as a whole is effusively dedicated. (Mather claims to have named one of his sons after John Hawkins.)

Like the "Letters," Mather's "Recollections" are primarily character studies in support of his conviction, spelled out in the final installment, that certain agencies are "necessary to the *permanence*" of the Washingtonian reformation: "1. Religious sentiment. This must be not only the chief, but the controlling agent. 2. Sympathy and associated action. This is a powerful agent, or rather a set of agencies, but there is some danger of relying upon them too exclusively. 3. Employment. I use this term in its widest sense. All the powers of the reformed man, moral, intellectual and physical, must be directed into the proper channels of action. 4. Removal of temptation in all its Protean forms. The principal obstacles to this are the cupidity of the seller, the appetite of the buyer, and the customs of social life."

LETTER III

𝒟ear Sir,

One morning I saw a country retailer going out of town with a loaded wagon, and as he seemed to be in some trouble, I went up to him and offered my assistance. I found that a rum cask had sprung a leak. A good many gathered around, and a variety of remarks were made. "It would be well if all the rum were poured out," said one. "What a stench," said another. "It smells good," said a ragged, pale-faced fellow, with an oath to his red-faced neighbour. "Pouring your rum into the street, eh? I'm glad to see it, Mr. Gridley," said a gentleman passing by. This occasioned a titter among the bystanders, and Mr. Gridley looked rather ashamed. I could point out every man there that was a drunkard, from the expression of his countenance; there was a longing look fastened on the muddy liquor not to be mistaken.

After leaving this scene, I went into a rumhole where I found two sailors, that I got acquainted with in New London. Here we charged high, and then we took a ride in a wagon together. They had driven the horse so outrageously that he was rather reluctant to go—but we soon got him well under way. We drove full tilt against a country wagon, with two buxom damsels in it, that had come in to do their Saturday shopping. And here I would say that if your public authorities authorize men to make drunkards, they ought to make the streets wide enough for drunkards to drive in. Well, the ladies were near being turned out, but experienced no other damage than the crushing of a band-box containing a go-to-meeting bonnet. But *we* struck against a post and were capsized upon the pavement. We were so drunk that we were not hurt by the fall. I apologized to the ladies for demolishing the bonnet, and told them that I had no funds, but would give them an order on the man that made us drunk, if that would do. I thought it was fair that he should endorse our driving. I expected that the constable and justice would make a good job out of our case, or the fees they would get for putting three of us in the work-house would make a sum not to be despised. But for some reason or other no notice was taken of the affair.

Rum-sellers often make a great *show* of being scrupulous about the individuals to whom they sell. I met a fellow the other day coming out of a shop swearing roundly because the keeper of it would let him have no rum. He was not very drunk—not enough to stagger, at least on even ground, and the shop I knew, by former experience, to be not the most decent that could be found, so that I wondered a little at the refusal. The riddle, however, was soon solved. I found there were some very respectable looking men in the shop, and this produced all at once a scrupulous fit in the rum-seller. After they went away, there came in a red-faced fellow, much more drunk than he that was sent away empty; but the *scruple* was gone and the *dram* was sold him. "Well Natty, was that good rum?" "Yes, yes," said he, smacking his lips; "I like something that I can hear from, and I'll swear there's no water in that. There's no mistake in rum and sugar"—and he staggered out of the shop. As I sat there I saw many come in to take their dram, and among them was a boy of fifteen, smoking his segar and swearing, and a lame old man of nearly eighty, and last of all came in the man who was so unceremoniously refused a little while before. He understood the matter; he knew that he would not be refused now that the cold-water men were gone.

Rum, like wine (I repeat it—*like wine*), makes men very wise, very eloquent, very brave, and very loving—that is, unless they get *too* drunk. I saw, the other day, examples of all these effects within a stone's throw of each other. I heard one man asserting that he could prove any thing in law, theology, or medicine. A little way on, I saw a fellow with animated gesture talking to a knot of idlers about priestcraft and the liberties of the people. Just then another, as he staggered along, said to his companion, "I'm not afraid of him, nor the constable, nor the—the devil," raising his voice to a pretty loud pitch at the climax; and then (O Cupid, how Bacchus and the modern god of rum do serve thy cause!) I saw an Irishman, just as he went aboard your steamboat, put his arms around a damsel and squeeze her most lustily, giving her a good smack, and as the boat went off, he stood in her stern waving his hat.

Drunkards are apt to be early risers. The gnawing within, after being so long without rum, wakes them and sends them forth to seek relief. As

I came along one morning to Mr. Brinker's shop, I found half-a-dozen or more waiting for him to come and cool their burnings. Such a sorry-looking set I never saw before. There they stood with their hands in their pockets, shivering and spitting, occasionally turning their eye, with a most woeful look in the direction in which he was to come. And as they saw him turn the corner there was almost a shout; they were a new set of men at once. One of the poor fellows, after taking his dram, fell down in a fit. The rum-seller and his company concluded that it was not caused by the rum that he drank there, because he had not had it down long enough. "Then," said I, "Mr. Brinker, you do think rum sometimes produces fits." "Y—es, sometimes," he said. "If a man takes too much," added a fellow half-seas over, "but I don't believe it hurts any body to drink moderately." "Nor I," echoed the whole company. One of them said, "he's subject to fits; it isn't drinking." This seemed to be a great relief to Mr. Brinker; but it was a still greater relief to him to have the poor fellow carried home. Rum-sellers dislike to have the results of their horrid traffic stare them in the face.

I have as yet described no night scenes in the rum-shops. They are often perfectly horrid. One night I became so drunk that the keeper of the shop was obliged to provide for me for the night. After having a good long nap, I awoke; and as no one seemed to be aware that I was awake, I lay there looking upon their midnight orgies. It was a Saturday night, and therefore they were more prolonged than usual. The shutters were closed, so that no light was to be seen by the passers by. The besotted faces of the drunkards, as they sat around the gambling table, made a frightful scene as the lights shone dimly on them. But gambling was not the worst thing done in this "suburb of hell." Two females were brought in by the keeper at midnight. Startle not, gentle reader, such abominations do verily exist in this community. I heard this same grog-shop keeper the other day, "agreeing exactly" with every respectable rum-seller, who said he was willing to join people in putting down intemperance, but that things were carried too far. O these *respectable* rum-sellers! they are a shield for the vilest pests of society. In truth they have a common interest with them in opposing temperance; for their "craft" is the same, and it is in danger to be set at naught. And if it would not endanger this respectability, they would join the dirty dram-sellers and ragged drunkards in the cry, Down with the cold-water men!

The next day (Sunday) I passed in this den of iniquity. Many, very many came there, entering by a back door, the front of the shop being perfectly closed. Among them was a Mr. Dilworth, a half-crazed, short, dapper, little man, who was constantly replying to every remark that he liked, "that's grammatically spoken." Old Dilly, as he was called, was a real grog-shop oracle. There was another fellow, whom they called Captain Pepper, with a big red nose and sore eyes, caused as he said by a 'sipelas humour [erysipelas: a painful skin rash —ed.], that was one of the great talkers of the company. There was a Mr. Smith, of about twenty, who, though so young, seemed to be an important character among the loafers; he was a very knowing man, and had a deal to say about priestcraft, aristocrats, &c. The rest of the company had nothing about them particularly observable, but exhibited the common characteristics of drunkards, a smutty face and ragged clothes. There came in a Mr. Ramsey, with a shoe on one foot and a boot on the other, and other things to compare, and he seemed to be quite welcome. He told them, however, that he could not stay long, for his wife was sick. "What's the matter with her," said Captain Pepper. "She's got a fever," said he, "and I thought some spirit would be good to put on outside, and so I've come after it." The Captain then told a long story about his wife once having a fever, and the doctors giving her over, and asserted that she was cured at last by putting a cloth wet in rum on her bowels. He concluded by saying, I really believe rum is a good thing in fevers"—to which old Dilly replied, "that's grammatically spoken." Though Mr. Ramsay seemed to believe all this, he staid by and put the rum into his own stomach, instead of applying it to his wife's skin. In fact he did not reach home until evening, and his wife died that night—probably the rum was not applied soon enough to save her. Captain Pepper said *his* wife was almost sick. "The old woman is very weakly," said he; "but since these cold-water times have come on, I can't get her to drink anything stimulating. This morning she almost fainted away fixing off the children for Sunday-school." "Sunday-school!" said Mr. Smith, with the most ineffable contempt, and he went on with a tremendous tirade against every thing that was good, all which the company applauded, and old Dilly pronounced to be "grammatically spoken." The conversation at length was turned upon temperance. Mr. Smith very gravely declared that he thought they carried things too far, and that 'Squire Lawson was right when he said that some people were very intemperate in their temperance. "That's grammatically spoken," said old Dilly. "That 'Squire Lawson is a liberal-minded fellow," said Captain Pepper, "we must have him up for the Gineral 'Sembly next year."

The conversation was very much of this sort through the whole day. But I have given you enough to show you what a grog-shop is on Sunday.

Old Dilly and Captain Pepper are now with me in the almshouse, and they may be introduced to the notice of your readers again.

We have had the past week a horrible case of delirium tremens in the house. The poor fellow chased dogs, cats, rats, and devils incessantly for several days and nights: and just before he died he thought he was in hell, and the devils were all around him, with all sorts of instruments of torture. "I'm in hell, in hell!" he would cry. "O! O! don't burn me so!— how that devil bites!" Such perfect terror I never witnessed.

LETTER VII

*D*ear Sir,

I will now, agreeably to the promise I made last week, relate my history.

I have said that I was from a noble family. My name is John Cotton Mather, and I am of the stock of Mather of Magnalia memory [*Magnalia Christi Americana* (1702): Cotton Mather's masterwork —ed.]. With such noble blood in my veins, I was not to be conquered by so mean an enemy as Rum. No; it was the *refined, the classic God of Wine*, whose praises have been sung by poets, and proclaimed by philosophers, that *first* overcame me—though of late it has been ungenteel, vulgar New England Rum that has held me as its easy prey. At fifteen years of age I entered College. My moral character was then without a stain. I was the pride of my father, and the joy of my mother. O! how has that pride been humbled, and that joy been destroyed! I was unsuspecting and knew nothing of the wiles of the world, so that temptation easily overcame me. Wine-drinking was then a general custom in College; so much so that a professor of religion might drink to the borders of intoxication, nay, even to intoxication itself, and be looked upon as committing, at most, but a very venial sin. I will not detail the steps by which I became a drunkard. That horrid result was arrived at in a little less than two years, and I was dismissed from College at length, on account of repeated and gross intoxication. My father tried various plans to reform me, but in vain. As a last resort, he sent me off upon a whaling voyage. On our return we were shipwrecked, and after suffering many hardships, I at last reached home. Vice had not yet destroyed my natural sensibilities, and the hardships I had endured had revived them in their original energy. As I entered my father's house, a poor weather-beaten sailor, I wept like a child, and as my parents and brothers and sisters gathered around me to greet me, I was speechless. As my father that night, before the evening altar, thanked God that the "lost was found," in the fulness of my feelings I resolved that I would wander no more, and that temptation should be resisted to the death.

For a year I tasted not even a drop of wine, though it was then made use of (it being long before the temperance effort was begun) as the common social beverage in the highest circles of society. I had not only my own appetite to resist, but the sparkling wine was continually before me. After a while, getting tired of being singular, the whole mass of society being in practice against me, I ventured to taste, and though a few, a very few, whispered the word *beware* in my ear, most of my friends did not seem to think that I was treading on dangerous ground, and as I was pleased to find that I could indulge myself without going beyond the bounds of moderation, I became less and less cautious. I was, however, for a long time free from actual intoxication. My father put me into mercantile business with an older partner, and in a few months after I was married to one of the most beautiful and lovely girls in the town. I was now most happily situated—in business with one of the best of men, surrounded with many friends, and above all, blessed with an excellent and lovely wife—but, reader, I was a *Wine Drinker*. There was near by a shop in which were sold Confectionery, Oysters, Wine, &c. There was a back room fitted up for an eating-room, and this was a common place of resort for young men. The most steady, and even the religious, were occasionally seen there, so that I felt no scruple as to the propriety of going there also. But my visits were more and more frequent, and once in a while I would go home from them, to say the least, unnaturally excited. My wife at first with tears remonstrated with me, and my partner and other friends did the same. This would do some good for a little time, but I was fairly within the current of the whirlpool, and in spite of the efforts put forth to save me, the circling flood was carrying me nearer and nearer to its centre with awful certainty. I soon wholly neglected my business, and my partner, after bearing with me with the patience of a father, dissolved his connexion with me. My father, after this, continued to find some employment of one kind or another for me; but though I would at times behave very well for a month or two, on the whole I was getting worse and worse. My wife lost all her bloom, and became thin and haggard. I saw it—I knew what was the cause—but though I loved her as I loved my own soul, I loved the wine cup more. She was gradually worn out by her troubles, and at length sickened and died. As that sweet spirit was going to heaven, I promised her with tears that I would repent and forsake my sins. Yet the very night after her burial I got intoxicated, and because I could find nothing else in the house to do it with, I took a bottle of Cologne that I found in her chamber. From that time I have been a wanderer. Occasionally I have been to my father's house, where I have always been welcomed with affection, notwithstanding all the evil that I have done. Hope has again and again been lighted up in the bosom, and they have made unwearied efforts to reform me; but I was an easy prey to temptation, and soon relapsed. I have been miserable, and have for years known nothing of happiness. My chains have galled me, and yet I have clung to them.

Such is the history of a wine drinker. Many of my companions who used to frequent that *respectable* eating shop have run a similar course. We there *began* a course of preparation for the vile and filthy scenes of the vulgar grog-shop. I would, therefore, warn every visiter of such a shop to beware, lest he take the first step in the downward road of intemperance. The drinker of wine, and ale, and cordials runs no small risk of becoming at length the besotted victim of rum. I would echo the solemn warning of the Bible—"Look not thou upon the wine when it is red;" for I can testify that "at the last it biteth like a serpent and stingeth like an adder" [see Prov. 23:31–32 —ed.].

One word more. I wish not to detract from the guilt which rests upon me, yet I verily believe that I should have succeeded in that first attempt at reformation, which I made after my return from sea, if the customs of society had not been wholly opposed to my efforts. There were in my case all the incentives that could possibly exist to prompt me to a course of virtue—my business was prosperous; I had a numerous circle of the best of friends around me; my natural qualities were such as to fit me to receive and impart enjoyment to a high degree in social intercourse; and the wife of my bosom was one who could exert almost the influence of a guardian angel—but all these were not adequate to withstand the influence of the *social* cup, addressing itself as it did at every step, with its bewitching allurements, to a propensity which had gathered strength by years of indulgence.

[RECOLLECTION] NO. V

I promised in my last number [not reprinted here —ed.] to give in my next a description of some cases of reformation in our village. We have had some of a very interesting character, and a sketch of them will afford a key to some of the principles on which the present temperance movement is based, and must depend for its success.

The reader will recollect that I said there were two taverns in the centre of the village—one kept by a Mr. Wightman, a lazy, slipshod, inoffensive sort of a man, and the other by a Mr. Branson, a vile, noisy, profane gambler, but shrewd and active, and of pretty good appearance. His tavern was of course the popular one. In front of it is a piazza running its whole length, and a long bench is fastened against the wall between the two doors. Under this piazza you might often see on a summer's day quite a little collection of village worthies telling stories, or discussing politics and other grave matters. Among them were some rather strongly marked characters. Reader, let me introduce you to them. That man with a weather-beaten face, of a frank, free-hearted expression, with a bold dash of the humorous, is Captain Carson, who has followed the seas his life. He is a jovial man, full of anecdote, and shrewd and sententious in his remarks. He is just now telling a story. See how his little audience swallow his yarn, with mouths wide open. Close by him sits a Mr. Clark, with his hat canted to one side, with an expression of countenance in which you can read his intention to beat the Captain's story as soon as he finishes it. He is a knowing man. He can talk theology with the parson, medicine with the doctor, law with the lawyer, in short, every thing, with every body, with perfect ease and assurance. Meanwhile he supports not his family, but they support him. Yet he walks about, flourishing his cane, which he does with a grace all his own, as if he was a man on whom not only a family, but the whole community depended. He is in the habit of telling large stories, especially when a little moved by the *spirit* within, and the Captain is always fond of quizzing him about his stories. Listen to him now. Captain Carson has just finished his story about a poor sailor, who suffered vastly from an inflamed foot, far away from land, the treatment of which he managed, of course, successfully. "Well," says Mr. Clark, "now Captain, you didn't manage that foot right. It might have been cured in less than half that time. I once had an inflammation in my foot. I applied a poultice made with catnip, and wormwood, and Indian posy and rum (describing very minutely the mode of preparation and application), and the result was that the inflammation all went into the great toe, and then when it went from there it popped like a pistol!"—giving a very graceful toss up of his cane—"Pon my word, it did." "Did it split your toe, and did it hit any body, Mr. Clark?" asked the Captain with the most quizzical look imaginable. But in spite of the ridiculousness of the story, and the burst of laughter which followed the Captain's inquiry, Mr. C. swore that it was true as gospel.

That bold-looking man that stands leaning against the pillar of the piazza is Mr. James, a thoroughly bad man, the most intimate friend of Mr. Branson, and like him, a gambler. He has some wit—enough to make a joke against every thing good—sufficiently witty to excite a laugh among the frequenters of a tavern. Next to him stands a roughly dressed man, Mr. Johnson, who was once a farmer, and owned a very large farm, which he lost by rum and the law. The geese of a neighbouring farmer were very troublesome, and he shot several of them. They then went to law about this and some other matters, and were in a constant quarrel for many years, keeping up their spunk all this time with rum—else they would have settled their difficulty almost at the outset. The conclusion was, that both lost their farms, and both became drunkards. Vastly more foolish were they than the geese they quarrelled about, and yet that Mr. Johnson, you can see by his face, is not naturally a fool. Rum often makes wiser men than he very foolish.

Now let me draw your attention to that grave-looking man that sits in an arm-chair opposite the captain. It is Squire Jones, a lawyer. He is seen in Mr. Branson's piazza only occasionally, and he is very cautious not to take his seat there except with company rather above the loafer order. You see a few of the ragged and dirty-shirted drinkers standing around. When they form any thing more than the out-skirts of the little company there assembled, he retires, though he is as much of a drunkard as any of them. He drinks mostly in private, and very seldom at a bar.

An amusing incident occurred some time since in relation to Squire Jones. At a temperance meeting Captain Carson was present, but Squire Jones was not, though many of his friends were and some of his immediate relatives. After the lecturer had finished his remarks, Captain Carson, who was rather tipsy, got up and said, "I spose, though I d—don't know, that I'm the only drunkard p—present in the s—sembly, but (raising his voice to a high pitch and looking all around) Squire Jones wh—where are *you*—I say, Squire Jones, where are *you?*" The effect on the audience you can imagine better than I can describe. It was placing the secret, genteel, parlor-drunkard just where he belonged, on a level with the open, bar-room sot. "But Squire Jones where are you," became at once a by-word in the village, and it is to this day at the tongues' ends of all the boys in the streets.

That short little man with a quick moving black eye, that stands behind the wise Mr. Clark's chair, is a Mr. Crowell, a shoemaker, and a first-rate one he is too. He is a periodical drinker for the most part. He loses enough of his time, and spends enough of his earnings, to make his family miserably poor; though, if it were not for this single habit, he would be as good a husband and father as there is in the village. He has long been the dupe of the vile Mr. Branson and his friend Mr. James, who continue to filch from him all his loose change whenever he gets on a spree. He is a social man, and you see he is enjoying the conversation to the full.

Now just notice for a moment that ragged, dirty, long-bearded man, that is hitching a horse to that post. It is Mr. Branson's hostler. He steps up into the piazza to join the group of drunkards, and dares to crack a joke even with the Squire, for he knows that the Squire loves brandy as well as he loves rum. How brutal he is in his whole appearance! He is gone by—you will say—there is no hope of him. But that same man, reader, has been in the high places of the earth in point of privileges, and he was dragged down from thence by intemperance into the miry filth of the bar-room and the grog-shop. Is there no power to bring him back again? Yes, blessed be God, there is.

So, I have introduced you, reader, to most of the characters in the group in Mr. Branson's piazza. Let me take you to the same spot again a few months after. The group you see is *smaller* now. Captain Carson is not there. Why? He is a reformed man, and the President of the Washington Total Abstinence Society, lately formed in our village, of which I have the honour to be Secretary. Mr. Crowell, the little shoemaker, is not there. He also is reformed, and his family are happy, and he is now at his last, working for their support, instead of idling away his time in gossip under Mr. Branson's piazza and drinking at his bar. Mr. Johnson, the farmer, is not there. He has ceased to be so much of a goose as to frequent Mr. Branson's bar, and is thinking about joining our Society. The hostler is not there, neither is he on Mr. Branson's premises. His rags he has cast off—he is changed back from the brute to the man—and that countenance which a few months ago was the seat of the stupid leer of the sot is now beaming with virtue and intelligence. Dr. Newton (for this same ragged hostler was once a physician of great promise) is now labouring as a lecturer in the service of our Society, and he intends soon to establish himself again in the practice of his profession. His history is an interesting one, and at another time I will give it to you. Even Squire Jones is not there. But it is not because he has reformed—he is as much a drunkard as ever. It is because it has become more disreputable since the formation of our Society to be seen lounging about a tavern.

But who do now compose the group in that piazza? A sorry company of dirty loafers, with the wise Mr. Clark for an oracle, and the vile Mr. James for his echo. Mr. Branson's "occupation" is nearly "gone," and it is the intention of our Washington Society that it shall be entirely so.

Now if we look carefully at the *characters* of the persons whom I have described, we shall see why it is that some of them are reformed, and not others. Reformation is not a haphazard business. This will be found to be true—that *character* has vastly more to do with the question of a drunkard's reformation than the degree to which the intemperate habit has reached. I use the word character in its widest sense, as including all that makes up the man.

Of that little group Mr. Clark is altogether too wise to learn any thing, especially to learn the simple lesson of teetotalism. He knows all about it. He knows how to promote the cause of temperance better than priests and priest-ridden men and women and reformed drunkards. He is a very Solomon. He never will "become a fool that he may be wise"— not he.

But why was not the Squire reformed? Could he not, with all his acuteness, see that he is running a career which, if persisted in, will ruin his respectability, his happiness, his soul? He may see this at times, and tremble at the prospect for the moment, but it is soon forgotten. He has created in himself, secretly for the most part, an appetite, which it needs influences from without to help him to overcome; but wrapped up in the dignity which his station throws around him, he shuts up the avenues by which these influences can reach him. He is left therefore to fight *alone* with temptation. His resistance is almost as a matter of course weak and soon given over. If he were the frank, open, social drunkard that Captain Carson was, he might then, like him, have been reached and perhaps recovered.

Compare now the case of Crowell, the shoemaker, with that of Branson's boon companion, the gambling Mr. James. Mr. Crowell was the more confirmed drunkard of the two, so far as the degree of appetite is concerned. He was often fairly in the gutter, while it is very seldom that Mr. James has been seen absolutely drunk. But Mr. Crowell had in his sober moments honourable feelings, a sense of respectability, affection for his family—these and other motives which could be appealed to. He was vicious only in consequence of his intemperance; while the intemperance of Mr. James was rather the *product* than the cause of his other vicious propensities.

This in my view is a very important distinction, in estimating the probabilities of reformation in different cases. It teaches us one very useful lesson. *Never despair of the reformation of any drunkard, however low he may have got in his intemperance—however strongly the disease, for it is such, is fastened upon him*, PROVIDED THAT WHEN HE IS SOBER, THERE ARE ANY GENEROUS FEELINGS IN HIS BOSOM, ANY GOOD MOTIVES, TO WHICH YOU CAN APPEAL WITH ANY SORT OF EF-FECT. If there be one chord that you can touch and awaken proper feeling, persevere in your efforts, though he fall again and again. But if the drunkard be a disorganizer, a hater of good doings, a bad citizen, a bad husband and father, *aside from intemperance*—if his heart be exceedingly depraved, and his drunkenness is merely a consequence of his badness of heart—there is no hope of his restoration, till his heart is changed, till the *source* of his intemperance and his other bad propensities is purged by religion. And this leads me to say that after all, *religion* must be made the *basis* of this temperance reformation now going on, if we wish it to be thoroughly and permanently successful. Motives from other sources may be and often are appealed to with great effect, such as regard for character, affection for one's family, self-respect and the desire for respectability, the love for rational happiness, &c., but still let it be written as with a sunbeam, that the "rock of salvation" is the same to the drunkard as to every other sinner, the only *sure* rock of safety on which his feet can be planted.

In this connexion I notice a very interesting fact, that the reformation of the drunkard is, in these days of wonders, often, very often, the means of introducing religion to his heart. How can it be otherwise? The man has been suddenly aroused from his delusive dream of vice. It seems to him, now that he has escaped from the spell with which the monster intemperance has so long bound him, that he has awakened to an entirely new world of thought and feeling. His bosom is accordingly opened to the influence of motives, and what motives are more calculated to act strongly upon him than those offered by religion? His heart too is softened by the kindness and sympathy, which have been extended to him by those who have prayed and laboured for his restoration. And as he looks back upon the degradation and misery from which he has been saved, how can he help breaking forth in thanksgiving to God, and devoting, with the deepest penitence and the warmest love, his future life to his service. I should like to dwell longer on this topic, but my limits warn me to close. I would merely add, let clergymen and all good men see to it, that they neglect not the wide field of usefulness laid open before them by the present temperance movement. Enter into it and reap the rich harvest.

6

from *An Autobiography by John B. Gough* (1845)

John Gough was born in Sandgate, England, on 22 August 1817, son of the village schoolmistress and a retired soldier. A precocious and bookish child, Gough was allowed to seek his fortune in America, where he arrived in 1829 in the company of English neighbors, to whom he was apprenticed. After a stint as a farm laborer near Utica, New York, he fled to New York City and learned the bookbinding trade. The course of Gough's drunken career is retraced in the following extended excerpt, which constitutes the first two parts of his *Autobiography*. In the third part, the narrative dissipates into a chronicle of Gough's early temperance lectures, of which he kept tediously detailed records.

Gough was spellbinding from the platform. An actor, a singer, a mimic, he combined tender mercies with temperance fire and brimstone. Hundreds felt compelled to sign the pledge. After hearing Gough speak in upstate New York in 1849, Susan B. Anthony exclaimed to her mother: "What a lecture, what arguments, how can a man or woman remain neutral or be a moderate drinker." As a Cincinnati newspaper reported, after Gough's triumphal lectures there: "He is comic, tragic, melo-dramatic, statesman-like, and everything that is rare, in his manner and speech."

Gough's *Autobiography*, an extended version of his stump speech, first appeared in 1845 in a privately published edition of a thousand copies. (Gough himself had a hand in the publication.) The book went through twelve printings between 1845 and 1853, as well as several issues in England, where Gough was also tremendously popular. An expanded (but more diffuse) version, first published in 1869 as *Autobiography and Personal Recollections*, was widely circulated as a subscription book, as were Gough's later collections of lecture material, *Sunlight and Shadow* (1880) and *Platform Echoes* (1885).

Much to the chagrin of his initial Washingtonian sponsors, Gough prospered greatly from his lecture fees; and long after he had broken with the Society and joined the temperance mainstream, his career was marked by controversy over the rectitude and magnitude of his earnings. In 1857, Gough accidently stepped into a vicious dispute between the suasionist and prohibitionist wings of the English temperance movement. In a private letter, he had bemoaned the recent repeal of the Maine law (the first enactment of prohibition at the state level), suggesting that the law had failed, in any case, to extinguish the liquor trade. The defeatist implications of Gough's letter, which was made public, led to violent attacks upon him from prohibitionists during his English tour. After one enemy, Dr. F. R. Lees, alleged that Gough was still drinking and, furthermore, mixing alcohol with other drugs, Gough sued him for libel and won a virtually uncontested judgment.

During his later years, long since happily remarried and settled on an estate outside Worcester, Gough continued to tramp the lecture trail, holding to a relentless schedule both at home and abroad. His life ended, as he might have wished, in harness. Having suffered a stroke during a lecture near Philadelphia, Gough lingered three days and then died in his sixty-ninth year, on 15 February 1886. Despite Gough's contemporary fame and importance—he was as well known in his own day as is Billy Graham in ours—no modern biography exists. Gough's papers may be found at the American Antiquarian Society in Worcester, Massachusetts.

PART FIRST

*I*t may be asked by many individuals, whose eyes will fall on these pages, why I have thought it requisite to add one to the already numerous autobiographies extant? I answer, that justice to myself, in some measure, demands an explicit statement of the principal incidents in an hitherto eventful life; those incidents, or, at least, many of them, having, in frequent instances, been erroneously described by the press generally. Besides this, many who have heard my verbal narrations have intimated a desire to become more fully acquainted with a career, which, although it has extended but little beyond a quarter of a century, has been fruitful of adventure. To gratify others, rather than myself, has been my object in reducing to a permanent form my somewhat eventful history. I make no pretensions to literary merit, and trust this candid avowal will dis-arm criticism. Mine is, indeed, a "short and simple annal of the poor"; and if the perusal of these pages should cheer some fainting wanderer on the world's highway, and lead him far from the haunts of evil, by the still waters of temperance, my labor will have been well repaid. Truth consti-tutes the merit of my tale, if it possess any merit; and most of us know that real life often furnishes stranger stories than romance ever dreamed of; and that facts are frequently more startling than fiction.

I was born on the twenty-second of August, 1817, at a romantic little watering-place, named Sandgate, in the county of Kent, England. My father had been a soldier in the fortieth and fifty-second regiment of foot, and was in the enjoyment of a pension of £20 per annum, having frequently fought during the Peninsular war, and been wounded in the neck. I remember as well as if it had been but yesterday how he would go through military exercises with me, my mimic weapon being a broom, and my martial equipments some of his faded trappings. I was not des-tined, however, to see how fields were won. With what intense interest have I often listened to his descriptions of battle-fields, and how have I shuddered at contemplating the dreadful scenes which he so graphically portrayed. He was present at the memorable battle of Corunna, and wit-nessed its hero, Sir John Moore, carried from that fatal field. "Here," he would say, "was such a regiment—there such a battalion; in this situa-tion was the enemy—and yonder was the position of the general and his staff." And then he would go on to describe the death of the hero—his looks, and his burial near the ramparts, until my young heart would leap with excitement. Apart from such attractions as these, my father pos-sessed few for a child. His military habits had become as a second nature with him. Stern discipline had been taught him in a severe school, and it being impossible for him to cast off old associations, he was not calcu-lated to win the deep affections of a child, although, in every respect, he deserved and possessed my love. He received his discharge from the army in the year 1823.

My mother's character was cast in a gentler mould. Her heart was a fountain, whence the pure waters of affection never ceased to flow. Her very being seemed twined with mine, and ardently did I return her love. For the long space of twenty years she had occupied the then prominent position of schoolmistress in the village, and frequently planted the first principles of knowledge in the minds of children, whose parents had, years before, been benefited by her early instructions. And well qualified by nature and acquirements was she for the interesting but humble office she filled, if a kindly heart and a well-stored mind be the requisites. Of course, I received my first lessons at home; but as I advanced in years, it became advisable that I should be sent to a school, and to one I was accordingly sent. There was a free school in the village, but my father possessed too much independence to allow him to send me to a charity school, and, though he could ill afford it, paid a weekly sum for my instruction at the seminary of Mr. Davis, of Folkstone. I progressed rapidly in my limited education, and became a teacher in the school; two classes, as was the custom, were placed under my care; the children of one of them I initiated into the art and mystery of spelling words of two syllables, and taught the Rule of Three to a class more advanced.

As most boys will, I sometimes got into petty scrapes, and once narrowly escaped a serious disgrace. I occasionally gave the reins to a temper which was naturally passionate, and on a certain occasion, when the order of "Teachers to your classes" was given, I exclaimed, "I wish the classes were at the devil!" One of the boys reported my remark to the master, saying, "Please, sir, I heard him." He called me to him. I denied that I had uttered such words; but one boy, and another, and another asserting that I did, with "Please, sir, I heard him, too," my falsehood was discovered. I then could deny no longer; and my master sternly ordered me, when the school closed, to take my slate and books home with me, and never return to the school. I sat down moodily in my place, pondering on what had occurred, and revolving within my mind what course I should pursue; for I justly dreaded my father's anger, and felt convinced that he would not pass my offence by lightly. After mature consideration, I went to my master, admitted my fault, reasoned with him, and stated how much I feared my father's anger, should I be discharged from the school. Nor were my entreaties without the desired effect; for the good man relented, and I was pardoned, my father never knowing any thing of the matter.

I was now about eight years of age, and having a keen taste for the beauties of nature, was often to be found roaming on Sandgate beach, gazing with wonder on the great deep, and, as I listened to its everlasting moan, little dreaming that three thousand miles beyond was a land in

114

which my lot would one day be cast. There was an old castle, too, in the vicinity, which had been built years ago—ages to my boyish mind—by Henry the Eighth. I became a great favorite of the keeper of this ancient place, and having acquired some knowledge of the history of the bluff king Hal, I used to wander through the desolate courtyards where the rank grass grew; sit in deserted, windowless chambers, where the bat nestled and the owl screamed, or gaze from turret and battlement on the surrounding scenery. And I would in fancy people the place with its old inhabitants, and see plumed cavaliers and ruffled dames pacing the corridors or surrounding the groaning board. Katherine of Arragon, and Ann Boleyn, with Henry's other wives, flitted by me. I lived, as it were, in the past; and thus, almost unconsciously, my imagination was cultured, and my mind imbued with a love of history and poetry.

My father belonged to the Methodist persuasion, and my mother was a Baptist, but the differences in doctrine existing between them never affected their happiness. As all in such cases should do, they agreed to differ. Among other circumstances connected with this period of my life, I well remember one which much impressed me. The venerable and devoted William Wilberforce resided, during a few of the summer months, at Sandgate, for the benefit of his health. I had heard much of the great philanthropist, and was not a little delighted when my father took me to his lodgings, where a prayer-meeting was held. How it was, I know not, but I attracted Mr. Wilberforce's attention. He patted me on my head, said many kind things, and expressed wishes for my welfare. He also presented me with a book, and wrote with his own hand my name on the fly-leaf. Having acquired some reputation as a good reader, he requested me to read to him. I did so, and he expressed himself as much pleased. The book presented to me, I long since lost, but never shall I forget the kindly words of the venerable giver.

I have remarked that I was considered to be a good reader. Often, whilst I have been sitting reading to my mother, as she sat working by our cottage-door, which faced the sea, have strangers stayed to listen, attracted by my proficiency in this art. There was a library in the village, kept by Mr. Purday, and to this place many of the visitors at our watering-place resorted, to learn the news. Very frequently I was sent for to read to ladies and gentlemen; and the school-mistress's son became a general purveyor of the gossip of the day, in return for which I was rewarded pretty liberally. On one occasion, a gentleman, to whom I had read some portions of a newspaper, was so pleased, that he took me to the library, fronting the reading-room, in the same building, and asked me what book I would like to take. Showing me a volume which contained hieroglyphical pictures, and a common prayer-book, he offered me either I might choose. Now, with all the love of a lad for pictures, I ardently desired the hieroglyphical designs, but, thinking I should be considered more favorably of if I decided on accepting the prayer-book, I chose, much against my will, the latter. My choice was applauded; and a bright half crown into the bargain consoled me for the self-mortification my vanity had imposed.

About this time I experienced a very narrow escape from death. I went to school, at Folkstone, and was returning from that place, one day, accompanied by some other boys, playing at wagon and horses, four boys personating quadrupeds, which I was driving at rather a rapid rate. It happened that a man, who was engaged in digging a trench by the side of the road, did not perceive the four lads I was driving, they having stooped as they passed; he threw up a spadeful of clay, for the purpose of tossing it to some little distance, and the sharp edge of the implement was driven with great force against my head. I instantly sunk down insensible and deluged with blood. I was carried home by the boys, who in reality became animals of burden, still unconscious, to my terrified parents, and for days my life was despaired of. Even when recovery seemed probable, few hopes of my returning reason were entertained, although, by the providence of God, I recovered; yet, to this day, I feel the effects of that blow. When excited in speaking, I am frequently compelled to press my hands on my head, to ease the pricking and darting sensation I experience; and never, I suppose, shall I be entirely free from inconvenience from this source. My father had a tender heart, notwithstanding his habitual sternness, and he never reverted to this circumstance in after days without tears.

During my father's absence in the wars, my mother's circumstances were very straitened, although, in addition to school-keeping, she worked industriously at making a kind of lace, then very fashionable, and in the manufacture of which article she greatly excelled. On one occasion, when our necessities absolutely required extra exertion, she took her basket of work, and travelled eight and a half weary miles, to the town of Dover. Arrived there, foot-sore and heart-weary, she threaded the streets and lanes with her lace, seeking for customers, but not one did she find; and, after reluctantly abandoning the pursuit, she once more turned her face towards her home—a home desolate indeed. Painful, bitterly painful, were my mother's reflections as she drew near her door, and when she rested her dreadfully tired frame, she had nothing in the house with which to recruit her strength. During her absence, a gentleman had sent for me to the Library, and was so pleased with my reading, that he made me a present of five shillings; and Mr. Purday, in addition, gave me sixpence. O! how rich I was. Never had I possessed so vast an amount of money before, and all imaginable modes of spending it flitted before my fancy. I went to play with some other boys until my mother's return from Dover; and, soon afterwards, on entering our house, I found her sitting in her chair, bathed in tears. I asked her what was the matter? when she drew me close to her, and looking in my face, with a mournful expression which I shall never forget, informed me that all her weary journey had been fruitless—she had sold nothing. O! with what joy I drew the crown-piece and the sixpence from my pocket, and placed them in her hand; and with what delightful feelings we knelt down, whilst she poured out her heart in thankfulness to God, for the relief so seasonably provided. My mother gave me a halfpenny for myself, and I felt far happier then than I did when I received the shining silver crown-piece: it was *all* my own, to do as I liked with—to keep or spend. What an inestimable privilege! I can, in all sincerity, say, that never have I received money since then, which has afforded me such solid satisfaction; and some of my most pleasant reminiscences are circumstances connected with that boyish incident.

I ought, before this, to have mentioned that I had a sister, two years younger than myself, of whom I thought a great deal. She was my chief playmate. I used to frequently personate a clergyman, being then very fond of imitation; and having rigged up a chair into something as much resembling a pulpit as possible, I would secure her services in the way of dressing up rag dolls, which constituted my congregation, for whose especial benefit I used to pour forth my mimic oratory, very much to my own amusement, if not to the edification of my dumb friends, who sat stiff and starched, perfect patterns of propriety. Then, as a diversion, I manufactured, from an old bottomless chair, a very respectable Punch and Judy box; and many a laugh have I raised among my young companions by my performances in this line. My puppets were of home manufacture, but they passed muster well enough, especially with the boys and girls, who had never been fortunate enough to have seen the genuine personifications of these remarkable characters.

About this time, my father returned home, and soon afterwards entered the service of the Rev. J. D. Glennie, a clergyman of the Church of England, and chaplain to Lord Darnley; and here I cannot but pay a passing tribute of respect to this pious and kind-hearted man, who always treated me with much consideration. His wife sent for me, and presented me with "Doddridge's Rise and Progress of Religion in the Soul," "The Economy of Human Life," and "Todd's Lectures to the Young"; works which shortly afterwards I perused at sea, when voyaging to America, they having been given to me the day before I left Sandgate.

A very important change in my fortunes now occurred. I was 12 years of age; and my father, foreseeing the difficulty of procuring me a trade, made an agreement with a family of our village, who were about emigrating to America, that they, in consideration of the sum of ten guineas, paid by him, should take me with them, teach me a trade, and provide for me until I was 21 years of age. After much hesitation, my mother, from a sense of duty, yielded to this arrangement. I, boylike, felt in high glee, at the prospects before me. My little arrangements having been completed, on the 4th of June, 1829, I took a last view of my native village. The evening I was about to depart, a neighbor invited me to take tea at his house, which I did. My mother remarked to me afterwards: "I wish you had taken tea with your mother, John"; and this little circumstance was a source of much pain to me in after years. The parting with my beloved parents was bitter. My poor mother folded me to her bosom, then she would hold me off at arm's length, and gaze fondly on my face, through her tearful eyes, reading, only as a mother could, the book of futurity for me. She hung up, on the accustomed peg, my old cap and jacket, and my school-bag, and there they remained until, years after, she quitted the house. At length the parting words were spoken, and I quitted the home of my childhood, perhaps forever.

A touching scene it was, as I went through the village towards the coach-office that evening. As I passed through the streets, many a kind hand waved a farewell, and not a few familiar voices sounded out a hearty "God bless you." There was one old dame, of whom I had frequently bought sweetmeats at her green grocery, named familiarly Granny Hogben; she called me into her shop, and loaded me with good wishes, bulls' eyes, cakes, and candies, although, poor affectionate soul, she could ill afford it. The inn was reached, and, in company with another lad, who was going out with our family to meet a relative, I mounted the roof of the London night coach, and was quitting the village, when, on turning round to take a last look at it, I saw a crouching female form, by a low wall, near the bathing-machines. My heart told me at once that it was my mother, who had taken advantage of half an hour's delay, at the inn door, to proceed a little distance, in order to have one more glance at her departing child. I never felt I was loved so much as I did from that time. When we arrived at Ashford, we were placed inside the vehicle. Amongst many things which impressed me on my journey was the circumstance of a poor, shivering woman begging alms at the coach door, at midnight, for whom I keenly felt. At Footscray, I again was placed outside the coach. On arriving near the metropolis, objects of interest increased every moment, and, when fairly in the great city, of which I had heard so much, I was almost bewildered with the crowds, and the multiplicity of attractive objects. A fight between two bellicose individuals was almost my first town entertainment.

Whilst I remained in London, I saw some of the great gratuitous attractions, such as St. Paul's, the Tower, the Royal Exchange, the Mansion House, and the Monument, to the summit of which I ascended, and surveyed from thence the "mighty mass of brick, and smoke, and shipping." On the 10th day of June, every thing being arranged, I sailed from the Thames, in the ship Helen. Passing Dover, we arrived off Sandgate, on Sunday, when it fell a dead calm, and the ship's anchors were dropped. I afforded some amusement to those around me, by the eagerness with which I seized a telescope, and the certainty with which I averred that I saw my old home. During that day, boat after boat came off to us from the shore, and friends of the family I was with paid them visits; but I was unnoticed—*my* relatives did not come. After long and wearily watching, I at last saw a man, standing up in a boat, with a white band round his hat. "That's him! that's my father!" I shouted. He soon got on deck, and almost smothered me with his kisses, from which I somewhat shrank, as his beard made very decided impressions on my smooth skin. I heard that my mother and sister had gone to a place of worship, at some distance from Sandgate, which I regretted much. When evening came on, our visitors from the shore repaired to their boats, which, when a few yards from the ship, formed in a half circle. Our friends stood up in them, and, o'er the calm waters sounded our blended voices, as we sang:

> Blest be the dear uniting love,
>   Which will not let us part;
> Our bodies may far hence remove,
>   We still are one in heart.

Boat after boat then vanished in the gloomy distance, and I went to my bed. About midnight, I heard my name called, and going on deck, I there found my beloved mother and sister, who, hearing, on their return home, that I was in the offing, had paid half a guinea (money hardly earned, and with difficulty procured, but readily and cheerfully expended) to a boatman, to row them to the ship. They spent an hour (O, how short it seemed!) with me, and then departed, with many tears. Having strained my eyes, until their boat was no longer discernible, I went back to my bed, to sob away the rest of the morning. I felt this to be my first real sorrow. Grief, however, will wear itself out; and, having slept somewhat, when I awoke in the morning, a breeze having sprung up, we were far out at sea. I never experienced any sea-sickness; and, had my expectations with respect to the family I was with been realized, I should have been comparatively happy. Occasionally, on looking over my little stock of worldly goods, I would find little billets, or papers, containing texts of Scripture, pinned to the different articles. In my Bible, texts of Scripture were marked for me to commit to memory; amongst them, I remember, were the 2d, 3d, 4th, and 5th chapters of Proverbs. As we voyaged on, I soon began to feel a difference in my new situation; and often did I bitterly contrast the treatment I received with that to which I had been accustomed at home. I wished myself back again; but the die was cast, and so I put up with disagreeables as well as I could. On the morning of the 3d of August, fifty-four days from the time of sailing, we arrived off Sandy Hook; and, O how I longed, as we sailed up the Narrows, to be on deck, and survey the scenery of the New World! I was not permitted to do this; for, whilst I could hear the shouts of delighted surprise which burst from the lips of the passengers who crowded the vessel's sides, I was confined below, occupied in blacking the boots and shoes of the family, in order that that they might be landed "sound, and in good order." We made the land at three in the morning, and were moored at the wharf, in New York, at three in the afternoon, rather an unusual thing, as ships are generally detained some time at Staten Island.

I had got so tired of biscuit* that I most ardently longed for some "soft Tommy," and was already munching it in imagination, when my guardians went on shore, leaving me behind. I had anticipated purchasing some dainties immediately, for, having received a little money for a cabbage-net I had made on board, I possessed the requisite funds. My capital was, however, not so large as it might have been, for I had, like other capitalists, negotiated a loan with the black cook, to whom I advanced an English crown. The principal and interest, to this day, remain unpaid, not an uncommon occurrence, I have been since told, in regard to foreign loans. To return. I was left on board all night, as my acquaintances did not return; and, during their absence, I sought for amusement in gazing from the vessel on the crowded wharfs. I well remember my surprise at seeing a boy, about my own age, inserting a plug of tobacco in his mouth; but I soon became accustomed to such things as these, and many, too, of a far stranger nature. When I *did* get an opportunity, I laid in a good stock of bread; and having stayed about two months in York City, during which time I often strolled about the streets, we started for Western New York. I was greatly delighted with the scenery on the Hudson river, which far surpassed any I had ever before witnessed. We went to a farm in Oneida county, where I remained two years, during which period I was never sent to either a Sabbath or

---

*I would here state that the family I travelled with had provided a quantity of fine white pilot bread for the voyage. In suppose I at first ate very heartily, and that fears were entertained of my diminishing the stock; for when we arrived at Portsmouth, the head of the family went on shore, and brought back with him a bag of the most suspicious-looking biscuit I ever laid eyes on. On this I was exclusively fed during the remainder of the voyage. To do Mr. —— justice, I do not think *he* was altogether to blame in this matter, for I believe him to have been naturally a kind-hearted man; but it is not always that husbands can do exactly as they please in this world.

day school. I felt this much, as I had an ardent desire to acquire knowledge; and, tiring of so unprofitable a life, and perceiving, also, that no chance existed of my being taught a trade, I sold a knife for the purpose of paying the postage of a letter to my father, in which I asked his permission to go to New York, and learn a trade. I sent off this letter clandestinely, because, hitherto, all my letters home had been perused by my guardians before they were despatched, and I did not wish their interference in this matter. In due course, I received a reply to my letter. My father said that as I was old enough now to judge for myself, I might act according to the dictates of my own judgment. Glad enough was I to have my fate in my own hands, as it were, and on the 12th of December, 1831, I quitted Oneida county for New York City. It may easily be imagined that I left my situation with but very little regret, for, although by some of the members I was treated with consideration and kindness, yet from those to whom I naturally looked for comfort and solace, I experienced treatment far different from that which my father anticipated when he intrusted me to their guardianship. In all conscientiousness, I can aver, that my situation, when I left this family, was worse than it was when I entered it. Here, I beg to make a remark, which is rendered necessary from the fact of it having been stated that I have represented the family as dissipated and drunken. Such a report never was made by me at any time, or in any place; nor did there exist foundation for such a rumor. Whisky and cider were used by the family, but not to excess, that I knew of. In pure self-defence I make this statement.*

Whilst with the family referred to, a revival of religion occurred in our neighborhood. My mind was much impressed, and I was admitted a member of the Methodist Episcopal Church. On my arrival in New York, I had half a dollar only in my pocket, and all the goods I possessed in the world were contained in a little trunk, which I carried. I stood at the foot of Courtland street, after I left the boat. Hundreds of people went by, on busy feet, heedless of me, and I felt desolate indeed. But, amidst all my lonely sorrow, the religious impressions I have just referred to, and, more especially, those which I had derived from the lips of my beloved mother, afforded some rays of consolation which glimmered

*I never should have referred to this subject, had not a meddlesome fellow in New York City busied himself about my affairs, impeached my veracity, and imputed to me motives which I never entertained. *Verbum, sat.*

through the gloom. Whilst I was standing, pondering whither I should bend my steps, a man came up to me, and asked where he should carry my trunk. Then, indeed, the strong sense of my forlornness came to me, and I scarcely ever remember to have experienced more bitterness of spirit than on that occasion. Fancy me, reader! a boy, just fourteen years of age, a stranger, in a strange city, with no one to guide him, none to advise, and not a single soul to love, or be loved by. There I was, three thousand miles distant from home and friends; a waif on life's wave, solitary in the midst of thousands, and with a heart yearning for kindly sympathy, but finding none. Whilst musing on my fortunes, all at once the following passage entered my mind, and afforded me consolation: "Trust in the Lord, and do good; so shalt thou dwell in the land, and verily thou shalt be fed." Shouldering my trunk, I entered the city; and, having left my load in charge of a person, I repaired to the Brown Jug, public-house, in Pearl street, in which place I remained until the Monday morning following, when I was recommended to apply to the venerable Mr. Dando, who was then the agent of the Christian Advocate and Journal. To this gentleman I told my story, after hearing which, he went with me to the Methodist book concern (then situated in Crosby street), where, after some conversation, I was engaged, to attend on the next Wednesday, as errand boy, and to learn the book-binding business; and, for my services, to receive two dollars and twenty-five cents per week, and to board myself. Mr. Dando recommended me, as a boarder, to a Mrs. M——, in William street, at the rate of two dollars weekly; and, low as were the terms, the reader will presently agree with me in thinking that it was far too much for the accommodation I received. To my surprise, I found, when the hour of rest approached, that I was to share a bed with an Irishman, who was lying very sick of a fever and ague. The poor fellow told me his little history, and I experienced the truth of the saying that "Poverty makes us acquainted with strange bed-fellows." He had emigrated to America, been attacked with the disease I have mentioned, and now was out of money, but daily in the expectation of receiving some from his friends. My companion shivered so much, and was so restless during the night, that I was wretchedly disturbed; and, next day, I told my landlady that I could not possibly sleep in the same bed with the Irishman again. Accordingly, the next night, she made me up a wretched couch, in the same room, under the rafters. It was hard enough, and what is called a cat's-tail bed; and so wretchedly situated was it, that when I stretched my hand out, to pull up the scanty supply of bed-clothes, my fingers would encounter the half glutinous webs of spiders, a species of insect to which I have had, from childhood, and still have, an unaccountable, but deeply-rooted, antipathy. Weary as I was, from want of sleep on the preceding night, I soon fell asleep in my uneasy bed, but was awoke, in the dead of the night, by frightful groans, uttered by my sick companion. I started, and found, to my surprise, that the man was up. I was dreadfully frightened, more especially, as he informed me that he feared he was going to die. I asked him to let me call assistance; but he positively forbade it, and then went and sat on the side of the bed. O! never have I heard such agonizing exclamations, as broke from the lips of that dying man, as he called, with terrible earnestness, on Christ to save him, and on God to be merciful to him. He seemed anxious to know the hour. I told him I thought it was near morning, as the cock had crowed. After some more moaning noises, he suddenly fell back on the bed. I heard a rattling, gurgling sound, and then all was silent. I *felt* the man was dead, although I could not see him, and knew that I was alone with Death, for the first time. O! how slowly dragged on the hours until dawn; and, when the faint light struggled through a little window in the roof, and gradually brought out the walls and furniture from the gloom, there lay the dead man on his back, his mouth wide open, and his eyes glazed, but staring only as dead eyes can. With a desperate effort, I started from my bed, gathered my clothes in a bundle, dressed myself outside the room door, and roused the woman of the house. She received the intelligence with about as much composure as if Death had paid her house an expected and customary visit, and only remarked, "Well, dear soul! he was very patient, and is gone to glory." After the poor man's death, his expected funds arrived; but, alas! too late.

I soon afterwards went to my work, and my business was to pack up bundles of books for Cincinnati. As I was working, I fell into a train of thought respecting my desolate situation, and, as I mused, the scalding tears fell, in large drops, on the paper I was using. Into the very depths of my sorrow a kind heart looked; for, whilst I was weeping, a young lady came to me, and asked me what was the matter? Her tone of kindness, and look of sympathy, won my confidence, and I informed her of the particulars of my little history. When I had finished my tale, she said, "Poor distressed child! you shall go home with me to-night." I did so; and, when I arrived at her house, I saw her mother, who was engaged in frying cakes on the stove. The young girl took her mother aside into an inner room, and, presently, the latter came out, and said to me, "Poor boy! I will be a mother to you." These words fell like refreshing dew on my young heart; and mother and sister, indeed, did the benevolent Mrs. Egbert and her daughter prove to me. Soon after this, I joined the church in Allen street; and, after remaining with the Egberts some months, I removed, and boarded with my class-leader, Mr. Anson Willis. I afterwards boarded with a Mrs. Ketchum; but frequently wished that I had remained with Mrs. Egbert. During this period of my life, circumstances induced me to leave the church, and also my place of employment; and I became exposed to temptation, and too soon grew thoughtless of religious things. I now worked at N. and J. White's, corner of William and Pearl streets, and, as my prospects were somewhat improving, I sent for my father, mother, and sister, to join me in this country. On Saturday afternoon, in August, 1833, a small note was brought, which informed me that my mother and sister were on board the ship President, then lying in the stream. I immediately left my work, intending to go to them, and was on my way down Fulton street, when the sole of my shoe got loose, and I stepped into the bindery of Burlock and Wilbur, where I had directed my relatives to call on their arrival, to get a knife to cut it off, when I learned that my mother had called at the store, a short time before, and had left to go to William street. I turned into that thoroughfare, and saw a little woman, rapidly walking, whom I recognized as her of whom I was in search. She looked every now and then at a slip of paper which she held in her hand, and frequently glanced from it to the fronts of the houses, as if to ascertain some particular number. Much as I desired to speak to her, I thought I would try whether she would recognize me or not; so I went behind her, passed on a little way, then turned, and met her; but she did not observe who I was. I again went behind her, and exclaimed, "Mother!" At the well-known sound she turned in a moment, and in an instant she had clasped me in her arms, and embraced me in a very maternal manner, heedless of the staring passers-by, who were very little used to have such public displays of affection got up for their amusement. I returned with my mother to the barge, in order to get her luggage, and, when there, was surprised by a great girl jumping into my arms, who was so altered from the time I saw her last, that I had some difficulty in recognizing my sister. My father did not accompany his wife and daughter, for he was loth to lose his hard-earned pension, and was in hopes to effect a commutation with the government, and receive a certain sum, in lieu of an annual payment.

At that time I was in the receipt of three dollars a week, wherewith to support myself; and, with the few articles my mother brought over, we went to housekeeping. O! how happy did I feel that evening, when my parent first made tea, in our own home. Our three cups and saucers made quite a grand show, and, in imagination, we were rich in viands, although our meal was frugal enough. Thus we lived comfortably together, nothing of note occurring, until the November following, when, owing to a want of business, and the general pressure of the times, I was dismissed from my place of work. This was a severe blow to us all, and its force was increased by my sister, who was a strawbonnet maker, also losing her employment. Our rent was a dollar and a quarter per week; but, finding it necessary to retrench in our expenditure, we gave up our two rooms, and made one answer our purpose, by dividing it into two compartments at night, by hanging up a temporary curtain. Our rent was now reduced to fifty cents a week, and all our goods and chattels were contained in the garret, which we continued to occupy until my mother's death. Things gradually grew worse and worse. Winter, in all its terrors, was coming on us, who were ill prepared for it. To add to our troubles, wood, during that season, was very high in price, and, in addition to want, we suffered dreadfully from cold. I obtained employment only at uncertain intervals, and for short periods, as errand-boy in a bookstore, in Nassau street, and in a bindery; but, even with this aid, we were sorely off, and painfully pinched. Thus was the whole of that dreary winter one continued scene of privation. Our sorrows were aggravated by my poor mother's sickness, and our apparel began to grow wretchedly scanty. I remember my mother once wishing for some broth, made from mutton. Not being able to bear that she should want any thing she required, I took my best coat, and having pawned it, procured her some meat, and thus supplied her wants, so far as practicable. Often and often have I, when we were destitute of wood, and had no money to procure any, gone a mile or two into the country, and dragged home such pieces as I might find lying about the sides of the road. Food, too, was sometimes wanting; and once, seeing my mother in tears, I ascertained that we had no bread in the house. I could not bear the sight of such distress, and wandered down a street, sobbing as I went. A stranger accosted me, and asked me what was the matter? "I'm hungry," said I; "and so is my mother." "Well," said the stranger; "I can't do much; but I'll get you a loaf"; and when I took this three cent piece of bread home, my mother placed the Bible on our old ricketty pine table, and, having opened it, read a portion of Scripture, and then we knelt down, thanking God for his goodness, and asking his blessing on what we were about to partake of. All these sufferings and privations my poor mother bore with Christian resignation, and never did she repine through all that dreary season.

As the spring came on, both my sister and myself got employment again, and our situation was bettered for a time. I now earned four dollars and a half a week; and was enabled to redeem my coat. A happy day was that, when I went in it with my sister to a place of worship. I would here mention that, during all that hard winter, we received no charitable assistance from any source. Once, and only once, my mother spoke of some wood which was to be given away to the poor, at the City Hall; but I refused to allow her to apply for relief there, knowing well that she would be subjected to the insulting questions of hard-hearted officials, who took advantage of their office to insult the unfortunate children of penury. Pity it is, that kind actions cannot always be performed in a kindly spirit; but, too often, such is not the case, in this cold-hearted world. Glad to this day am I, that I prevented her from being mortified by a contumely, which I cannot bear to think she should have borne.

And now comes one of the most terrible events of my history, an event which almost bowed me to the dust. The summer of 1834 was exceedingly hot; and as our room was immediately under the roof, which had but one small window in it, the heat was almost intolerable, and my mother suffered much from this cause. On the eighth of July, a day more than usually warm, she complained of debility, but as she had before suffered from weakness, I was not apprehensive of danger, and saying I would go and bathe, asked her to provide me some rice and milk against seven or eight o'clock, when I should return. That day my spirits were unusually exuberant. I laughed and sung with my young companions, as if not a cloud was to be seen in all my sky, when one was then gathering which was shortly to burst in fatal thunder over my head. About eight o'clock I returned home, and was going up the steps, whistling as I went, when my sister met me at the threshold, and seizing me by the hand, exclaimed, "*John, mother's dead!*" What I did, what I said, I cannot remember; but they told me, afterwards, I grasped my sister's arm, laughed frantically in her face, and then for some minutes seemed stunned by the dreadful intelligence. As soon as they permitted me, I visited our garret, now a chamber of death, and there, on the floor, lay all that remained of her whom I had loved so well, and who had been a friend when all others had forsaken me. There she lay, with her face tied up with a handkerchief:

> By foreign hands her aged eyes were closed;
> By foreign hands her decent limbs composed.

[See Pope, *Elegy to the Memory of an Unfortunate Lady.* —ed.]

O! how vividly came then to my mind, as I took her cold hand in mine and gazed earnestly in her quiet face, all her meek, enduring love, her uncomplaining spirit, her devotedness to her husband and children. All was now over; and yet, as through the livelong night I sat at her side, a solitary watcher by the dead, I felt somewhat resigned at the dispensation of Providence, and was almost thankful that she was taken from the "evil to come." Sorrow and suffering had been her lot through life; now she was freed from both; and loving her as I did, I found consolation in thinking that she was "not lost, but gone before."

I have intimated that I sat all night watching my mother's cold remains; such was literally the fact; and none but myself and God can tell what a night of agony that was. The people of the house accommodated my sister below. When the morning dawned in my desolate chamber, I tenderly placed the passive hand by my mother's side, and wandered out into the as yet almost quiet streets. I turned my face towards the wharf, and, arrived there, sat down by the dock, gazing with melancholy thoughts upon the glancing waters. All that had passed seemed to me like a fearful dream, and with difficulty could I at certain intervals convince myself that my mother's death was a fearful reality. An hour or two passed away in this dreamy, half-delirious state of mind, and then I involuntarily proceeded slowly towards my wretched home. I had eaten nothing since the preceding afternoon, but hunger seemed like my other senses to have become torpid. On my arrival at our lodgings, I found that a coroner's inquest had been held on my mother's corpse, and a note had been left by the official, which stated that it must be interred by noon of the following day. What was I to do? I had no money, no friends, and what was perhaps worse than all, none to sympathize with myself and my sister, but the people about us, who could afford the occasional exclamation, "poor things!" Again I wandered into the streets, without any definite object in view. I had a vague idea that my mother was dead, and must be buried, and little feeling beyond that. At times, I even forgot this sad reality. Weary and dispirited, I at last once more sought my lodgings, where my sister had been anxiously watching for me. I learned from her that, during my absence, some persons had been and brought a pine box to the house, into which they had placed my mother's body, and taken it off in a cart, for interment. They had but just gone, she said. I told her that we must go and see mother buried; and we hastened after the vehicle, which we soon overtook.

There was no "pomp and circumstance" about that humble funeral; but never went a mortal to the grave who had been more truly loved, and was then more sincerely lamented, than the silent traveller towards Potter's Field, the place of her interment. Only two lacerated and bleeding hearts mourned for her; but as the almost unnoticed procession passed through the streets, tears of more genuine sorrow were shed, than frequently fall when

> Some proud child of earth returns to dust.

We soon reached the burying-ground. In the same cart with my mother was another mortal whose spirit had put on immortality. A little child's coffin lay beside that of her who had been a sorrowful pilgrim for many years, and both now were about to lie side by side in the "narrow house." When the infant's coffin was taken from the cart, my sister burst into tears, and the driver, a rough-looking fellow, with a kindness of manner that touched us, remarked to her, "Poor little thing; 't is better off where 't is." I undeceived him in his idea as to this supposed relationship of the child, and informed him that it was not a child but our mother for whom we mourned. My mother's coffin was then taken out and placed in a trench, and a little dirt was thinly sprinkled over it. So was she buried!

There was no burial-service read—none. My mother was one of God's creatures, but she had lived, died, amongst the poor. She had bequeathed no legacies to charitable institutions, and how could the church afford one of its self-denying men to pray over her pauper-grave? She had only been an affectionate wife, a devoted mother, and a poor Christian; so how could a bell toll with any propriety as she drew near to her final resting-place? No prim undertaker, who measured yards of woe on his face according to the number of hatbands and gloves ordered for the funeral, was there, and what need, then, of surpliced priest? Well, it was some comfort to me that my poor mother's body could "rest in hope," without the hired services of either; and I could not help feeling and rejoicing that he who wept at the grave of Lazarus was watching the sleeping dust of his servant. O! miserable indeed is the lot of the poor—a weary, struggling, self-denying life, and then a solitary death and an unblessed grave!

From that great Golgotha we went forth together; and, unheeded by the bustling crowd, proceeded sadly to our now desolate chamber, where we sat down and gazed vacantly around the cheerless room. One by one the old familiar objects attracted our notice. Among other articles, a little saucepan remained on the extinguished embers in the grate, with rice and milk burned to its bottom! This was what my mother was preparing for me against my return from bathing, and the sight renewed my remembrances of her care, which it so happened was exercised for me in her latest moments. I afterwards was informed that she was found lying cold on the floor, by a young man who passed our room-door, on the way to his own, and saw her lying there. She seemed to have been engaged in splitting a piece of pine-wood with a knife, and it is supposed that, whilst stooping over it and forcing down the knife, she was seized with apoplexy, and immediately expired.

Whilst we were sadly contemplating our situation and circumstances, and calling to mind many sayings and doings of our lost mother, I began to think about our future course, and said to my sister, "Now, Mary, what shall we do?" She remarked something, I forget what; and I, in turn, made an observation, to the effect, as well as I can remember, that we could take all our furniture on our backs! when we, both of us, broke out into a violent fit of laughter, which lasted for several minutes; and I never, either before or since, remember to have been so entirely unable to control myself. It was a strange thing to hear that hitherto silent chamber, in which, for hours, we had scarcely spoken above a whisper, echoing such unaccustomed sounds, but so it was; and I am unable to explain why, unless it be on the principle of reaction. And yet it was not the laugh of joy, but more like the fearfully hysterical mirth of saddened hearts, in which, for the time, all the feelings of youth had been imprisoned, but by one wild effort had broken forth, shouting with natural but unbidden glee.

On that Wednesday night, I could not bear to remain in the house, so I sauntered out, and passed the long hours of darkness in the streets— to lie down I felt was impossible, so great was my weight of woe. The next day I passed wearily enough, and at night I procured a little sleep; but from the afternoon of my mother's death, not a morsel of food had passed my lips. I loathed food, and it was not until the Friday evening that I was persuaded to take any. Every thing about us so forcibly and painfully reminded us of her we had lost, that my sister and myself determined to remove from our lodgings; and, having disposed of our feather-bed and a few little matters to the woman of the house, we paid a week's board in advance at a house in Spring street. I now began to feel the effects of my night-watchings and neglect of food, and was taken so sick, that a city physician attended me for three or four days. As soon as I recovered, I inquired for my old and kind friends, the Egberts. They were in the city, and I proceeded to their house, in Suffolk street, where I was received cordially, and kindly nursed, with all the care of a mother and sister, during the weak time which followed my indisposition. My sister and I had separated, as she boarded where she worked, in the upper part of the city.

As soon as I had sufficiently recovered, I scraped together what money I could, and went on a visit to the family with whom I left England. With them I remained two months, and received many condolences on the subject of my mother's death and my lonely situation; but after, and, indeed, during this time, I could not help feeling that my absence would not be regretted, so I made preparations for quitting them. Whilst in the country, I spent a few days with Mr. Elijah Hunt, who, together with Mrs. Hunt, were extremely kind to me. As my wearing apparel was getting shabby, Mr. Hunt, in the kindest manner, provided me with a twenty-five dollar suit, trusting to my honor for repayment when it lay in my power. Never shall I forget the kindness of him and his family to me at that time. I started for New York about September, and there went to work for Mr. John Gladding, who always behaved kindly towards me. I boarded in Grand street; and about this time laid the foundation of many of my future sorrows.

I possessed a tolerably good voice, and sang pretty well, having also the faculty of imitation rather strongly developed; and, being well stocked with amusing stories, I got introduced into the society of thoughtless and dissipated young men, to whom my talents made me welcome. These companions were what is termed respectable, but they drank. I now began to attend the theatres frequently, and felt ambitious of strutting *my* hour upon the stage. By slow but sure degrees I forgot the lessons of wisdom which my mother had taught me, lost all relish for the great truths of religion, neglected my devotions, and considered an actor's situation to be the *ne plus ultra* of greatness. I well remember, in my early days, having entertained, through the influence of my mother, a horror of theatres; and once, as I walked up the Bowery, and watched the multitudes passing to and fro from the steps of the play-house there, which I had mounted for the sake of a better view of the busy scene, this passage of Scripture came to my recollection, "The glory of the Lord shall cover the face of the earth as the waters cover the sea"; and I mentally offered up a prayer that that time might speedily arrive. Not very long afterwards, so low had I fallen and so desperately had I backslidden, that at the very door of that same theatre, which I had, five years before, wished destroyed, as a temple of sin, I stood applying for a situation as actor and comic singer! No longer did I wish a church should be built on the site of the theatre; that very place of entertainment had become at first a chosen, and now, to support excitement, an almost necessary place of resort. I afterwards performed at the Franklin Theatre, under the assumed name of Gilbert, which my mother bore before she married, when a comic song of mine was so encored that I was encouraged to pursue the course I entered on, but I did not at that time.

During this period, I worked pretty steadily at my business, but such were my growing habits of dissipation that, although receiving five dollars a week, I squandered every cent away, and was continually in debt.

132

My proceedings, too, became characterized by a hitherto unfelt reck-lessness. One morning a young man came to me and informed me that a great fire had broken out down the street. (I had belonged to a volun-teer fire-engine company, and also to a dramatic society, which held their meetings at the corner of Anthony street and Broadway, and which had greatly tended to increase my habits of irregularity.) I passed by the information lightly and selfishly, saying, "Let it burn on, it wont hurt me." When I had finished my breakfast, some one informed me the fire was in the neighborhood of the shop where I worked. This alarmed me; and I proceeded towards my place of business, where I arrived just in time to see the flames bursting through the workshop windows. By this disaster, although I had so little anticipated it, I lost what I could ill afford, an overcoat and some books; and worse than this, I was thrown out of employment; so that I *was* injured by the fire, which I had so con-fidently thought "could not hurt me."

Mr. Gladding, after the fire, determining to remove to Bristol, Rhode Island, and set up in business there, invited me to accompany him. I therefore left New York, and remained in his employ for about a year, during which time nothing of importance transpired. In February or March, 1837, however, Mr. Gladding failed, and as I was again obliged to seek for occupation, I proceeded to Providence, and there continued my drinking habits. I succeeded in procuring work at Mr. Brown's, in Market Row, and experienced much kindness at his hands. Here I might, and ought, to have done well, but for my unfortunate habits of dissipation, which gradually increased, and which were every day trea-suring up misery for me.

It happened that, at this time, a company of actors were performing at Providence. I got acquainted with them, and being strongly advised by them to make an essay on the stage, I acceded to their wishes and fol-lowed my own inclinations with respect to the matter. It could not be ex-pected that, connected with the stage, I could follow steadily a more so-ber occupation. Nor did I; for I worked only at uncertain intervals, frequently was absent for days together, and, as a necessary consequence, incurred the displeasure of my employer, who soon after discharged me from his shop, on the ground of inattention to my business, although I was acknowledged by him to be an excellent workman. I now entirely gave myself up to the stage, and gained some reputation for the manner in which I performed a low line of character. Brilliant, however, as I thought my prospects to be, I was doomed to disappointment; for, before long, the theatre came to a close, and I, in common with the other members of the company, failed to receive remuneration for my services. Thus was I again thrown on my own resources, and, with a tarnished reputation, my situation was far worse than it had hitherto been. I tried to obtain employment, but none could I obtain; and although I wished to get out of the town, I was unable to do so from want of funds. My clothes had grown shabby, and I was guiltless of wearing more than one suit. Worse than this, my appetite for strong drink was increasing, and becoming a confirmed habit—the effect of almost unlimited indulgence. I was now reduced to absolute want. My boarding-house account had assumed an unpleasant aspect, and, more than once, had I received threatening notices to quit. One night I was reduced to extremities, and so poorly was I off, that I was compelled to wander about the streets, from night until almost morning, in order to keep myself warm. In pure desperation, I repaired to one of the very lowest class of hotels, where I obtained a miserable lodging. It happened, at this time, that a person visited Providence who wanted to engage some performers for a theatre which was to open, for a short season, in Boston. To this person, whose name was Barry (and who, afterwards, was lost, with his whole stock company, whilst going to Texas), I was introduced; and he was, at the same time, informed of my necessity. Mr. Barry, with a kindness, which was well meant, said he would take me to Boston with him, on his own responsibility, and use his influence in my behalf. I left Providence, on a Sunday morning, and succeeded in getting an engagement in Boston. During this time, my sister was working at her trade in Providence. I performed low comedy parts, until the theatre closed, in 1837, when I was again deprived of pay, and once more thrown, like a football, on the world's great highway, at the mercy of every passing foot. My appearance was now shabby enough, as that of a strolling player generally is. All my little stock of money was spent as fast as I received it; and, once more, I was absolutely in want. Like many others, similarly circumstanced to myself, I experienced, in my adversity, kindness from woman. A Mrs. Fox, with whom I boarded, was quite aware of my destitute situation, and benevolently afforded me a home and subsistence until I could once more obtain work. This I at last did, at Mr. Benjamin

Bradley's, and in his employ I continued until the month of January, 1838, when I was discharged. The reason assigned by Mr. Bradley for my dismissal was what might have been expected from a knowledge of my habits. He said I was too shabby in appearance for a shop, and it was his opinion, as well as that of others, that I drank too much. I had paid my board at Mrs. Fox's up to that time, but was now again without a cent, and was in the depths of trouble, until I accidentally heard that a person at Newburyport was in want of a binder, to whom he was willing to give six dollars a week wages. Small as was this remuneration, I need scarcely say that I eagerly accepted the offered salary, and travelling, partly by stages, and partly in cars, entered Newburyport late in the evening of the 30th of January. The next morning I commenced work in my new situation, and, for a few weeks, by a desperate effort, I managed to keep free from the intoxicating cup. I was now comparatively steady, and gave satisfaction to my employer; but this state of things, unhappily, did not last long, for, I regret to say, I had a longing for society, and soon formed an acquaintance with companions who were calculated to destroy any resolutions of amendment which I had formed. I joined a fire-engine company, and, before long, I was again on the high-road of dissipation, neglecting my business, destroying my reputation, which was already damaged, and injuring my health.

Work grew slack towards the July of that year, and, as I could not earn sufficient to support myself at my trade, I embraced another occupation, and entered into an arrangement, with the captain of a fishing-boat, to go a voyage with him down Chaleur bay. My sea experiences were somewhat severe, as will presently be seen; but as there was no rum on board, I was forced to keep sober, and that, at least, saved me a considerable amount of suffering. When, however, I went on shore, I made up for my forced abstinence by pottle-deep potations, and my visit to another vessel was generally accompanied by a carousal, if rum was by any means to be obtained. In consequence of what is commonly called a "spree," my life was, at one time, placed in considerable jeopardy. Several of our crew, with myself, had been on board a neighbouring vessel, and, on our return at night, I was, as might be expected, very drunk. The boat was rowed to the side of our craft, and I was so much intoxicated that, unnoticed, I lay at the bottom of the boat. As customary, when the rest of the crew got on board, the hook was fastened in the bow of the boat, which was drawn up. In consequence of this, as the bow was hoisted with a jerk, I was flung violently, from where I was lying, to the stern, and the force of the blow effectually awakened me. I called out, and alarmed my companions, just in time to prevent being thrown overboard; and was soon rescued from my perilous position. It seemed that they had not noticed me in the boat when they left it, and supposed, in the dark scramble, I had got safely on board. So was my life again saved by an all-wise Providence; but I was so closely wrapped up in my garb of thoughtlessness, that I passed by the matter with little thought or thankfulness.

And yet, at this time, I did not consider myself to be what in reality I was—a drunkard. Well enough did I know, from bitter experience, that character, situations, and health had been periled, in consequence of my love of ardent spirits. I felt, too, an aching void in my breast, and conscience frequently told me that I was on the broad road to ruin; but that I was what all men despised, and I, among them, detested, I could not bring myself to believe. I would frame many excuses for myself—plead my own cause before myself, as judge and jury, until I obtained, at my own hands, a willing acquittal. O! how little does the young man dream that he is deceiving himself, though not others, whilst pursuing so fatal a course as was mine. He, as I did, abhors the name of "drunkard," whilst no other word so aptly and accurately defines his position.

The purpose of our voyage having been answered we prepared for our homeward sail, and were making for port when a violent storm burst over us. It was a Southeaster, and in our perilous position off Cape Sable none of us expected to weather it. For hours we expected to go to the bottom, and scarce a hope remained to cheer us, the captain having given up every thing for lost. We could discern the sea breaking violently over the Brazil rock four miles and a half off from us, and we were rapidly drifting to the coast; but in that dreadful season, strange to tell, I suffered but very little, if any thing, from alarm or anxiety. What to attribute this feeling, or rather absence of feeling to, I know not; but so it was, that owing to callousness or some other cause, I felt not the slightest fear, although some old "Salts" were dreadfully anxious, and prayed in agonizing accents for deliverance. I sat as calmly as ever I remember to have done in my life whilst wave after wave dashed over the frail vessel, making every timber creak, and her whole frame to quiver as if with mortal agony. By the mercy of God, however, the wind shifted to the westward, and by means of the only rag of a sail which remained to us we managed to crawl off. Next morning at daylight having discovered land we made towards it, and about noon anchored in Shelburne bay, Nova Scotia, where we remained long enough to replace a lost sail, and repair our damaged vessel. We soon set sail once more, and I arrived in Newburyport on the first Sunday in November, glad enough to be freed from my imprisonment for three and a half months in a small vessel of fifty tons burden.

Once more on land I engaged to work at my own business, and did so for some time with Mr. Tilton. Not long afterwards I entered into the matrimonial state, and commenced housekeeping, having earned money sufficient by my fishing voyage to purchase some neat furniture. In my new condition I might have done well, for I had every prospect of success, had it not been for my craving after society, which in spite of having a home of my own I still felt. Alas! forgetful of a husband's home duties I again became involved in a dissipated social network, whose fatal meshes too surely entangled me, and unfitted me for that active exertion which was now rendered doubly necessary. I continued at my work until the month of June, when business becoming slack, I again went on a fishing excursion with my wife's brother, the captain of the boat, into the Bay of Fundy. We were away this time for only six weeks, and returned in safety, without having encountered any thing worthy of note.

During my residence at Newburyport, my early serious impressions on one occasion in a measure revived, and I felt some stingings of conscience for my neglect of the Sabbath and religious observances. I recommended attending a place of worship, and for a short time I attended the Rev. Mr. Campbell's church, by whom, as well as by several of his members, I was treated with much Christian kindness. I was often invited to Mr. Campbell's house, as well as to those of some of his hearers, and it seemed as if a favorable turning-point or crisis in my fortunes had arrived. Mr. Campbell was good enough to manifest a very great interest in my welfare, and frequently experienced a hope that I should be enabled, although late in life, to obtain an education. And this I might have acquired had not my evil genius prevented my making any efforts to obtain so desirable an end. My desire for strong liquors and company seemed to present an insuperable barrier against all improvement; and, after a few weeks, every aspiration after better things had ceased, every bud of promised comfort was crushed. Again I grieved the Spirit which had been striving with my spirit, and ere long became even more addicted to the use of the infernal draughts which had already wrought me so much woe, than at any previous period of my existence.

And now my circumstances began to be desperate indeed. In vain were all my efforts to obtain work, and at last I became so reduced, that at times I did not know, when one meal was ended, where on the face of the broad earth I should find another. Further mortification awaited me, and by slow degrees I became aware of it. The young men with whom I had associated in bar-rooms and parlors, and who wore a little better clothing than I could afford to put on, one after another began to drop my acquaintance. If I walked in the public streets I too quickly perceived the cold look, the averted eye, the half recognition—and to a sensitive spirit, such as I possessed, such treatment was almost past endurance. To add to the mortification, caused by such treatment, it happened that those who had laughed the loudest at my songs and stories, and who had been social enough with me in the bar-room, were the very individuals who seemed most ashamed of my acquaintance. I felt that I was shunned by the respectable portion of the community also, and once, on asking a lad to accompany me in a walk, he informed me that his father had cautioned him against associating with me. This was a cutting reproof, and I felt it more deeply than words can express. And could I wonder at it? No. Although I may have used bitter words against that parent, my conscience told me that he had done no more than his duty in preventing his son being influenced by my dissipated habits. Oh! how often have I laid down and bitterly remembered many who had hailed my arrival in their company as a joyous event. Then plaudits would ring in my ears, and peals of laughter ring again in my deserted chamber; then would succeed stillness only broken by the beatings of my agonized heart, which felt that the gloss of respectability had worn off and exposed my threadbare condition. To drown these reflections I would drink, not from love of the taste of the liquor, but to become so stupefied by its fumes as to steep my sorrows in a half oblivion; and from this miserable stupor I would wake to a fuller consciousness of my situation, and again would I banish my reflections by liquor.

It has been said that no one is ever utterly forlorn and friendless. Whether this be the case or not, it is not for me to decide. In my own case, and in what seemed my last extremity, I obtained some assistance. There resided in Newburyport a countryman of mine, named Low. He was an Englishman, and perhaps felt some interest in me as an old-countryman. Mr. Low was a warm-hearted and generous-minded man, and perceiving that I possessed some abilities, which he regretted to see thrown away, he very kindly manifested a desire to afford me assistance. He was a rum-seller, and I had spent many a shilling at his bar, so that he had frequent opportunities of becoming acquainted with my "ways and means." It occurred to me, that if I could get some tools, it was just possible I might get into business, and, by perseverance and sobriety, succeed in redeeming myself from the fallen state I was in, and, in some measure, at least, retrieve my fallen, ruined fortunes. Mr. Low assisted me very materially in my endeavors to regain a respectable position in society, by furnishing me with sufficient funds for procuring tools, so that I might work on my own account.

Despite of all that had occurred, my good name was not so far gone, but that I might have succeeded, by the aid of common industry and attention, in my business. I was a good workman, found no difficulty in procuring employment, and, I have not the slightest doubt, should have succeeded in my endeavors to get on in the world, but for my unhappy love of stimulating drinks, and my craving for society. I was now my own master—all restraint was removed, and, as might be expected, I did as I pleased in my own shop. I became careless, was often in the bar-room, or carousing in the parlor, when I should have been at my bindery; and, instead of spending my evenings at home, in reading or conversation, they were, almost invariably, passed in the company of the rum bottle, which became almost my sole household deity. Five months only did I remain in business, and, during that short period, I gradually sunk deeper and deeper in the scale of degradation. I was now the slave of a habit which had become completely my master, and which fastened its remorseless fangs in my very vitals. Thought was a torturing thing. When I looked back, Memory drew fearful pictures, in lines of lurid flame; and, whenever I dared anticipate the future, Hope refused to illumine my onward path. I dwelt in one awful present. Nothing to solace me—nothing to beckon me onwards to a better state. I knew, full well, that I was proceeding on a downward course, and crossing the sea of Time, as it were, on a bridge perilous as that over which Mahomet's followers are said to enter Paradise. A terrible feeling was ever present, that some evil was impending, which would soon fall on my devoted head; and I would shudder, as if the sword of Damocles, suspended by its single hair, was about to fall, and utterly destroy me.

Warnings were not wanting; but they had no voice of terror for me. I was intimately acquainted with a young man in the town, and well remember his coming to my shop one morning, and asking the loan of ninepence, with which to buy rum. I let him have the money, and the spirit was soon consumed. He begged me to lend him a second ninepence, but I refused; yet, during my temporary absence, he drank some spirit of wine, which was in a bottle in the shop, and used by me in my business. He went away, and the next I heard of him was that he had died shortly afterwards. Such an awful circumstance as this might well have impressed me; but habitual indulgence had almost rendered me proof against salutary impressions. I was, to tell the truth, at this time, deeper in degradation than at any period, before or since, which I can remember.

My custom now was to purchase my brandy, which, in consequence of my limited means, was of the very worst description, and keep it at the shop, where, by little and little, I drank it, and continually kept myself in a state of excitement. This course of proceeding entirely unfitted me for business, and it not unfrequently happened, when I had books to bind, that I would, instead of attending to business, keep my customers waiting, whilst in the company of dissolute companions. I drank during the whole day, to the complete ruin of my prospects in life. So entirely did I give myself up to the bottle, that those of my companions who fancied they still possessed some claims to respectability gradually withdrew from my company. At my house, too, I used to keep a bottle of gin, which was in constant requisition. Indeed, go where I would, stimuli I must, and did, have. Such a slave was I to the bottle, that I resorted to it continually, and in vain was every effort, which I occasionally made, to conquer the debasing habit. I had become a father; but God, in his mercy removed my little one at so early an age, that I did not feel the loss as much as if it had lived longer, to engage my affections.

A circumstance now transpired, which attracted my attention, and led me to consider my situation, and whither I was hurrying. A lecture was advertised, to be delivered by the first reformed drunkard, Mr. J. J. Johnson, who visited Newburyport, and I was invited by some friends, who seemed to feel an interest, to attend, and hear what he had to say. I determined, after some consideration, to go, and hear what was to be said on the subject. The meeting was held at the Reverend Mr. Campbell's church, which was greatly crowded. I went, and heard the speaker depict, in forcible and graphic terms, the misery of the drunkard, and the awful consequences of his conduct, both as they affected himself, and those connected with him. My conscience told me that the truth was spoken by the lecturer, for what had I not suffered from intemperance? I remained only about ten minutes, and, as I left the chapel, a young man offered me the pledge to sign. I actually turned to sign it, but, at that critical moment, the appetite for strong drink, as if determined to have the mastery over me, came in all its force, and remembering, too, just then, that I had a pint of brandy at home, I deferred signing, and put off, to a "more convenient season," a proceeding which might have saved me so much after sorrow. I however compromised the matter with my conscience, by inwardly resolving that I would drink up what spirit I had by me, and then *think* of leaving off the use of the accursed liquid altogether.

"Think of it!" O! had I *then acted*, what misery would have been spared me in after days. One would have imagined that I had had my fill of misery, and been glad to have hailed and grasp any saving hand which might be held out. But, O! such was the dominion which rum had over me, that I was led captive by it, as at will. It had impaired every energy, and almost destroyed the desire to be better than I was. I was debased in my own eyes, and, having lost my self-respect, became a poor, abject being, scarcely worth attempting to reform. *Did* I *think* of it? O, no. I forgot the impressions made upon me by the speaker at the meeting I have alluded to. Still I madly drained the inebriating cup, and speedily my state was worse than ever. O, no, I soon ceased to think about it, for my master passion, like Aaron's rod, swallowed up every thought and feeling, opposed to it, which I possessed.

My business grew gradually worse, and, at length, my constitution became so impaired, that, even when I had the will, I did not possess the power to provide for my daily wants. My hands would, at times, tremble so, that I could not perform the finer operations of my business—the finishing and gilding. How could I letter straight with a hand burning and shaking, from the effects of a debauch? Sometimes, when it was absolutely necessary to finish off some work, I have entered the shop with a stern determination not to drink a single drop until I completed it. I have bitterly felt that my failing was a matter of common conversation in the town, and a burning sense of shame would flush my fevered brow, at the conviction that I was scorned by the respectable portion of the community. But these feelings passed away, like the morning cloud or the early dew, and I pursued my old course.

To what shifts was I reduced, in order to conceal my habit of using intoxicating drinks! Frequently have I taken a pitcher, with a pint of new rum in it, purchased at some obscure groggery, and put about one third as much water as there was spirit in it, at the town pump, in the Market square, in order to induce persons to think that I drank water alone. This mixture I would take to my shop, and, for days and days together, it would be my only beverage. In consequence of this habit, I would frequently fall asleep, or, if awake, be in so half torpid a state, that work, or exertion of any kind, was quite out of the question; and, after an indulgence in this practice for some time, I was compelled to remain at home, from sheer inability to enter on active duty. I grew, of course, poorer and poorer, and my days dragged wearily on. At times, I almost wished that my life, and its miseries, would close.

The reader will remember that I have before referred to my sister. She had been for some time married, and was then residing at Providence, Rhode Island. One day, I received a letter from her, in which she stated that she was severely afflicted with salt rheum, and requested my wife would visit her, for the purpose of nursing her and her infant. My wife deciding on going. I accompanied her to the cars, and then returned home. It was the first time, since our marriage, that we had ever been separated, and the house to me looked lonely and desolate. I thought I would not go to work, and a great inducement, to remain at home, existed in the shape of my enemy, West India rum, of which I had nearly a gallon in the house. Although the morning was by no means far advanced, I sat down, intending to do nothing until dinner time. I could not sit alone, without rum, and I drank, glass after glass, until I became so stupefied, that I was compelled to lie down on the bed, where I soon fell asleep. When I awoke, it was late in the afternoon, and then, as I persuaded myself, too late to make a bad day's work good. I invited a neighbor, who, like myself, was a man of intemperate habits, to spend the evening with me. He came, and we sat down to our rum, and drank together freely, until late that night, when he staggered home; and so intoxicated was I, that, in moving to go to bed, I fell over the table, broke a lamp, and lay on the floor for some time, unable to rise. At last, I managed to get to bed; but, O! I did not sleep, for the drunkard never knows the blessings of undisturbed repose. I awoke in the night, with a raging thirst. My mouth was parched, and my throat was burning; and I anxiously groped about the room, trying to find more rum, in which I sought to quench my dreadful thirst. No sooner was one draught taken, than the horrible dry feeling returned; and so I went on, swallowing repeated glassfuls of the spirit, until, at last, I had drained the very last drop which the jar contained. My appetite grew by what it fed on; and, having a little money by me, I with difficulty got up, made myself look as tidy as possible, and then went out to buy more rum, with which I returned to the house. The fact will, perhaps, seem incredible, but so it was, that I drank spirits continually, without tasting a morsel of food, for the next three days. This could not last long; a constitution of iron strength could not endure such treatment, and mine was partially broken down by previous dissipation.

I began to experience a feeling, hitherto unknown to me. After the three days drinking, to which I have just referred, I felt, one night, as I lay on my bed, an awful sense of something dreadful coming upon me. It was as if I had been partially stunned, and now, in an interval of consciousness, was about to have the fearful blow, which had prostrated me, repeated. There was a craving for sleep, sleep, blessed sleep! but my eyelids were as if they could not close. Every object around me, I beheld with startling distinctness, and my hearing became unnaturally acute. Then, to the singing and roaring in my ears, would suddenly succeed a silence, so awful, that only the stillness of the grave might be compared with it. At other times, strange voices would whisper unintelligible words, and the slightest noise would make me start, like a guilty thing. But the horrible, burning thirst was insupportable, and, to quench it, and induce sleep, I clutched, again and again, the rum-bottle, hugged my enemy, and poured the infernal fluid down my parched throat. But it was of no use—none. I could not sleep. Then I bethought me of to-bacco; and, staggering from my bed to a shelf near, with great difficulty I managed to procure a pipe and some matches. I could not stand to light the latter, so I lay again on the bed, and scraped one against the wall. I began to smoke, and the narcotic leaf produced a stupefaction. I dosed a little; but, feeling a warmth on my face, I awoke, and discovered my pillow to be on fire! I had dropped a lighted match on the bed. By a desperate effort, I threw the pillow from the bed, and, too exhausted to feel annoyed by the burning feathers, I sank again into a state of somno-lency. How long I lay, I do not exactly know, but I was roused from my lethargy by the neighbors, who, alarmed by a smell of fire, came to my room to ascertain the cause. When they took me from my bed, the under part of the straw with which it was stuffed was smouldering, and, in a quarter of an hour more, must have burst into a flame. Had such been the case, how horrible would have been my fate, for it is more than prob-able that, in my half-senseless condition, I should have been suffocated, or burned to death. The fright produced by this accident, and very nar-row escape, in some degree sobered me; but what I felt more than any thing else was the exposure. Now, all would be known, and I feared my name would become, more than ever, a by-word and a reproach.

Will it be believed that I again sought refuge in rum? Scarcely had I recovered from the fright than I sent out, procured a pint of rum, and drank it all in less than half an hour? Yet so it was. And now came upon me many terrible sensations. Cramps attacked me in my limbs which racked me with agony, and my temples throbbed as if they would burst. So ill was I, that I became seriously alarmed and begged the people of the house to send for a physician. They did so, but I immediately re-pented having summoned him, and endeavored, but ineffectually, to get out of his way when he arrived. He saw at a glance what was the matter with me, ordered the persons about me to watch me carefully, and on no account to let me have any spirituous liquors. Every thing stimulating was rigorously denied me, and then came on the drunkard's remorseless Torturer—delirium tremens, in all its terrors, attacked me.

For three days I endured more agony than pen could describe, even were it guided by the mind of a Dante. Who can tell the horrors of that horrible malady, aggravated as it is by the almost ever-abiding con-sciousness that it is self-sought. Hideous faces appeared on the walls, and on the ceiling, and on the floors; foul things crept along the bed-clothes, and glaring eyes peered into mine. I was at one time surrounded by millions of monstrous spiders, who crawled slowly, slowly over every limb, whilst the beaded drops of persperation would start to my brow, and my limbs would shiver until the bed rattled again. Strange lights would dance before my eyes, and then suddenly the very blackness of darkness would appal me by its dense gloom. All at once, whilst gazing at a frightful creation of my distempered mind, I seemed struck with sudden blindness. I knew a candle was burning in the room, but I could not see it. All was so pitchy dark. I lost the sense of feeling too, for I endeavored to grasp my arm in one hand, but consciousness was gone. I put my hand to my side, my head, but felt nothing, and still I knew my limbs and frame *were* there. And then the scene would change. I was falling—falling swiftly as an arrow far down into some terrible abyss, and so like reality was it that as I fell I could see the rocky sides of the horrible shaft, where mocking, jibing, mowing, fiendlike forms were perched; and I could feel the air rushing past me making my hair stream out by the force of the unwholesome blast. Then the paroxysm sometimes ceased for a few moments, and I would sink back on my pallet, drenched with perspiration, utterly exhausted, and feeling a dreadful certainty of the renewal of my torments.

By the mercy of God I survived this awful seizure; and when I rose a weak, broken-down man, and surveyed my ghastly features in a glass, I thought of my mother, and asked myself how I had obeyed the instructions I had received from her lips, and to what advantage I had turned the lessons she taught me. I remembered her countless prayers and tears, thought of what I had been but a few short months before, and contrasted my situation with what it then was. Oh! how keen were my own rebukes; and in the excitement of the moment I resolved to lead a better life, and abstain from the accursed wine-cup. For about a month, terrified by what I had suffered, I adhered to my resolution; then my wife came home, and in my joy at her return, I flung my good resolutions to the wind, and foolishly fancying that I could now restrain my appetite, which had for a whole month remained in subjection, I took a glass of brandy.

That glass aroused the slumbering demon, who would not be satisfied by so tiny a libation. Another, and another succeeded, until I was again far advanced in the career of intemperance. The night of my wife's return I went to bed intoxicated. I will not detain the reader by the particulars of my every-day life at this time; they may easily be imagined from what has already been stated. My previous bitter experience, one would think, may have operated as a warning, but none save the inebriate can tell the almost resistless strength of the temptations which assail him.

I did not, however, make quite so deep a plunge as before. My tools I had given into the hands of Mr. Gray, for whom I worked, and received at the rate of five dollars a week. My wages were paid me every night, for I was not to be trusted with much money at a time, so certain was I to spend a great portion of it in drink. As it was, I regularly got rid of one third of what I daily received for rum. I soon left Mr. Gray, under the following circumstances. There was an exhibition of the Battle of Bunker Hill to be opened in the town, and the manager knowing that I had a good voice and sung pretty well, thought my comic singing would constitute an attraction; so he engaged me to give songs every evening, and to assist in the general business of the Diorama. In this occupation I continued about three weeks or a month, and when the exhibition closed in Newburyport, by invitation, I remained with the proprietor and proceeded with him to Lowell. As it was uncertain when I should return, the manager wishing me to travel with him, I sold off what few articles of furniture yet remained in my possession, and my wife arranged to stay, during my absence, with her sister. I stayed in the town of Lowell for the space of three months, my habits of intemperance increasing, as might be expected, for in a wandering life my outbreaks were not so much noticed as when I was residing at home. As had been the case often before, rum claimed nearly all my attention, and consequently the business I was called upon to perform was entirely neglected or carelessly attended to. On several occasions when I repaired to the place where the Diorama was exhibited, I was in such a state that I could do nothing required of me, and severe were the rebukes I received in consequence from my employer. These remarks incensed me highly, and only made me drink more, so that ere long my name and that of an incorrigible drunkard were synonymous. We next proceeded to Worcester, and there remained a fortnight. I experienced great difficulty in procuring the meagre salary which was promised me, and many privations had I to endure in consequence; my stock of wearing apparel was scanty enough, and hardly fit to appear in the street. This was in the month of October, and as the winter was drawing on fast, I miserably contemplated what my situation would be through the approaching severe season. Want and cold appeared before me in all their frightful realities, and I again resolved to abstain from the maddening influences which governed me with despotic rule.

I sent to my wife, requesting her to return, and transmitted her three dollars, for her expenses to Worcester, being the first money I had sent to her for four months, except five dollars which I received as part of the proceeds of a concert I gave at Lowell. I adhered, in a great measure, to my resolution not to become intoxicated, and had written to my wife, telling her of my determination to reform. On the day I expected her to return home, I met with an acquaintance, who asked me to stroll about with him, in order that he might see the town. We drank together; and our walk ended by my getting drunk, and forgetting the good resolutions which I had made. In the evening, when I was reeling along from the hotel towards the exhibition, I chanced to see a stage, and approached it, in order to see if my wife was there. She had arrived; and I took her with me to the hotel, where she discovered I had been drinking, and when she reminded me of the promise I had made her to abandon the destructive habit, I felt thoroughly ashamed of my weakness. I then went to the performance, and managed to get through my work. Soon after this, I quitted the service of the proprietor of the Diorama; and, putting as sober a face upon matters as I could, I applied to Messrs. Hutchinson and Crosby for employment. These gentlemen agreed to take me on trial, stating that, if they were satisfied with my work, they would engage me. My work was approved of; and, once more installed in a good situation, I had a chance of pushing my fortune.

My wife now began to exhibit symptoms of declining health, and my prospects as before were none of the brightest. I managed to keep my situation, and fancied that my intemperate habits were known only to myself, as I carefully avoided any open or flagrant violation of propriety—but drunkenness, more than any other vice, cannot long be hidden. It seems as if the very walls whispered it; and there is scarcely an action of the drinking man which does not betray him. I did not, however, long remain cautious; for one morning, after having drank freely the evening before, I felt unable to work, and was compelled to remain at home during that day and the next. All my property, which I could by any means render available, I had disposed of, in order to procure money for purchasing drink; and the man in whose house I boarded, having watched my proceedings with a very vigilant and interested eye, became, I suppose, fearful that I should not be able to pay for my board, and informed my employers, Messrs. Hutchinson and Crosby, that I was detained at home in consequence of what is called a drunken spree. I do not think the information was given from any motive of kindness towards myself, but believe it was a selfish motive which prompted the interference.

I felt wretched enough when I proceeded to the shop to resume my work. Mr. Hutchinson was a man of great moral purity of character, but he had a strong hatred of intemperance, and looked not very lightly on my transgression. As soon as he saw me, he sternly informed me that he did not want any men in his employ who were in the habit of being the worse for liquor; and threatened me with instant dismissal, should I ever again neglect my business for the bottle. I assured him that he should not again have occasion to complain of my inebriety, and I inwardly resolved to profit by the warning I had received. Having a sick wife, and being almost utterly destitute of means, reflection would force itself upon me. I was startled at the idea of her and myself coming to want, entirely in consequence of my evil habit, and I resolved again to attempt the work of reformation.

In order to render myself less liable to temptation, and to avoid the dissipated society which I was constantly falling into at the hotel, where I lived, I left it, and engaged board at the house of a gentleman, who happened to be the president of a temperance society. Here I attempted to restrain my appetite for drink, but the struggle was terrible; so mighty a power would not be conquered without contesting every inch of his dominion; and I, trusting to my own strength, assailed it with but a feeble weapon. I felt as if I *could* not do without the draughts which I had been so long accustomed to, and yet I was ashamed to display the weakness which prompted me to indulge in them. To procure liquor, I was compelled to resort to every kind of stratagem, and the services of my inventive faculties were in constant requisition. Many a time would I steal out, when no one noticed me, and proceed, with a bottle in my pocket, to the farthest extremity of the town, where I would purchase a supply of rum, which I would take home with me. Occasionally I would procure spirit at the apothecary's shop, alleging, as an excuse, that it was required in a case of sickness; and the pint I would generally divide into three portions, one of which I took in the morning, another at noon, and the remainder I disposed of in the evening. My habits were not naturally of a deceptive character, and I always felt degraded in my own esteem, whenever I had occasion to resort to the expedients I have mentioned—but what will not a drunkard do, in order to procure the stimulus he so ardently desires? Have it I would, and get it I did; and I always seemed to desire it the more when the difficulty of procuring it was increased.

My wardrobe, as had, indeed, been nearly always the case with me whilst I drank to excess, was now exceedingly shabby, and it was with the greatest difficulty that I could manage to procure the necessaries of life. My wife became very ill. O! how miserable I became. Some of the females who were in attendance on my wife told me to get two quarts of rum. I procured it, and as it was in the house, and I did not anticipate serious consequences, I could not withstand the strong temptation to drink. I did drink, and so freely, that the usual effect was produced. How much I swallowed, I cannot tell, but the quantity, judging from the effects it produced, must have been considerable.

Ten long, weary days of suspense passed, at the end of which my wife and her infant both died. Then came the terribly oppressive feeling, that I was utterly alone in the world; and it seemed, almost, that I was forgotten of God, as well as abandoned by man. All the consciousness of my dreadful situation pressed heavily indeed upon me, and keenly as a sensitive mind could, did I feel the loss I had experienced. I drank, now, to dispel my gloom, or to drown it in the maddening cup; and soon was it whispered, from one to another, until the whole town became aware of it, that my wife and child were lying dead, and that I was drunk! But if ever I was cursed with the faculty of thought, in all its intensity, it was then. And this was the degraded condition of one who had been nursed on the lap of piety, and whose infant tongue had been taught to utter a prayer against being led into temptation. There, in the room where all who had loved me were lying in the unconscious slumber of death, was I gazing, with a maudlin melancholy imprinted on my features, on the dead forms of those who were flesh of my flesh and bone of my bone. During the miserable hours of darkness, I would steal from my lonely bed to the place where my dead wife and child lay, and, in agony of soul, pass my shaking hand over their cold faces, and then return to my bed, after a draught of rum, which I had obtained, and hidden under the pillow of my wretched couch. At such times, all the events of the past would return, with terrible distinctness, to my recollection, and many a time did I wish to die, for Hope had well nigh deserted me, both with respect to this world and the next. I had apostatized from those pure principles which once I embraced, and was now—

> A wandering, wretched, worn, and weary thing,
> Ashamed to ask, and yet I needed help.

I will not dwell on this painful portion of my career, but simply remark, that all the horrors, which I believe man could bear, were endured by me at that dreary time. My frame was enervated, my reputation gone; all my prospects were blighted, and misery seemed to have poured out all her vials on my devoted head. The funerals of my wife and child being over, I knew not what course to pursue, for, wherever I went, I failed not to see the slow moving finger of scorn pointed at me, and I writhed in agony, under the sense of shame which it produced. Every one looked coldly at me, and but few hesitated to sneer at my despicable condition. What *had* I done to deserve all this torturing treatment? I was naturally of a kind and humane disposition, and would turn aside from an unwillingness to hurt a worm: frequently have I reasoned with boys who inflicted cruelty on dumb animals. I would have hugged the dog that licked my hand, and taken to my bosom even a reptile, if I thought it loved me. What *had* I done, to make me so shunned and execrated by my kind? Conscience gave me back an answer—I drank! and in those two words lay the whole secret of my miserable condition.

It was not to be expected that, whilst I persisted in my drinking habits, I should attend to my work. My employers perceived that I neglected their interests, as well as my own, and I was informed by them that they were no longer in need of my services. What was I to do? I had incurred some debts, which I wished to discharge, and I expressed a desire to that effect. After some hesitation, I was reëngaged, on the understanding that I should receive not one farthing of money for my labors, lest it should be spent in liquor. My employers said they would purchase me tobacco, and take my letters from the post-office for me; and, under these stipulations, I went to work again. I kept, in a great degree, sober for a few days; but felt, all the time, indescribably miserable, from the consciousness that all confidence in me had been lost, and that I was a suspected man. This impression nettled me to the quick, and, ere long, I began to feel indignant of the control exercised over me. I thought that as I had battled with the world, single-handed, for twelve years, and had received nothing (with one or two exceptions) but unkindness and misery, I had a right to do as I chose, without being watched wherever I went. My proud spirit would not brook this system of espionage, so I speedily made up my mind to do as I pleased. If I wanted drink, I considered I had a perfect right to gratify my inclinations, and drink I determined to have.

Have it I did, though secretly, and to my employers it was a matter of wonder how I managed to get drunk so often. My funds, as I said, were all expended, and I was driven by my ravenous appetite to a course which, at any other time and under any other circumstances, I should have shrunk in horror from. I had in my possession some books which I once had valued, some of them presents; and I also retained a few articles, the once highly valued mementos of dear and departed friends. As I looked eagerly over these frail remnants of what I once possessed, my all-absorbing passion for drink exercised its tyrannizing power, and one by one, until none remained, every relic was disposed of, and the proceeds arising from the sale of them spent for rum. Could there be a more striking instance of the debasing influence which alcohol exerts? Why, at one time, I would almost as soon have parted with my life as with those precious remembrancers of

The loved, the lost, the distant, and the dead.

Now, however, all fine feeling was nearly obliterated from the tablet of my affections, and if I felt any pang in parting with articles I once so prized, the glass was my universal panacea. At length nothing remained on which I could raise a single cent, and I found in the lowest depths of poverty "a lower still."

I have, in several parts of this narrative, referred to my vocal talents and my ventriloquial acquirements. After every other resource had failed me, in my utmost need, I was compelled, as the only means of getting a little rum, to avail myself of these aids. Accordingly, my custom was to repair to the lowest grogshops, and there I might usually be found, night after night, telling facetious stories, singing comic songs, or turning books upside down and reading them whilst they were moving round, to the great delight and wonder of a set of loafers who supplied me with drink in return. Who would have recognized in the gibing mountebank, the circle of a laughing, drunken crowd, the son of religious parents, one who *had* been devoted and affectionate not so very long before; one, too, who had felt and appreciated the pleasures which religion alone can bestow? At times my former condition would flash across my mind, when, in the midst of riot and revelry, conviction would fasten its quivering arrow in my heart, making it bleed again, although I was forced to hide the wound. And through the mists of memory, my mother's face would often appear, just as it was when I stood by her knee and listened to lessons of wisdom and goodness, from her loving lips. I would see her mild reproving face, and seem to hear her warning voice; and, surrounded by my riotous companions, at certain seasons, reason would struggle for the throne whence she had been driven, and I would, whilst enjoying the loud plaudits of sots,

> See a hand they could not see,
> Which beckoned me away.

Sabbaths which, from my childhood, I had been taught to reverence, were now disregarded. Seldom did I enter God's house, where prayer was wont to be made, as I had done during a portion of the time I resided in New York. The day of rest was no Sabbath to me, and my usual way of spending it was to stroll into the country, where I might be alone, with a bottle of intoxicating liquid in my possession. When this was empty, I would crawl back to the town, under cover of the darkness, and close the sacred hours in some obscure groggery, in the society of those who, like myself, disregarded the command of the Almighty to keep holy the Sabbath day.

Again the dreary winter was about to resume its rigorous reign, and with horror I anticipated its approach. My stock of clothing was failing fast. I had no flannels or woollen socks, no extra coats, and no means of procuring those absolutely necessary preservatives against the severities of an American winter. I had no hope of ever becoming a respectable man again—not the slightest—for it appeared to me that every chance of restoration to decent society, and of reformation, was gone forever. I wished, and fully expected, soon to die. Hope had abandoned me here, and beyond the grave nothing appeared calculated to cheer my desponding spirit. O, what a deep and stinging sense I had of my own degraded position, for my feelings were keenly alive to the ridicule and contempt which never ceased to be heaped on me. Utterly wretched and abandoned, I have stood by the railway track with a vague wish to lie across it, drink myself into oblivion, and let the cars go over me. Once I stood by the rails, with a bottle of laudanum clattering against my lips, and had nearly been a suicide; but the mercy of God interposed, and I dashed the poison on the ground, and escaped the sin of self-murder. All night long have I lain on the damp grass which covered my wife's grave, steeped to the very lips in poverty, degradation, and misery; and yet I was a young man, whose energies, had they been rightly directed, might have enabled me to surmount difficulty, and command respect.

I had long since ceased to correspond with my sister, and so careless had I become, that I never thought of communicating again with the only relative I had remaining. Frequently was I tempted to take my life, and yet I clung instinctively to existence. Sleep was often a stranger to my eyelids, and many a night would I spend in the open air, sometimes in a miserable state of inebriation, and, at other times, in a half-sober condition. All this time I often resolved that I would drink no more— that I would break the chain which bound me, but I still continued in the same course, breaking every promise made to myself and others, and continuing an object of scorn and contempt. I felt that very few, if any, pitied me, and that any should love me was entirely out of the question. Yet was I yearning intensely for sympathy; for, as I have before stated, my affections were naturally strong and deep; and often, as I lay in my solitary chamber, feeling how low I had sunk, and that no one eye ever dropped a tear of pity over my state, or would grow dim if I were laid in the grave, I have ardently wished that I might never see the morning light. Fancy, reader, what my agony must have been, when, with the assurance that no drunkard could enter the kingdom of Heaven, I was willing, nay, anxious, for the sake of escaping the tortures to which I was subjected in this life, to risk the awful realities of the unseen world. My punishment here was greater than I could bear. I had made a whip of scorpions, which perpetually lashed me. My name was a byword. No man seemed to care for my soul. I was joined, like Israel of old, unto idols, and it seemed as if the Lord had said respecting me, "Let him alone."

Before I conclude this portion of my history, let me urge on every young man, whose eye may glance over these pages, to learn from my miserable state a lesson of wisdom. Let him beware of the liquor that intoxicates. Poets may sing of the Circean cup—praise in glowing terms the garlands which wreathe it—wit may lend its brilliant aid to celebrate it, and even learning invest it with a charm; but when the poet's song shall have died, and the garlands have all withered; when wit shall have ceased to sparkle, and the lore of ages be an unremembered thing; the baneful *effects* of the intoxicating draught will be felt; and then will the words of wisdom be awfully verified in the miserable doom of the drunkard:

> Wine is a mocker—strong drink is raging.
>
> *   *   *   *
>
> Who hath woe? who hath sorrow? who hath contentions? who hath wounds without cause? who hath redness of eyes?
>
> They that tarry long at the wine; they that go to seek mixed wine.
>
> Look not thou upon the wine when it is red, when it giveth its color in the cup, when it moveth itself aright.
>
> *At the last it biteth like a serpent, and stingeth like an adder.*

[See Prov. 20:1, 23:29–32. —ed.]

PART SECOND

Hitherto my career had been one of almost unmitigated woe; for, with the exception of the days of my childhood, my whole life had been one perpetual struggle against poverty and misery, in its worst forms. Thrown at a tender age upon the world, I was soon taught its hard lessons. Death had robbed me of my best earthly protector, and Providence cast my lot in a land thousands of miles from the place of my birth. Temptation had assailed me, and trusting to my own strength for support, I had fallen, O, how low! In the very depths of my desolation, wife and children had been torn from my side. In the midst of thousands I was lonely, and, abandoning hope, the only refuge which seemed open for me was the grave. A dark pall overhung that gloomy abode, which shut out every ray of hope; and although death to me would have been a "leap in the dark," I was willing to peril my immortal soul and blindly rush into the presence of my Maker. Like a stricken deer, I had no communion with my kind. Over every door of admission into the society of my fellow-men, the words, "No Hope," seemed to be inscribed. Despair was my companion, and perpetual degradation appeared to be my allotted doom. I was intensely wretched; and this dreadful state of things was of my own bringing about. I had no one but myself to blame for the sufferings which I endured; and when I thought of what I might have been, these inflictions were awful beyond conception. Lower in the scale of mental and moral degradation I could not well sink. Despised by all, I despised and hated in my turn, and doggedly flung back to the world the contempt and scorn which it so profusely heaped on my head.

Such was my pitiable state at this period—a state apparently beyond the hope of redemption. But a change was about to take place—a circumstance which eventually turned the whole current of my life into a new and unhoped for channel.

The month of October had nearly drawn to a close, and on its last Sunday evening I wandered out into the streets, pondering as well as I was able to do, for I was somewhat intoxicated, on my lone and friendless condition. My frame was much weakened by habitual indulgence in intoxicating liquor, and little fitted to bear the cold of winter, which had already begun to come on. But I had no means of protecting myself against the bitter blast, and as I anticipated my coming misery, I staggered along, houseless, aimless, and all but hopeless.

Some one tapped me on the shoulder. An unusual thing that, to occur to me; for no one now cared to come in contact with the wretched, shabby-looking drunkard. I was a disgrace—"a living, walking disgrace." I could scarcely believe my own senses when I turned and met a kind look; the thing was so unusual and so entirely unexpected, that I questioned the reality of it—but so it was. It was the first touch of kindness which I had known for months; and simple and trifling as the circumstance may appear to many, it went right to my heart, and like the wing of an angel troubled the waters in that stagnant pool of affection, and made them once more reflect a little of the light of human love.

The person who touched my shoulder was an entire stranger. I looked at him, wondering what his business was with me. Regarding me very earnestly, and apparently with much interest, he exclaimed:

"Mr. Gough, I believe?"

"That is my name," I replied, and was passing on.

"You have been drinking to-day," said the stranger, in a kind voice, which arrested my attention, and quite dispelled any anger at what I might otherwise have considered an officious interference in my affairs.

"Yes, sir," I replied, "I have."

"Why do you not sign the pledge?" was the next query.

I considered for a minute or two, and then informed the strange friend, who had so unexpectedly interested himself in my behalf, that I had no hope of ever again becoming a sober man, that I was without a single friend in the world who cared for me, or what became of me, that I fully expected to die very soon—I cared not how soon, nor whether I died drunk or sober—and, in fact, that I was in a condition of utter recklessness.

The stranger regarded me with a benevolent look—took me by the arm, and asked me how I should like to be as I once was, respectable and esteemed, well clad, and sitting as I used to in a place of worship, enabled to meet my friends as in old times, and receive from them the pleasant nod of recognition as formerly—in fact, become a useful member of society?

"Oh!" replied I, "I should like all these things first rate; but I have no expectation that such a thing will ever happen. Such a change cannot be possible."

"Only sign our pledge," remarked my friend, "and I will warrant that it shall be so. Sign it, and I will introduce you myself to good friends, who will feel an interest in your welfare and take a pleasure in helping you to keep your good resolutions. Only, Mr. Gough, sign the pledge, and all will be as I have said; ay, and more too."

Oh! how pleasantly fell these words of kindness and promise on my crushed and bruised heart. I had long been a stranger to feelings such as now awoke in my bosom. A chord had been touched which vibrated to the tone of love. Hope once more dawned, and I began to think, strange as it appeared, that such things as my friend promised me *might* come to pass. On the instant I resolved to try, at least, and said to the stranger:

"Well, I will sign it."

"When?" he asked.

"I cannot do so to-night," I replied, "for I *must* have some more drink presently; but I certainly will to-morrow."

"We have a temperance meeting to-morrow evening," he said; "Will you sign it then?"

"I will."

"That is right," said he, grasping my hand, "I will be there to see you."

"You shall," I remarked; and we parted.

I went on my way much touched by the kind interest which, at last, some one had taken in my welfare. I said to myself, "If it should be the last act of my life, I will perform my promise, and sign it even though I die in the attempt, for that man has placed confidence in me, and on that account I love him." I then proceeded to a low groggery in Lincoln square hotel, and in the space of half an hour, drank four glasses of brandy; this, in addition to what I had taken before, made me very drunk, and I staggered home as well as I could. Arrived there, I threw myself on the bed and lay in a state of drunken insensibility until morning.

The first thing which occurred to my mind on awaking was the promise I had made on the evening before, to sign the pledge; and feeling, as I usually did on the morning succeeding a drunken bout, wretched, and desolate, I was almost sorry that I had agreed to do so. My tongue was dry, my throat parched—my temples throbbed as if they would burst, and I had a horrible burning feeling in my stomach which almost maddened me and I felt that I *must* have some bitters or I should die. So I yielded to my appetite, which would not be appeased, and repaired to the same hotel, where I had squandered away so many shillings before; there I drank three or four times, until my nerves were a little strung, and then I went to work.

All that day, the coming event of the evening was continually before my mind's eye, and it seemed to me as if the appetite which had so long controlled me exerted more power over me than ever. It grew stronger than I had at any time known it, now that I was about to rid myself of it. Until noon I struggled against its cravings, and then, unable to endure my misery any longer, I made some excuse for leaving the shop, and went nearly a mile from it in order to procure one more glass wherewith to appease the demon who so tortured me.

The day wore wearily away, and when evening came, I determined, in spite of many a hesitation, to perform the promise I had made to the stranger the night before. The meeting was to be held at the lower Town Hall, Worcester, and thither, clad in an old brown surtout, closely buttoned up to my chin, that my ragged habiliments beneath might not be visible, I repaired. I took a place among the rest, and when an opportunity of speaking presented itself, I requested permission to be heard, which was readily granted.

When I stood up to relate my story, I was invited to the stand, to which I repaired; and, on turning to face the audience, I recognized my acquaintance who had asked me to sign. It was Mr. Joel Stratton. He greeted me with a smile of approbation, which nerved and strengthened me for my task, as I tremblingly observed every eye fixed upon me. I lifted my quivering hand, and then and there told what rum had done for me. I related how I was once respectable and happy, and had a home; but that now I was a houseless, miserable, scathed, diseased, and blighted outcast from society. I said, scarce a hope remained to me of ever becoming that which I once was; but having promised to sign the pledge, I had determined not to break my word, and would now affix my name to it. In my palsied hand I with difficulty grasped the pen, and, in characters almost as crooked as those of old Stephen Hopkins, I signed the total abstinence pledge, and resolved to free myself from the inexorable tyrant—rum.

Although still desponding and hopeless, I felt that I was relieved from a part of my heavy load. It was not because I deemed there was any supernatural power in the pledge, which would prevent my ever again falling into such depths of woe as I had already become acquainted with, but the feeling of relief arose from the honest desire I entertained to keep a good resolution. I had exerted a moral power, which had long remained lying by, perfectly useless. The very idea of what I had done strengthened and encouraged me. Nor was this the only impulse given me to proceed in my new pathway: for many who witnessed my signing, and heard my simple statement, came forward kindly, grasped my hand, and expressed their satisfaction at the step I had taken. A new and better day seemed to have dawned upon me.

As I left the hall, agitated and enervated, I remember chuckling to myself, with great gratification, "I have done it—I have done it." There was a degree of pleasure in having put my foot on the head of the tyrant who had so long led me captive at his will; but, though I had "scotched" the snake, I had not killed him, for every inch of his frame was full of venomous vitality, and I felt that all my caution was necessary to prevent his stinging me afresh.

I went home, retired to bed; but in vain did I try to sleep. I pondered upon the step I had taken, and passed a restless night. Knowing that I had voluntarily renounced drink, I endeavored to support my sufferings, and resist the incessant craving of my remorseless appetite as well as I could; but the struggle to overcome it was insupportably painful. When I got up in the morning, my brain seemed as though it would burst with the intensity of its agony, my throat appeared as if it were on fire, and in my stomach I experienced a dreadful burning sensation, as if the fires of the pit had been kindled there. My hands trembled so, that to raise water to my feverish lips was almost impossible. I craved, literally gasped, for my accustomed stimulus, and felt that I should die if I did not have it; but I persevered in my resolve, and withstood the temptations which assailed me on every hand.

Still, during all this frightful time, I experienced a feeling, somewhat akin to satisfaction, at the position I had taken. I had made at least one step towards reformation. I began to think that it was barely possible that I might see better days, and once more hold up my head in society. Such feelings as these would alternate with gloomy forebodings, and "thick coming fancies" of approaching ill. At one time hope, and at another fear, would predominate; but the raging, dreadful, continued thirst was always present, to torture and tempt me.

After breakfast, I proceeded to the shop where I was employed, feeling dreadfully ill. I determined, however, to put a bold face on the matter, and, in spite of the cloud which seemed to hang over me, to attempt work. I was exceedingly weak, and fancied, as I almost reeled about the shop, that every eye was fixed upon me suspiciously, although I exerted myself to the utmost to conceal my agitation. How I got through that day, I cannot now tell, but its length seemed interminable, and as if it would never come to an end. I felt I was undeserving of confidence after I had so often broken my promises of amendment; but I determined to make another effort to procure the respect of my employers, and going to one of the gentlemen in the shop, I informed him that I had signed the pledge.

He looked at me very earnestly, and said, "I know you have."

"And," I added, "I mean to keep it."

"So they all say," he replied; "and I hope you will."

As he spoke doubtingly, I reiterated my determination to abide by the resolution I had made, never more to touch intoxicating liquors, and said to him, "You have no confidence in me, sir."

"None, whatever," he replied; "but I hope you will keep your pledge."

I turned to work again, saddened in mind and subdued in spirit; for the conversation I had just held with my employer showed me how low I had sunk in the esteem of prudent and sober-minded men. Whilst brooding over my misfortunes, I heard my name mentioned, and, turning round, saw a gentleman, who had entered unobserved by me. He said, "Good morning, Mr. Gough. I was very glad to see you take the position you did last night, and so were many of our temperance friends. It is just such men as you that we want, and I have no doubt but you will be the means of doing the cause a great deal of good."

This greatly encouraged me; and the gentleman, whose name was Mr. Jesse W. Goodrich, then and now practising as an attorney and counsellor at law in Worcester, added, in a very kindly tone, "My office is at the Exchange, Mr. Gough, and I shall be very happy to see you, whenever you like to call in—very happy."

It would be impossible to describe how this act, trifling as it appeared, cheered me. With the exception of Mr. Joel Stratton, who was a waiter at the temperance hotel, and who had asked me to sign the pledge, no one had accosted me for months in a manner which would lead me to think any one cared for me, or what might be my fate. Now, however, I was not altogether alone in the world; there *was* a probability of my being rescued from the slough of despond, where I had so long been floundering. I saw that the fountain of human kindness was not utterly sealed up; and again a green spot, an oasis, small, indeed, but cheering, appeared in the desert of life. I had something now to live for. A new desire for life seemed suddenly to spring up; the universal boundary of human sympathy included even my wretched self in its cheering circle. And all these sensations were generated by a few kind words.

What a lesson of love should not this teach us? How know we, but some trifling sacrifice, some little act of kindness, some, it may be, unconsidered word, may heal a bruised heart, or cheer a drooping spirit. Never shall I forget the exquisite delight which I felt when first asked to call and see Mr. Goodrich; and how did I love him from my very heart for the pleasure he afforded me in the knowledge that *some one* on the broad face of the earth cared for me—for me, who had given myself up as a castaway; who, two days before, had been friendless in the widest signification of the word, and willing, nay, wishing, to die. Any man who has suddenly broken off a habit, such as mine was, may imagine what my sufferings were during the week which followed my abandoning the use of alcohol. Any attempt to describe my feelings would inevitably fall far short of the reality, and I shall mention only one or two circumstances in connection with this eventful period of my life.

On the evening of the day following that on which I signed the pledge, I went straight home from my workshop, with a dreadful feeling of some impending calamity haunting me. In spite of the encouragement I had received, the presentiment of coming evil was so strong, that it bowed me almost to the dust with apprehension. The unslakable thirst still clung to me, and water, instead of allaying it, seemed only to increase its intensity. I feared another attack of delirium tremens, and not without reason; for, on that very evening, when I took the iron pin to screw up the binding-press, it seemed to turn to a writhing, creeping snake in my hands. I dropped it in horror, and it was nothing but a bar of iron! These and similar illusions terrified me, and ere long my worst apprehensions were realized. I was fated to encounter one struggle more with my enemy before I became free.

Fearful was that struggle. God, in his mercy, forbid that any other young man should endure but a tenth part of the torture which racked my frame and agonized my heart. As, in the former attack, horrible faces glared upon me from the walls—faces ever changing, and displaying new and still more horrible features—black, bloated insects crawled over my face, and myriads of burning, concentric rings were revolving incessantly. At one moment the chamber appeared as red as blood, and in a twinkling it was dark as the charnel-house. I seemed to have a knife with hundreds of blades in my hand, every blade driven through the flesh of my hands, and all were so inextricably bent and tangled together, that I could not withdraw them for some time; and when I did, from my lacerated fingers the bloody fibres would stretch out all quivering with life. After a frightful paroxysm of this kind, I would start like a maniac from my bed, and beg for life, life! What I of late thought so worthless, seemed now to be of unappreciable value. I dreaded to die, and clung to existence, as feeling that my soul's salvation depended on a little more of life. A great portion of this time I spent alone; no mother's hand was near to wipe the big drops of perspiration from my brow; no kind voice cheered me in my solitude. Alone I encountered all the host of demoniac forms which crowded my chamber. No one witnessed my agonies, or counted my woes, and yet I recovered; *how*, still remains a mystery to myself, and still more mysterious was the fact of my concealing my sufferings from every mortal eye.

In about a week, I gained, in a great degree, the mastery over my accursed appetite; but the strife had made me dreadfully weak. Gradually my health improved, my spirits recovered, and I ceased to despair. Once more was I enabled to crawl into the sunshine; but, O! how changed. Wan cheeks and hollow eyes, feeble limbs, and almost powerless hands, plainly enough indicated that, between me and death, there had indeed been but a step.

A great change now took place in my condition for the better, and it appeared likely enough that the anticipations of my friend, Mr. Stratton, who induced me to sign the pledge, as to my becoming once more a respectable man, were about to be realized. For a long period, of late, I had ceased to take any care with respect to my personal appearance, for the intemperate man is seldom neat; but I now began to feel a little more pride on this head, and endeavored to make my scanty wardrobe appear to the best advantage. I also applied myself more diligently to business, and became enabled to purchase articles which I had long needed, and assume a more respectable appearance. Unfortunately, however, work soon began to slacken, and my circumstances, in consequence, were but poor.

I, generally, regularly attended the weekly temperance meetings, and my case being well known, I was at length invited to speak on the subject. After some hesitation, I consented to do so, and addressed an audience for about fifteen minutes, stating what my course had been, and what temperance had effected for me, and also expressing my firm determination to adhere to the total abstinence pledge. I well remember the individual who first engaged me for a regular speech. It was a good man, and devoted friend of the cause, Mr. Hiram Fowler, of Upton. He heard my address at one of the temperance meetings, and thinking I should do good, was very anxious to secure my humble services.

One afternoon, not long after I joined the society, a gentleman invited me to speak on temperance, in the schoolhouse, on Burncoat plain. That evening I shall never forget. I was not, from scarcity of funds, enabled to procure fitting habiliments in which to appear before a respectable audience, and so I was compelled to wear an old overcoat, which the state of my under clothing obliged me to button closely up to my chin. The place assigned to me was very near a large and well-heated stove. As I spoke, I grew warm, and after using a little exertion, the heat became so insufferable, that I was drenched in perspiration. My situation was ludicrous in the extreme. I could not, in consequence of the crowd, retreat from the tremendous fire, and unbuttoning my coat was out of the question altogether. What with the warmth imparted by my subject, and that which proceeded from the stove, I was fairly between two fires. When I had done my speech, I was all but done myself, for my body contained a greater quantity of caloric than it had ever possessed before or since. I question whether Monsieur Chabert, the fire king, was ever subjected to a more "fiery trial."

Not long after this, it began to be whispered about that I had some talents for public speaking; and my career, as an intemperate man, having been notorious, a little curiosity as to my addresses was excited. I was invited to visit Milbury, and deliver an address there. I went, in company with Doctor Hunting, of Worcester. Mr. Van Wagner, better known, perhaps, as the Poughkeepsie blacksmith, was also to speak. I spoke, for the first time, from a pulpit at this place; and my address, which was listened to very attentively, occupied about a quarter of an hour or twenty minutes. At this time, nothing was farther from my intentions than becoming a public speaker. In my wildest flights, I never dreamed of this. I can sincerely say that I was urged to give these early addresses solely by a hope that good, through my instrumentality, might be done to the temperance cause, to which I owed my redemption.

Prior to delivering this address at Milbury, I had purchased a new suit of clothes, the first which I had been able to get for a long period. They came home on the day fixed for my speaking. Now, I had been so long accustomed to my old garments, that they had become, as it were, a part and parcel of myself, and seemed to belong to me, and feel as natural as my skin did. My new suit was very fashionably cut, and as I put on the articles, one by one, I felt more awkwardness than, I verily believe, I ever exhibited, before or since, in the course of my life. The pantaloons were strapped down, over feet which had long been used to freedom, and I feared to walk in my usual manner, lest they should *go* at the knee. I feared, too, lest a strap should give, and make me lop-sided for life. The vest certainly set off my waist to the best advantage; but it did not seem, on a first acquaintance, half so comfortable as my ancient friend, although the latter had long been threadbare, and *minus* a few buttons. And, then, the smartly cut coat was so neatly and closely fitted to the arms, and the shoulders, and the back, that, when it was on, I felt in a fix as well as a fit. I was fearful of any thing but a mincing motion, and my arms had a cataleptic appearance. Every step I took was a matter of anxiety, lest an unlucky rip should derange my smartness. How I tried the pockets, over and over again, and stared at myself in the glass! Verily I felt more awkward, for some time, in my new suit, than I did whilst roasting before the fire in my old one.

On the evening following my visit to Milbury, I delivered a second address, in another church there, which was well attended. Invitations now began to pour in on me from many quarters, and I had been asked, several times, to go to the same old school-house, on Burncoat plain, where I had before spoken; when, on the 26th of December, 1842, Dr. Kendall, of Stirling, applied for some person to deliver a temperance address. I was recommended as a suitable person, and went with him, occupying the whole of the evening, for the first time. Mr. Van Wagner spoke the next night, and I was detained until the Sunday morning. On my return to Worcester, I found that several applications for my services had been made from other towns. Mr. Genery Twichell was desirous that I should go with him to Barre, where a New Year's Day celebration, or temperance jubilee, consisting of singing and addresses, was to be held. In compliance with Mr. Twichell's wish, I attended the anniversary, and felt much gratification; after which I again returned to Worcester.

I now, finding that my engagements were increasing fast, applied to my employers for leave of absence for a week or two, in order to enable me to perform them. The required permission I obtained. When I went away, I left a pile of Bibles on my bench unfinished, promising to finish them on my return; but unforeseen circumstances occurred, and I never returned to complete them.

My time was now almost entirely employed in lecturing on the temperance cause; and, as good appeared to be effected by my labors, I was encouraged to proceed. I visited, about this time, in succession, the towns of Grafton, Webster, Leicester, Milbury, West Boylston, Berlin, Bolton, Upton, Hopkinton, and Mendon, together with many other places in Worcester county, the names of which it is not necessary to record. My audiences gradually increased in numbers, and, as I acquired more confidence in speaking, my labors were rendered the more useful and acceptable.

I must now refer to a circumstance which occurred about five months after I signed the pledge, and which caused infinite pain to myself, and uneasiness to the friends of the cause. I allude to a fact, notorious at the time—my violation of the pledge. This narrative purports to be a veritable record of my history, and God forbid that I should conceal or misstate any material circumstance connected with it. If the former portion of this Autobiography be calculated to operate as a warning against the use of alcoholic liquors, the event which I am now about to record may not be without its use, in convincing many who have flung away the maddening draught, that they need a strength, not their own, to enable them to adhere to the vows they make. Well, and wisely, has it been said by the inspired penman, "Let him that thinketh he standeth, take heed lest he fall"; for unassisted human strength is utterly unable to afford adequate support in the hour of weakness or temptation. We are only so far safe when we depend on a mightier arm than our own for support. Our very strength lies in our sense of weakness, and this was to be demonstrated in my experience.

I had known all the misery which intoxication produces, and, remembering it, could fervently offer up a prayer, such as the following, which, although first breathed by other lips than mine, aptly expressed my feelings:

ALMIGHTY GOD, if it be thy will that man should suffer, whatever seemeth good in thy sight impose on me. Let the bread of affliction be given me to eat. Take from me the friends of my confidence. Let the cold hut of poverty be my dwelling-place, and the wasting hand of disease inflict its painful torments. Let me sow in the whirlwind, and reap in the storm. Let those have me in derision who are younger than I. Let the passing away of my welfare be like the fleeting of a cloud, and the shouts of my enemies be like the rushing of waters. When I anticipate good, let evil annoy me; when I look for light, let darkness come upon me. Let the terrors of death be ever before me. Do all this, but save me, merciful God, save me from the fate of a Drunkard. Amen.

I loved the temperance pledge. No one *could* value it more than I; for, standing, as I did, a redeemed man, enabled to hold up my head in society, I owed every thing to it. Painful as I said this event of my life was in the act, and humiliating in the contemplation, I proceed to state every particular respecting it.

I was, at this time, delivering addresses in the town of Charlton, Worcester county. Laboring so indefatigably, and indeed unceasingly, almost immediately, and for some time, after suddenly breaking off the use of a stimulus to which I had been accustomed for years, I became very weak in health; and, being of an extremely nervous temperament, I suffered much more than I otherwise should have done. I had an almost constant hæmorrhage from my stomach, and gradually became so excited, and nervously irritable, that I entirely lost my appetite, and could neither eat nor sleep. The engagements that I had made at Charlton came to a termination on Fast day, and in order to prepare for an address the next evening at Sutton, that town being the next on my list of appointments (numbering now more than thirty in succession), I returned to Worcester. Whilst there, and on my way there from Charlton, I felt sensations to which I had before been a stranger. It was a most distressing feeling, but one impossible to define. It will be remembered that, in a former page, I have given an account of an accident which I received when a boy, my head having been wounded by a spade. In the neighborhood of this old injury I experienced considerable pain. A restlessness, too, accompanied these symptoms, for which I could not account, and which I could not by any effort subdue. It was noticed, with some uneasiness, by my friends, that I acted and talked very strangely; but I was not at all conscious that, in my every day habits, there was any thing to excite or attract more than ordinary attention.

I boarded with a Mrs. Chamberlain, as good, kind, and considerate a woman as I ever knew. She observed my illness, and strongly urged me to remain at home, and go to bed. But I was in so nervous a state, that to remain still for five minutes together was a thing utterly impossible. I could neither sit in one position long, or remain standing; and this restless feeling was far more distressing to myself than can be imagined by those who have not suffered in a similar way. It appeared to me that I must be going *somewhere,* I knew not, and cared not whither, but there was a certain impulsive feeling which I could not restrain, any more than an automaton can remain motionless when its machinery is wound up. I left Mrs. Chamberlain's house, much against her wish, saying I should return shortly, and intending to do so; but when I had wandered about for a little time, I heard the fifteen-minute bell, at the depôt, announce that the train was about to start for Boston, and almost without thinking of what I was about to do, I proceeded to the station, entered the cars, and, without any earthly aim or object, set out for Boston; all I felt was an irresistible inclination to move on, I cared not where.

Several gentlemen, into whose company I fell, noticed the extreme strangeness of my deportment and conversation whilst in the cars. On arriving in Boston, I strolled for some time about the streets, uncertain how to employ or amuse myself. Evening drew on, and it occurred to me that I might dissipate my melancholy, and quiet myself down, by going to the theatre; I resolved to pursue this course, and accordingly entered the playhouse. I had not been there long before I fell in with some old companions, with whom I had been intimate many years before. We talked together of old times; and, at last, observing my manner, and noticing that I talked strangely and incoherently, they inquired what ailed me. I told them that I felt as if I wanted to move on, that move on I must, but cared not whither—in fact that I was very ill. After being pressed to accompany them and take some oysters, I consented, and we all repaired to an oyster-room. It was during the time of taking this refreshment that a glass of wine or brandy was offered me. Without thought, I drank it off. And then, suddenly, the terrible thought flashed across my mind that I had violated my pledge. The horror I felt at the moment, it would be impossible for me to describe. Ruin, inevitable ruin, stared me in the face. By one rash and inconsiderate act, I had undone the work of months, betrayed the confidence reposed in me by friends, and blasted every hope for the future. To say that I felt miserable would only give a faint idea of my state. For five months I had battled with my enemy, and defied him when he appeared armed with all his terrors; but now, when I fondly fancied him a conquered foe, and had sung in the broad face of day my pæans of victory, to hundreds and thousands of listeners, he had craftily wrought my downfall. I was like some bark,

> Which stood the storm when winds were rough,
> But in a sunny hour, fell off;
> Like ships that have gone down at sea
> When heaven was all tranquility.

My accursed appetite, too, which I deemed eradicated, I found had only slept; the single glass I had taken roused my powerful and now successful enemy. I argued with myself that as I *had* made one false step, matters could not be made worse by taking a few more. So, yielding to temptation, I swallowed three or four more potations, and slept that night at the hotel. With the morning reflection came; and fearful, indeed, appeared to me my situation. Without drinking again, I started in the cars for Newburyport, painfully feeling but not exhibiting any signs of having indulged in the intemperate cup on the previous evening. At Newburyport an unlooked for trial awaited me—I was invited to speak for the temperance society there. I felt that I had no claim *now* to be heard, although I bitterly repented my retrograde movement; but at length I consented to speak, and did so, both on the Sunday and the following Monday. To Worcester I dreaded returning, so agonized was I in mind. It was there I came forward as a redeemed drunkard, had there, time and again, solemnly vowed that the intoxicating cup should never press my lips again, had there been received by the kind and the good with open arms, and encouraged to proceed; but, alas! how had I fallen! and with what countenance could I meet those to whose respect and sympathy I felt I had now no longer claim?

I returned, in consequence of entertaining such sentiments as these, again to Boston, there intending to remain until I should decide as to what my future course should be. I became faint, hungry, and sick; and my heart remained "ill at ease." Again I drank, although not to excess, and at length resolved, at all hazards, to return to Worcester, which place I reached on Saturday, where, as might be expected from my conduct previous to leaving, my friends were very much alarmed at my absence.

On my arrival home, I immediately sent for my friend, Mr. Jesse W. Goodrich, the same gentleman, it will be remembered, who kindly invited me to call on him the day after I signed the pledge. I also sent for Dr. Hunting, who had greatly interested himself in my welfare. When these gentlemen came to see me, I at once made them acquainted with what had transpired in Boston, and my violation of the pledge, and then expressed to them my determination to leave the town, county, and State, never more to return to it. I then re-signed the pledge, and commenced packing up my books and clothes, with the full determination of leaving Worcester the following Monday.

My friends, who did not desert me, even in these dark hours of my existence, again rallied round me, and persuaded me to remain, in order to attend the temperance meeting on the Monday I had fixed as the day of my departure. My candid statement had, in a measure, revived their confidence in me. In accordance with their desires, I did remain, and went, at the time mentioned, to the upper Town Hall, where a very large audience was assembled, who appeared to feel a great interest in the proceedings. I was almost broken-hearted, and felt as if I were insane; but I humbly trust that I sincerely repented of the false step I had taken, and, cheered by the considerate kindness of my friends, I determined, God helping me, to be more than ever an uncompromising foe to alcohol.

As this portion of my history is of some importance, I shall, instead of entering into any detailed description of the meeting I have just spoken of myself, quote in this place the report of the proceedings which appeared at the time in the public journals.

The following article appeared in the *Cataract and Washingtonian:*

> Mr. John B. Gough, as soon as he was known to be in the hall, was called for in all directions, and received in a manner which showed the true spirit of Washingtonian sympathy, kindness, and charity, to be still predominant in the bosom of this great Washingtonian fraternity. Feeble in health, and with an utterance half choked by the intensity of his feelings, he briefly alluded to, and promptly acknowledged

his late misfortune, saying that he *had*, within a few days past, deemed himself a crushed and a ruined man; but that the enemies of the great cause he had attempted to advocate need not rejoice. That he had rallied, had re-signed the pledge, and then felt, and should prove himself, a more uncompromising foe to alcohol than he had ever been before; and, after invoking, in tones that came *from* and went *to* the heart, the blessing of Heaven upon his friends, this society, and the cause, attended by his physician and some friends, retired from the hall, subdued, even to tears, by the trying ordeal through which he had been passing.

The following is extracted from a more extended report in the same journal:

"The Washingtonian Society of Westboro" met at the Town Hall, on Thursday evening, April 20, 1843. The hall was full to overflowing. The meeting was called to order by the President of the Society, and opened with prayer by the Rev. Mr. Harvey; after which the President introduced Mr. J. B. Gough, the well-known, eloquent, and successful advocate of temperance, who, in a very feeling and appropriate manner, stated that, within a short time, he had broken his pledge, but he had signed it again, again risen up to combat King Alcohol, and that he appeared before them the uncompromising foe to alcohol in all its forms, willing to devote all the energies of his body and mind to the noble cause of temperance; and, with all humility, threw himself upon the kindness of his friends, stating it was for them to say whether or not he should proceed, and have their kindness and support, when the following resolutions were offered, and unanimously adopted, almost by acclamation:

"*Resolved*, That as intemperance is the cause of most of the misery and suffering that affect our fellow-men, drying up and poisoning the streams of domestic happiness, it is therefore our imperative duty to exert our united efforts against the monster, and stand, shoulder to shoulder, until the evil is banished from the land.

"*Resolved*, That we highly appreciate the former services of Mr. J. B. Gough, as a Washingtonian lecturer, and, notwithstanding the unhappy circumstances which have lately occurred, we do most cordially greet him in the Washingtonian spirit of kindness and sympathy, and most cheerfully do we give him our countenance and support in the glorious cause of temperance."

Mr. Gough again rose, evidently much embarrassed, and was received by the audience with *decided* marks of approbation. He stated, that to be thus received was more than he felt able to bear. Scorn and contumely he should be enabled to endure, but to kindness he had not always been accustomed, and he was completely unmanned. Recovering his self-possession, he went on, and most eloquently warned all, particularly the young men, who had become Washingtonians, *to abandon their old associates,* and not place themselves *in the way of temptation.* He portrayed, in most glowing colors, the criminality of those who endeavor, whatever may be their motive, to induce any one to violate his pledge, leaving them to their own consciences and their God. After holding the undivided attention of his audience for near an hour, he concluded with a most powerful appeal to all to come out and sign the pledge, hoping that no one would offer as an excuse that the speaker had violated his, but come out, and, each and all, give their support to a cause which is worthy of the best effort of our powers.

A similar resolution was passed at Sutton. It was as follows:

Resolved, That we deeply sympathize with Mr. Gough in his misfortune, in having violated his pledge, and heartily express our satisfaction with his apology, and highly approve of his determination to continue his labors in the temperance cause.

Never shall I forget the kindness shown me at this time by my friends, amongst whom I would especially mention Mr. Goodrich, Dr. Hunting, and Mr. George M. Rice, of Worcester.* It would be impossible for me to enumerate here all from whom I received the most considerate attentions, but they are not forgotten by me, and never will be.

Although freely and fully forgiven by the Society, I still felt keenly on the subject of my lapse; but my intention of leaving the town was not carried into effect; as my friends, one and all, urging me to remain, I felt it my duty to accede to their wishes. I was waited upon in Worcester by Mr. Ellsworth Childs, of Westborough, with a request from the good

---

*Although by the generosity of my friends I was kindly forgiven, yet by some few I was, and still am, regarded in no very favorable light. I regret this, but do not blame them for not recognizing me on the true Washingtonian principles; they have my good will and wishes, whatever may be their disposition towards me.

friends of that place that I should visit them, and I felt it to be a duty to go to the different towns where I had made engagements, and to which I had been reinvited, freely and frankly to confess the circumstances which led me to break my appointments, and solicit their forgiveness, which was willingly accorded in every case.

I trust that I now had a full sense of my own insufficiency to keep myself from sinking. Hitherto I had relied too implicitly on my own strength for support, and my utter weakness had been painfully exemplified in my violation of a sacred promise. It was a humiliating blow, but it taught me that I derived my strength from on high, and that when He withdrew it I was utterly powerless to think of myself any good thing. Whatever my future situation in life may be, I hope ever to possess a strong sense of my utter weakness, and cherish a humble dependence on Him who is able to keep me from falling, and render my labors honorable and useful.

This account of my violation of the pledge will, I doubt not, be entirely new to many of my readers, although in my own neighborhood the fact was notorious enough. It is my earnest wish to send forth this narrative to the world in as complete and perfect a manner as practicable; omitting nothing, nor adding to any thing, so that it may be as faithful a record of my life as can be presented. I have not shrunk from depicting the dark days of my life, because I wished to warn my fellow-men against the wine-cup, and to strip the false and fading flowers from the manacles which amuse the inebriate whilst they cripple his energies; and in referring, as I shall have occasion to do, in the remaining pages, to the time since the dark pall was lifted up, I trust, forever, and hope's brilliant star shed on me its lustre, I hope I shall not be deemed egotistical—than this nothing can be more foreign to my views and sentiments. My readers must take the picture as it is, remembering that I have not adopted the style of any academy or school, but endeavored to present to the mind's eye a graphic delineation of what may be often met with in our daily paths—a painting of human nature FROM THE LIFE.

ANDRUS V. GREEN

from *The Life and Experience of A. V. Green* (1848)

Born on the Fourth of July in 1795, Andrus Green moved as a youth from his native Rhode Island to the Mohawk River valley of upstate New York. Apprenticed to a blacksmith at fifteen, he soon engaged in sprees excessive enough for him to swear off alcohol. But the drinking customs of the trade overcame Green's abstemious intentions, and he fell into occasional inebriety—transferring his allegiance from rum, the working man's standby, to whiskey. At the end of his indentures, he returned to Schoharie, New York, to open a blacksmith shop. He subsequently spent a year in school, vainly courted a young woman of means, and then found a more suitable wife.

Even while he prospered, Green believed, he was already in the grip of King Alcohol: "for when a man has got an appetite for rum, he is as sure to become a drunkard as he is to become a man, if he indulges himself in the practice of common dram drinking." In part for relief from sectarian religious wrangling, Green and his family headed west in 1829, settling on a farm in Cuyahoga County, Ohio.

As he rose in the esteem of his neighbors, Green became an itinerant preacher, an officer in the state militia, and a justice of the peace, with good prospects for political advancement. His misfortunes began, however, with the loss of his farm to its mortgage holder and the subsequent acceleration of his inebriety. From town leader, Green fell to town drunkard, and his family suffered accordingly. His ultimate reformation by the Washingtonians is recorded in the following excerpt. Green's public stature was restored, this time as a temperance lecturer.

Life and Experience offers a vision of the Washingtonian movement that is unusually rambunctious and vernacular. In his preface, Green frankly admits he is writing, not only "for the purpose of giving a warning to others," but also to enable the debilitated author "to get a house and home for his family, as he has lost all the property that he had earned, twice in his life." Green proposed that to make things interesting he would "use plain and easy language."

THE FIRST LESSON

I was born in the State of Rhode Island, July 4th, 1795, and was accustomed to the use of barley bread and johnny cake, clams and oysters, but never got drunk on either; and when but a youth, my father moved to the State of New York, and settled in the county of Schoharie, in the town of Middleburgh. He had for a neighbor a man by the name of Jesse Swan. He was a drunkard maker, and he worked well at his trade; for he kept a store, tavern, ashery, gambling shop, and almost every thing that was calculated to draw his neighbors; and it was a place of every evil work, and my father was soon a companion of the rum bottle, and set the example for his boys, who were then growing up under his care, and at an early day of my life, I was fond of the common beverage, which was rum. Numerous were the friends of my father, and too often drank his health in a bottle of rum, one of the most unnatural places for health, for it lays the foundation for diseases of every kind. When I was about nine years of age, my father sent me to Swan's to get him some tobacco, and told me to tell Swan he must treat his customer, as that was the fashion; and Swan got some rum and told me to drink it all, and I did so, to obey him and my father also. This fashion of merchant's treating and giving liquor to gain custom has been a profitable source of making drunkards, in all ages of the world. But I got home some how, very drunk. My beloved mother, O! how sweet the name! soon began to chastise father for bringing up his children to follow the fashion of drinking; but the old man laughed to see me stagger around the house. This was the starting point of my life. Oft with my father, I soon found that I loved the taste of that thing called rum; and as I grew in years, I drank more and loved it better; and truly, I think I loved it as well as the young man said he loved his wife, and he loved her so well that he come very near eating her; and he was sorry since that he did not eat her all up, when he would have got rid of an awful scold. I think about two

174

years after this time, I went with my father and brothers and friends, to a Yankee husking bee, and seated myself by the side of my then-called uncle, who by the by would get very brindle, and when the bottle came around, I drank with him, and soon found myself very sick. I got up, thinking to go home, but I could not stand; so I crawled into the husks and was soon all covered over with them, and knew no more until the next day. When they went to stacking the husks, they pitched me out nearly dead, and deprived of my senses in a great degree. They carried me home, and I remained sick for some time, under the watchful care of my mother. Here some will say I was a fool, and drank too much. I ask, sir, who made me a fool, and who told me how much to drink? The fashion of that country in those days knew no bounds, and no one set bounds for them. Sure they told me I must not get drunk, but never told me I must not drink at all, if I did it would ripen into drunkenness by the moderate habit or use of a little; for now I consider the use of dram drinking the only way to manufacture drunkards.

LESSON XI

The Loss of My Farm

In this lesson the reader will find me turned out of house and home, and the cars of destruction rolling me faster on to the dishonored grave of the drunkard.

I then went to work to make my family as comfortable as I could. By this time, a neighbor of mine told me that I should have to leave my farm in the spring. I wanted to know the reason; he told me that I had sold my farm, and the man that had got it was going to let it out in the spring, and I should have to leave. I was struck as with a thunderbolt, but did not believe it. He told me that I had given a deed of my farm. This set me to thinking: I concluded it was nothing more than a Yankee hoax, and paid no more attention to it, until I went into Cleveland, and went to the Clerk's Office and found that I had given a deed, and it was recorded, and the man had transferred the farm in his own name. I went to see him, and asked him how he came by a deed of my farm. He asked me if I did not understand the bargain. I told him that I had given him a mortgage, and that I was to have my own time to redeem it. Well, well, said he, Mr. Green, you shall have no trouble about it. I always meant to be honest, and I thought that every other person was until I found them to be of the contrary. I went home, and in a few weeks on came a man, who said he had hired the farm, and should move on in a few days. He then was with me in my barn. I told him he should not come on to my premises: he swore that he would. I then ordered him out of my barn; he swore he would not go. Then I took up a pitchfork, and told him to clear. He came at me, and began to beat me and bruise my body, until he saw fit to stop and went out of the barn. I prosecuted him in behalf of the State, in a case of assault and battery; as there was no witness present he plead guilty in self defence, and the court was fool enough to discharge him. . . .

Soon after this, I concluded to get together all that I could, and buy a small place for my family. I concluded to go up the Ohio Canal, and look for a home; so I got my wife to go with me, and we went to Cleveland, took a canal boat, and started. We had a night ride to start upon. Some time in the night there was a drunken man fell overboard; my wife ran out, supposing it was me, for we did not pretend to lie down to sleep. Our first stop was at Akron; here the drunkery keepers were at the boat to get customers, and one of them got me right away; so I went to a large brick house standing on the corner of the street, close by the Pennsylvania Canal and there called for a room, with the expectation of looking around that section of the country. We stayed there some time. . . .

Now I have come to the time when my life seems to me like a dream, for after this time, for three years to come, it would be hard for me to say that I breathed a sober breath; and if I had been without for a week at a time, and did not get my beverage, the old tub which I carried around would always furnish me with the smell of whiskey, which would always vomit a stone wall; therefore, if I should not give the plain truth as things took place, my friends and readers may charge it to insanity by alcohol. . . .

I will give you one circumstance that always appeared to me like a dream or a vision. I was going home one night from the grog shop, some ten o'clock in the night: the moon shone very bright, and my house in sight, but I had to stop and rest very often by the road side, and I thought I never should get home. At length I saw a stone some two or three rods from my house, and it appeared to be elevated some eight or ten inches above the ground. I thought if I could get to that stone, I would sit down on it, and wait for some help to get in. So I hobbled along until I came to the stone—it appeared to look very white; I came up to it and sat down, and lo and behold, I had sat down in a mud hole of water, where the hogs had rooted and made a place to wallow. Here I had a chance for reflection. Now, Green, what will become of you? To-day a man told me I could live but a short time—six weeks at the most; now compare your present condition with that of former times, when you were a minister of the gospel and a magistrate; how often have you been in and with the most respectable company and people, and have joined together some one hundred of the youth of our land, in the solemn bands of matrimony; and where are you now? what has become of your once boasted talents and mind? Now you are here, in the pleasant village of Medina, and don't know a stone from a hole in the ground! Well, then I made an effort to get out, and rolled over upon the grass, and got off all the mud that I could and crept into the house, and lay down and soon fell asleep, and awoke and felt out for my water, but no water was there. What now shall I do? The chimney is all on fire and no water. I crawled out to find the water pail in the dark, and got it by the ears and began to drink, smacked my lips together but thought it tasted rather greasy. I soon found that I had been drinking out of the swill pail!

Cold weather now began to come on, and I had to move again to some other place; so I went to my old friend Smith and asked him for a room in his house. It was granted, and I soon was in the house with the old Judge. In the course of that winter, I found that matters and things did not go very well in his family; but I was determined to say nothing about it. Oft was I interrogated respecting some flying reports, but would not be found talking about my neighbors; however, the Judge and myself were on the most friendly terms, for we would get our grog in a bottle on Saturday, to last over the Sabbath.

Trouble with Judge Smith

This winter was soon gone. Our number of hard drinkers increasing, the boys began to play their pranks with the old men, and were indulged in the same by their parents, and some of the married men set the example; for at one time the Judge had been out to get some straw to put into his bed, and on his return he stopped at the white house to get his drink, and after he had got it, he went out, got his straw slung over his back, when out came one of the drunkery keepers, with a brand of fire behind him, and set the straw to burning, while the Judge was on his return home. Such examples the boys soon took the advantage of; for at one time they had gave me whiskey so that they thought that they would have some fun with me, as I sat in the bar room of the white house; so the boys had assembled and had got their ropes put into a snare around the steps, to take me when I came out of the house. Men in town stood at their doors to see the sport, and to encourage the boys to abuse the poor drunkard. So out I came, and not being as drunk as they supposed, I jumped over the rope, and had got almost across the street, when on came about twenty boys after me, and hauled me up fast to the post on the side walk. I took my knife out and cut the rope, and called for Esquire Albro to fetch me a whip. He soon was out of his store with a good whip, with a long lash; I took the whip, and after the boys; sometimes on my head and sometimes on my hands and feet. That soon made a scattering among the boys, and a loud shout among the men.

The spring opened very warm and pleasant, and the drunkery keepers at the white house had made a showering house in one part of their wood house, where many would go in warm weather and get showered. So they told the Judge they thought it would do him good to be showered (as the Judge was complaining of being out of health). So the Judge consented to it; and now, said he to the Judge, you had better take a good drink of brandy before you take off your clothes, so that you will not take cold. Of course he got his drink and went into the house, stripped himself, and hallooed out I am ready. No sooner than the word came, down came a pailfull of hog's swill, and showered the Judge all over. However, they made it all right again, if such things can be made right. This spring the wife of the old Judge began to get uneasy, and petitioned the court to grant her a bill of divorce from her husband, stating that he had been a drunkard for more than three years, and she could not put up with his insults any longer. She therefore swore the peace against him, and had him put in jail. Here he stayed for some time. At length he got bail and came out. Smith was sent off to baffle her in the trial. They now lived separate, for he too came back and boarded with his mother. At

178

this time I had moved out of his house but understood the game. Sure enough, Smith was insane, just as all other men are when under the influence of the spirit of alcohol. Notwithstanding Mr. Smith was a complete traveling swill tub, yet I never knew him to fetch a limb to the ground when he was drunk; and all this time Smith thought himself no more than a common drinker. However, at the time of the trial, his wife obtained a bill of divorce from her once beloved husband. They had three children, two of them small, and running around the streets as if they had no friend or home. At this time Mrs. Smith had so managed that she had got about all of Smith's property in her hands, together with the homestead, by the decree of the court. I shall leave the Judge here, and remark upon him again when he sees better times, and that will soon come. . . .

LESSON XII

The Delirium Tremens

In this Lesson, my language will fail me to describe the horrible scene before me; and no person, unless he has been in the same scene, or has passed through the same ordeal, can picture to himself how he would have felt to have ten thousand devils after him at once. But such was my case. About this time provisions were scarce, and the tavern-keepers had to ride far and near to supply themselves and their tables with fresh meat. It so happened that I had got one cow left, and a large fat calf. This calf I designed to have killed for the purpose of getting some bread-stuff for my family. He said he would take half of the calf, and pay me the money for it at the market price. I then went and got my calf dressed off in good style, and took the one half of it to this man. The calf was very fat and heavy; he took the veal, and now, said I, there is three drinks of whiskey I owe you for; take out that and let me have the balance in money, to get bread for my family. He said he had not got the money, but the next morning, if I would come in, he would pay me. I stepped out, and then he said to his bar tender, don't you give Green any money for his meat, for he will soon drink it all up, and when he has drunk up the amount of his calf, then don't you trust him with any more. So I went several times to get the money; they would set down the bottle and give me whiskey, but no money; and soon they told me that I had drank up my veal and they did not owe me any more.

Here my calf was gone, and my family without bread. However, others would trust me for whiskey, but I was so discouraged that I had rather die than live. I soon became very drunk again, and was picked up on the side walk, some time in the night, by a man who was out late, and carried home. I never could tell how I got to the house, nor who helped me. The next day those devils were after me; some of them were black and some white—of all colors, and in all shapes. This appears to me like a dream: but they were all around me with pitch forks and fire-brands and gaveling irons and pincers; and if I cast my eyes down, there were ten thousand snakes and serpents hissing at my heels. One of the blue devils had in one hand a brand of fire, and in the other a small pair of pincers. At this time I tried to get out of their way, but could not. Then I wanted they should kill me right out; but this blue-bottle, fiery-eyed devil said they were not going to kill me in that way, but with the pincers he would pull off my finger nails; then my toe nails; then a finger; then a toe; then pull off one of my arms; then the other; then pull off my legs, and with that brand of fire they should burn up my body. At this time my wife came up stairs and found me in the chamber with a rope over a rafter and around my neck, upon an old drunken chair, ready to swing off, when she caught me and got me down stairs, and upon the bed. I knew nothing as I ought for some time—crazy and wild. I hope that the reader will not think that this is all literally true—it was all imaginary, with the exception of hanging myself; this was true as near as I can recollect. Once before this I had tried to make way with myself by hanging, but thank God I have escaped them so far. One of my old neighbors hung himself on an apple tree, while he was deranged with hard cider.

Thus my reader will see how drunkards are made. When they first begin to tipple in small drinks, or drams, then they commence where I did; then they step upon the old boat Jollification; from thence to point Just Enough; thence to Tipsy Bay; then down to Blackeye town, and off into Peelshin Alley, and to Hog Pond; stop occasionally at Hickup Tavern—then sail off down stream to Death River; and from there stop at the wharves of One Drink More; and thence away off into Puke City—and here they find me again, for I was so far gone, that unless I could get about one pint before breakfast, my victuals would not stay in my stomach, and often the smell of whiskey would make me heave.

One time early in the morning, I went into a tavern and called for some bitters; the landlord set down the bottle, and I poured out a good common drink and turned it down the red lane, and it came up again and I catched it in the glass and drank it again; so I did for three times, and the last time I catched it in the glass and set it on the counter, and stepped back and sat down on the bench. Soon in came an old soap stick and called for bitters. He told him there was some in that glass, and he might have it. He took the glass and swallowed the contents—then exclaiming, that just touched the spot, took out his money to pay for it; I told him that he was welcome, for that drink, for I had drank it down three times, and it would not stay with me. He was mad, but could not fetch it back again. This same man is now a tee-totaller. Had I been like some men when drunk, I think my wife would have broken my head before this time; but to the contrary, when I was drunk I was very good humored, and would quarrel with nobody, if they did not provoke me; if they got me mad then I would [as] soon fight a horse as a man.

Not far from this time we had a man by the name of Simmons came to Medina, and introduced himself as a Baptist preacher, and he wanted to hold a protracted meeting in the place; so the Methodists opened their house to him. He commenced and proceeded, but did not stop when he got through. However, the good people of this place crowded the house night and day—I think it held for some six weeks. During this time I attended the effort almost every day, for about two weeks. I found out that he was a son of thunder, and therefore it suited me the better; for I always did like to hear a man preach hell fire and brimstone—hell and damnation; the hotter it come the better it suited me; yet I was full of hell fire all the time, and therefore did not think he meant me; for I would get pretty blue before I went, and would get very dry before meeting was out. I saw that he had his eyes upon me, and thought that he meant me all the time—unless he said something about the drunkard—then I thought that he meant somebody else, for I would not own that I was a drunkard; and I have often thought since, if he had given the drunkard maker a portion of his fire and brimstone, and showed some pity for the victim, he might have had some effect on me. But I was full of the devil's dyestuff all the time, and therefore had no room for more; for his preaching, nor any other's, would have no more effect upon me than oil would on a goose's back. Then the time had nearly come when I had to move my family again; so I went to my old friend again, and asked Smith for a room in one part of the old house, where his mother lived. This also was granted, and I soon took my family there. This was moving about once in six months. The Judge then boarded with his mother. Here Smith and myself often would hold counsel over a bottle of whiskey, to cheer each other in our unhappy state.

A Riot

About this time Judge Smith had trouble respecting his college house. As I am a little before my story, I must return: It being just before the court sat, wherein the rights and wrongs were to be tried for a divorce, most every night Smith would lose some articles of his household furniture; therefore he went and armed himself, and would get some one with him, to watch his house and property. I watched with him some nights, when we both were drunk, and at the same time some persons would come in at some part of the house, and carry off his property. At length the furniture was all gone, and his mansion was left alone. He then concluded that his wife would not trouble him any more, and therefore came to the conclusion that he would repair the house, and fix it up for sale. His wife found it out, and came to him and told him if he would repair the house and paint it over again, she would come back and live with him again. Of course the Judge went at it. Then Smith came to me and told me his calculations: now, said he, Mr. Green, if you will help me I will pay you. I told him I would do him all the good I was able to do. Well, said he, we will go and take off the window blinds and have them painted over again, to start on. So we commenced the work. Soon some of his neighbors came, that had taken sides with Mrs. Smith, and told him and me if we did not let that house alone they would have us both in jail. It set Smith to swearing, and they went off and left him. This made enemies for me, but I did not know it at the time. Not many days after that, this riot or mob commenced, but kept still from me. Smith had heard something said in town, and came and told me he thought there was more trouble ahead. They watched their opportunity

182

when Smith and myself were very brindle. One night after myself and family were all asleep, I would think about eleven o'clock at night, I was aroused from my sleep by a noise at the door; the next moment the door was broken down, and some ten or twelve or more, I should think, were in my house; and then they came to my bedroom, pushed open the door, and some five or six rushed in where we slept. My wife sprang to the floor, and was seized by a ruffian, and she screamed aloud. By this time three or four broke my bedstead down, and got me by one of the legs and pulled with the vengeance of a tiger. This awoke my daughter, and she not knowing what the matter could be with her mother, she hallooed murder. This alarmed the Judge and his mother, and they came into my room with a lighted candle. Then the blood hounds left the house, and soon they commenced throwing stones, brickbats, and any thing they could find, at the house. They broke in my windows, and they soon broke my looking glass, and other furniture, and almost covered my beds with brickbats. Some half bushel fell upon the bed where my two youngest children lay. At the same time, a woman went to the house where the Mayor lived, and aroused him; but he would not stir a foot towards quelling the riot. Whether he was afraid of his own life, or did not care about ours, that I do not know. The cries and noise soon spread all over the village, and the streets and lanes were crowded. At this time the mobites were still. Several of the men came into the house with lights, to see if we were dead or living. We slept no more that night, notwithstanding the human devils were around my house all night, but made no more attempts to come in. The next morning some of the neighbors came in, and appeared to be very sorry for the abuse and insult we had received. I soon began to walk around the town and see the people, and I saw quite a number that looked as guilty as if they had just came out of the State's Prison; but no one was guilty by consent. I asked them what all this meant, in a Christian and professed moral community. They said it was because I took sides with and helped Judge Smith; but I think they were sorry for it; if they were not, I was sorry for them. Neither do I think that any of them would be found in such a rebellion against a peaceable citizen, if they had been sober themselves. However, things went on without troubling us any more.

Not long after that I moved my family out of the town a little west. There I remained in the town of York, until the star of temperance made its appearance. This was a novelty; never before did I hear of a man that had gone down so low by intemperance that every nerve was un-strung—sometimes had to get about on crutches and at other times lie confined to his bed in drunken fits, unable to get on his own clothes, or feed himself at times, poor and crippled, flesh consumed, appetite gone, heart broken, and yet withal, a strong, burning, craving appetite for al-cohol, that ever did or could break right off sudden and reform again. But such was my case, and such was my condition. Neither did I think that there was any help or chance for me; for I concluded that if I stopped the use of all kinds of stimulus, death must be my portion very soon, for I had become so very poor in flesh, as well as in purse, that I concluded nothing but a miracle could ever save me.

LESSON XIII

Life from the Dead

Joyful news we bring to-day!
   Glory! glory! to our king;
Temperance spreads its onward way,
   Wafted as on angel's wings.

Lo! another Jubilee!
   Thousands hail it with delight;
Thousands, once in chains, now free
   From the drunkard's damning blight!

The news from Baltimore had come to Ohio, that the drunkards had taken the cause into their own hands, and had formed a society called the Washingtonian Society, and had adopted a pledge of total absti-nence; and the most degraded and hardest sots, yet once the most re-spectable part of community, were coming out and signing the total ab-stinence pledge. Some doubted it, others derided it, while other shouted for joy. Soon Mr. John A. Foot, Esq., came to Medina and gave them a lecture, and they soon had a small society formed. Then others began to speak out upon the subject, and soon they obtained the consent of some hard cases to make an effort; and these drunkards soon went to preach-ing. This awakened an interest in community, and some of the preachers came forward to back them up, while others kept back. They came after me, and told me what was going on, and wanted I should come to their meetings; but to no purpose. I told them that it would be stooping too low for me to go to a temperance meeting. I told them that I was not a drunkard, and would not disgrace myself so much as to join a society with the reformed drunkards, for I could drink, or I could let it alone; there was no danger of me. Let those sign that could not live without it. Several weeks passed on. At length they came after me, and said they would carry me if I would go that night. I told them no, I should not go after them poor deluded creatures. They said that Judge Smith had signed the pledge. This was a thunderbolt to me; but I would not go.

After they had gone and left me, I began to think, and made up my mind that Smith would die soon, for I did not believe that Smith nor myself could live long without taking our social drams; but, said I to myself, if Judge Smith can stand it one month and not drink, and live through it, then I will try the pledge myself. One of my boys and one of my girls had been to their meetings, and had put their names to the pledge, and they would tell me all that was going on; and oft did I enquire about Smith: the reply was, he has become a sober man, and you will see a great change in him. It would go through me like electric shocks. Some nights I would sleep awake all night.

About this time I had a very singular dream: In the vision of the night, when a deep sleep was upon me, I found myself at the foot of a long hill or mountain, and I was trying to get up the hill, but had to crawl upon my hands and knees; and as I ascended the hill, it grew very narrow, and the path very rough. At length I came to the top of the mountain, and the road very narrow—not more than two feet wide— there I stopped and looked around, and on one side of me it was very steep, apparently some three hundred feet down, and at the bottom a wide spread river, with flowing water; and on the other side, about the same distance down, but full of old logs, stumps, and stones, and at the foot of the hill a wilderness; and it was death on either side; so I crawled along until I began to descend, and then rose to my feet and began to run down the hill. It appeared as if I could not stop, and I made long and large leaps down, down, down, until the road began to grow wider all the way, and was full of ruts, gullies, and holes. When I had came almost to the foot of the hill, I saw a large crowd of people standing there, and a wide stream of water running along with rapidity, and the bridge was gone, and the people could not get across; and as I came down, I screamed out from the top of my voice, clear the way! clear the way! the people parted and let me go through, and as I came to the water, I arose and had wings as large as a great eagle, and flew clear over the river of water, and then came down upon my feet. I looked around, and saw the people all on the other side, at the foot of the mountain, and the side that I was on was level, smooth, and as handsome a road as I ever saw in my life; and a rich country around it, abounding with all kinds of fruit. A beautiful country, and very pleasant people. They asked me which way I came from; I told them the wilderness mountain. They wanted to know how I came across the muddy river; I told them when I came to the bottom of the hill, I had wings and flew across. Well then you have come to the right place, and we will conduct you to the house of a friend.

At this time I awoke from my sleep, and wondered what this should all mean. Then I was anxious to see my old friend, now the four weeks had gone that I had allotted for Mr. Smith to die in. So I took my staff and one of my boys and went into the town; as soon as I came in, I found Smith, and he took me by the hand, and said, Mr. Green, this is a new heaven and a new earth, and my health is better than it has been for years. I fastened my eyes on him and surveyed him from head to foot. His long slim form began to straiten up, and his whole person appeared to me as if it had all been modeled over anew. Now, Mr. Green, if you will take hold with me and sign the pledge, we can reform the whole State of Ohio. This was a new idea to me. Well, Judge, said I, can you live without taking something to drink, for your stomach sake and your often infirmities? Yes, said Smith, with an oath—damn the stuff, it only helps to kill in the room of helping to cure; for, said he, the doctors have been waiting for my bones three years, to set up in their office; but they shall not have them, for I will outlive them all, if I let their stuff alone. Smith then left me.

Now, said I to myself, how shall I go to work to get my name on the pledge? my hands and fingers are all of a tremble, and I cannot write my name. I therefore went into one of the grog shops and called for a horn; they sat down the bottle, and I turned out the glass as full as I could carry it to my face, being so nervous that I spilt some of it, and the rest of the poison I turned down the red lane, where many a barrel had gone. I then went to another tavern and called for more; down came the bottle, and this time I think I drank half a pint, sat down, and watched the motion of my fingers. I concluded that I could not write my name yet, so I went to the third tavern, and drank half a pint more, sat down, and watched the operations of that. Not enough yet; I then went to the tavern where I took the first moderate drink, and drank the fourth half pint. By this time I had got something like one quart; waited about fifteen minutes, then concluded that I could hold a pen and write my name. So I went out upon the sidewalk; I found that my feet were dancing an eight reel, but my hand was steady.

I then inquired of a man, if he could tell me who had the pledge of the Temperance Society. He said W. Cole, the Auditor of the county. I went to his office and asked him for the pledge that Mr. Smith had signed; then commenced a controversy between him and myself. I saw that Cole looked very cross at me, for he and myself had a quarrel once, when I was drunk, and I expected he would quarrel with me again. What do you want of that pledge? said Cole. I am going to put my name there. Oh, Green, you are drunk again. Well, you need not tell me of that, read me that pledge; so he read it. Now sir, let me have it. No, no, said Cole, you are too drunk to sign the pledge; go out of my shop. I shall not do it until I sign that pledge. Green, said he, you are too hard a case; if you do sign the pledge you will not keep it for you are drunk now. I don't care for that, let me have the pledge. Green, said he, we have got a good society here now, and we calculate to keep it so; but if you sign this pledge, you will get drunk every chance you have, and make us trouble. At this time I began to get mad, and thought I would put him out of the office and then I could get the pledge. But he, seeing my revolutionary spirit begin to rise, gave me the pledge book. I took his pen and put my name there, in large capital letters, clear across the book. There, Cole, said I, that is the Declaration of Independence. Now, said I, you must give me a receipt. A receipt, said Cole, that is something new; no man has ever called for a receipt before; Green, you are crazy—go along out of my shop. I shan't do so, until you give me a receipt in full of all demands from the beginning of the world until the end. My object was to have something to show to my wife, for I had promised her so many times to quit drinking that I knew she would not believe me unless I had something to show. He therefore gave me a receipt, and I put it into my pocket and went out into the street.

I found that I was staggering yet, and never was so ashamed of myself in all my life. What, said I, you have signed the pledge and got a receipt; and here you are reeling and staggering in the street. I thought that I would get out of town as soon as I could. I found my son and we started. I told the boy we would go through the woods (for I was ashamed to be seen on the same street where I had been drunk ever so many times before, but never thought of being ashamed before). We soon were in the woods, and I began to feel much better, for it seemed to me that I had got rid of a heavy load, and felt as light as any of the boys. We came to a stream of water, and my boy jumped it like a squirrel; I thought that I could jump as far as any of the boys, so I made a leap and went into the drink, head and heels. My boy came and helped me out, then said to me, O, pa (with the big tears on his rosy cheeks), I wish you were a Washingtonian. Well, said I to the boy, my son, I am a Washingtonian, as you call them. Yes, said he, you need not tell me so, for I never saw one of that society stagger as bad as you do, and you cannot jump two feet. However, we soon came to our log cabin, and we went in, and my little wife turned her eyes upon me—and now, reader, you guess what she said. Why she said just nothing at all, until I presented my receipt—then she stood and gazed on me for some time, then got me by the hand, and gave way to a flow of tears. Now, said she, you are safe and never will again deceive my rising hopes. My daughter came and threw her arms around me, and said, pa, you will never get drunk again!

Turns Missionary and Begins to Travel

This was the greatest time of rejoicing that I ever witnessed in my family. In about ten days, the people of Medina gave out notice that Mr. Green would lecture on temperance, in the Court House. I came, by their request, and took the Judge's seat; but was trembling, and my knees smote together like the head of an old flax-break. The house was crowded with the ladies and gentlemen of the place. I arose amid the shouts and cheers of the congregation, and I thought that they were all making fun of me. I asked them what they wanted of me; they said, tell your experience. *That* I knew they were all acquainted with, for there were the men that had gave me the devil's dyestuff, together with the lawyers and doctors of the place. I spoke about one hour, and told them they had better give up the traffic in whiskey, for I never calculated to drink any more. Many took the pledge, and that very week all the taverns in the place turned out their liquor. In about two weeks I gave them another lecture; by this time, invitations came from different places, for me to come and talk to them. I then commenced traveling. The people of the town of York hired me to lecture in every school district in their town; I done so with great success. At the same time, Judge Smith had begun to travel and lecture. As I had no horse, the people got an old horse and buggy for Smith, and he and I commenced our missionary travels. We went off and formed societies where we could. At this time excitement was up very high—other men were in the field also—the reformed drunkard was listened to with great interest, and it did appear to me that the whole world would soon be converted, notwithstanding some would stand aloof; many church members, and some preachers, were very cold and indifferent, and would not lend us their aid; and I did think that it would be more tolerable for Sodom and Gomorrah, in the day of judgment, than for them; for I did know that many of them were dram drinkers, and would take the drunkard's draught. However, they soon began to take hold of the work.

I now must make a few more remarks upon the character of Mr. Smith: The fourth of July now began to be talked of, for a temperance celebration, for I had now been a sober man from the 26th of February, 1842, until this time; therefore, as I had not seen a sober day on the fourth of July in thirty years, I was thought best to celebrate my birthday on a sober scale, to commence my after life. So we assembled at the white house, at this time kept by S. Bradley, said to be the best temperance house in town. Here we had an oration by Dr. Warner, and some stump orators of the day—a first rate time—Smith and myself blowing off steam, percussion, in difference directions. One day, as we were talking together, I told Smith that he would be married to his old gal again. Not so, said Smith; but if I do, she will have to do the courting, for I done it once, and now it is her turn. We then had made some calculations of having a temperance convention, in the month of September, and bring out from Oberlin their big tent; so we had all things in readiness; the tent came and was pitched on the village green. At the day appointed, the people began to assemble from every direction, and we commenced our operations. Some three thousand people had come together in the tent. Here was an interesting time; some fifteen preachers, and as many more reformed drunkards, were the speakers that took part in the enterprise, our pledges going around at the same time, and an excellent choir of singers from Oberlin. The first day passed away with great applause, so we concluded to hold the meeting one day longer; so we got a guard to watch the tent through the night, to keep off the enemy, for we had gobs of them.

A Cold Water Wedding

The second day was very pleasant; the people came together early, and our tent was well filled up. The forenoon passed off with great profit. In the afternoon some time, there was a silence in the tent, as the crowd opened to the right and left, to witness a novel scene. All eyes fixed on the tent door, as if to see an elephant; when lo! and behold! Judge Smith came marching into the tent, and upon one arm there was his old gal, again holding on to him as if they were young folks. They stepped upon the stand, and all eyes fastened upon them, with as much astonishment as if they were going to be swallowed up by a whale. In the room of that [tent] a man of God soon pronounced them man and wife again; then, said the priest, what God has joined together, let not man nor alcohol put asunder. They were married the second time, and, reader, don't you think that there was in that crowd three children that saw their father and mother married. Reader, look back, and see if you can remember of seeing your parents married. This was another miracle, brought about by the Washingtonians. This was five years ago, and as I don't expect to call Smith into question again, let me say that they gathered up their scattered property, all that they could, and moved off to Wisconsin, and still live together, and the Judge still keeps a sober man; and report says they are doing well. This convention came to a close that night, and all went off with increasing encouragement. From that time I began to travel into different counties, and lectured day and night—some times as many as from one to two hundred would take the pledge in one night.

8

GEORGE HAYDOCK

from *Incidents in the Life of George Haydock* (1847)

George Haydock was born in Salem, Connecticut (near the New York border), on Christmas Eve, 1805. He moved a year later to Schoharie County, New York, where his father pursued his work as a woolen manufacturer. At seventeen, Haydock entered the same trade as a journeyman in Bloomfield, New Jersey; and falling in with a hard-drinking lot called the "Paterson Gang," he nearly killed a man in a bar-room brawl. He almost died himself when he passed out in the road and barely escaped being crushed by a passing wagon's wheel. He was fired from his job for drinking before he turned twenty-one. Drunken wandering ensued. He finally settled in Hudson, New York, northeast of Albany.

In 1828 Haydock took a job as a rock blaster, dangerous work that resulted in terrible injuries from an accident: his skull was crushed, his right eye blown out, and his left leg smashed. Disabled for manual labor, Haydock was set up in business by his sympathetic friends: *the business of selling poison in the shape of rum, to my fellow men, to my brethren!* While the saloon supported his family, Haydock vainly sought "deliverance from the power of Alcohol" in religion.

True redemption arrived in 1841 with the Washingtonian delegates, J. F. Pollard and W. E. Wright, who were starting their sweep of upstate New York. The intensity and sincerity of the men from Baltimore struck a resounding chord. One Hudson observer reported that "the spell which had bound so many seemed to dissolve under the magic eloquence of those unlettered men. They spoke from heart to heart. The drunkard found himself unexpectedly an object of interest. He was no longer an outcast. There were some who still looked upon him as a man." Within a few weeks, three thousand (more than half) of the citizens of Hudson, including Haydock, had signed the pledge.

Haydock immediately began a new career as a temperance lecturer, proving his proficiency by garnering eight thousand signatures during his first year. By the time he published his temperance narrative, the Washingtonians had long since dispersed into the plethora of fraternal societies that are celebrated in "The Temperance Family," the conciliatory conclusion of *Incidents*. The Baltimore society first raised the temperance army; thus despite the differing regimental colors, Haydock insists, "We are all Washingtonians."

INCIDENTS IN THE LIFE OF GEORGE HAYDOCK

*I*t was the custom in those times, about the year 1840, for unfortunate and miserable individuals in desperate circumstances, and poor laboring men who worked for a living, when they could find it to do, or when sober enough to do it, to congregate together as associates, and Sunday was generally passed by us in this manner, viz: drinking together like a band of brothers, joined in the cause of intemperance. If one had not the means to defray expenses, the other had, and so the game went on, Sunday after Sunday, and there seemed no end to it in those times.

To give some of the scenes which transpired in one notorious house of resort, in the lower part of Hudson, where we used to meet, I will state that we formed a drinking club, called the "Garret Society," where rules and regulations were as follow:

1st. Men in order to be good members of this society must attend to every body's business except his own.

2nd. They must pay their rum bills in preference to their bread bills.

3rd. Must know what their neighbors had for breakfast, and whether it was paid for or not, and,

4th. Never to speak well of any religious order.

Of this society I was chosen President. My duties as President was to examine the society, and drink at the overhauling of any member. But whenever I sat down and any thing like consciousness returned to my mind, I would have to get up and pour down that poison, in order to drown any thing like feeling. I would endeavor with all my might to believe in infidelity, but one moment's reflection would make me miserable, and I destroyed self-reproach by pouring down the direful drug. I give these scenes of fact to arouse some fathers and mothers in this city;

I have seen boys scarce 18 years of age, of respectable parents, allowed on Sunday in these grog holes of perdition, some of which yet exist in this city, to get drunk for the money as often as they pleased, and remain there in the loft, stowed away until they were sober. A fine school this for morality, I must confess—a great school to initiate criminals in—a regular passport to state prison or the gallows.

I continued on drinking until my wife had become much alarmed and made up her mind that the best course for her to pursue was to part from me, for she saw nothing surer than that she must go to the county house, if I continued on in the way I had. She one afternoon took occasion to tell me this, with tears in her eyes. I mistook her motive, as no man who is in the habit of drinking rum can judge aright, drunk or sober, unless he has been sober for some days. I told her coolly she might go in welcome, if she so pleased. This was in the Summer of 1841, about one week before Pollard and Wright came to the city of Hudson.

When those men came to this city and threw out their advertisements, it caused considerable excitement here, by reason that their method being so much out of the ordinary way of lecturing, as in houses, or churches; whereas they proposed lecturing on the public square, in the open air. I was in the steam-boat office when one of their advertisements was put up, stating that Pollard and Wright, the Baltimore reformed drunkards, would give a lecture on the Public Square, at 6 o'clock that evening. *Reformed drunkards* being somewhat of a novel title to us at that period, as it was in fact in many places throughout the state. For example—in one place out west, where these philanthropists had sent their advertisements, stating that they would be there to lecture on the subject of temperance, a colored man coming along, and reading the same passed on, and meeting one of his companions called Sambo, said to him, "There are two of these reformed drunkards from Baltimore coming here to lecture on the subject of temperance reformation." The other became frightened, and in the greatest consternation exclaimed, "By gosh, you don't catch dis nigger out of door after dark!" and in the same way, in a certain degree, it was received here, for said I to my drinking companions, "*Let us go and see what kind of cattle these are!*"

Accordingly we went up to *see* and *hear* them. Our intention was to go and make fun of them; and the rum-sellers' plan was, if possible, to break up their meetings. Pollard was on the stand, and speaking to the following effect—that a man could work as well in a hot summer's day without liquor as he could with. I immediately replied, "I guess if you had ever sawed a load of wood on a hot summer's day, you would like a *smasher* too, as well as myself." This created a laugh; with that he commenced to tell his own experience. Going into detail of his own miseries—the various incidents which composed his life—he gave in that relation a true and actual picture of my own life, and drinking habits, which had upon me considerable effect. It became, even in spite of myself, interesting.

At this period a rum-seller came up to me and says: "George, if you'll go home and get your bell, and kick up a row here, I'll give you a dollar."

I told him it wouldn't pay. (It must be understood that at this time I was common crier for the city of Hudson, attending auctions, peddling books, sawing wood, drinking rum, &c. for a living.)

A drunkard who was made so for this purpose, standing by, kept continually calling Pollard and Wright *liars!*

I told him to stop his noise—I didn't want to hear but one talking in a crowd at a time!

To this he replied, "*You are a drunkard as well as I am!*"

I admitted it, and says, "*It is no credit to me, and if you open again you are down.*"

He commenced calling names again, as before, and I immediately floored him. Some of the rum-sellers found fault with me for so doing; but I told them, "I would keep order any way they could fix it." One of the Washingtonians came up to me after the meeting was over, and shaking hands, thanked me very kindly for stopping the noise. I told him to attend to his own business—not wishing to show any humiliation.

This course of lecturing, telling the drunkard that he was indeed a man among men, instead of despising and denouncing him, appeared to me quite a new method of talking—and seemed to suit my feelings exactly.

The next day one of those demons in human shape, a rum-seller, came to me and said, "George, if you will go and sit in a cart, and give away Rum to-day on the Public Square, I will make it as good as 25 dollars to you!" My reply was, "I will not do it." He then offered me 10 dollars to go and speak against Pollard and Wright. I told him, "*I would not do it at any price.*"

I heard them that afternoon, and the next morning made up my mind to two things: one was to sign the Pledge before I went to sleep that night, and the other was to get drunk before I did sign it. Accordingly I got very blue, and then went to the Temperance lecture. A man I found there drunk, calling Pollard a liar (the second one so doing), as usual employed for that purpose by rum-sellers. I went up to him with my cane, in a menacing attitude, and says to him, "If you ain't out of this in a minute, *I'll hit you a rap over the head.*"

A rum-seller says to me, "*That man can whip you in a minute.*"

I says to him, "It's a job you and him had better let out."

They were both silenced, not daring to proceed. Thus Satan's kingdom seemed to me to be divided against itself, and ready to fall down! After the meeting was over, I, with several more of my drinking companions, signed the Pledge.

I then started for home. When I arrived, my wife, seeing the condition that I was in, looked melancholy and down-hearted, as she had often done before. My little girl, about four years of age, went into one corner of the room, to get out of my way. I myself felt well and contented, at this time, though drunk—that glorious Pledge, giving me Temperance Freedom, was signed.

I looked up at my wife, and spoke about as follows, nearly in these words: "*Old woman I've signed the Pledge!*"

"Well" said she, "you look like a Pledge subject."

I continued to repeat again "*that I had signed the Pledge!*"

She looked up, and perceiving, in spite of the disguise of liquor I was in, that I was in earnest, she placed her hand upon my shoulder, and all the wife was in that affectionate look, and while the tears streamed down her cheeks, she exclaimed, "Then George, I am a happy woman, for I am satisfied that you will never break it!" Those words shall never be proved false by me, and those expressions seem to make the Pledge stronger, even yet, as I reflect upon them.

The next morning I felt miserably bad; I could eat no breakfast, for the want of my usual dram. At two in the afternoon every limb began to tremble in agitation, and ideas of horror and desolation pervaded my mind. I was the most wretched feeling man, as I supposed, in existence. Every nerve appeared to be unstrung; I had no idea that I was so far advanced in drinking, until that period; for the Pledge is the touchstone of a man's real situation—this situation, though I had not felt it before, had in truth for a long time been mine—I was just on the edge, I suppose, of the Drunkard's Delirium Tremens—that situation in which Earth appears to be an infernal region full of fiends and horrors dire—ideas and fancies which have no name, above or below—but in all this I had but one thought, one idea, ruling over all—live or die, I'll take no Rum, but will adhere to the Pledge!

In three days after signing, they had me up speaking Temperance in the Hall. I myself, as I told them, having as yet the shakes of Rum upon me, and consequently said very little. They continued every evening to call me up to the stand, for the first fortnight. I kept counting every day the hours as they passed, for the rum-sellers prophesied that I would not keep the pledge good for a fortnight—and some old drinkers gave me three months; but here the friends of Temperance took me by the hand, and showed such confidence in me, and used me so kindly, noticing and respecting me, perhaps more than I ever had been, that it was, as it were, impossible for me to do different than to keep the Pledge. Indeed from the first hour I signed it, I never desired to violate that sacred engagement.

After the first fortnight of speaking in public, I then began going to the surrounding neighborhood. At this time rum-sellers were endeavoring to send out their votaries to create fights. I was called upon one Sunday afternoon to address the people of the village of Athens in the open air; coming down to the ferry to go across the river, I was obliged to wait a short time for the small boat. I saw a man and his wife coming down the hill; the woman with a child in her arms, followed by a little girl about six years of age. I saw that the man and woman were both intoxicated; they were making their way as well as they were able to that slaughter house of human reason—the grog shop. I thought I would watch as near as I could to see if the fiend in human shape, the rum-seller, could have conscience to sell liquor to those people under existing circumstances. He did so; the woman, after drinking, soon began to behave like a maniac, endeavoring to fight her husband. She would take up her little infant and hold it out by its arm, and throw it back again on her own arm; at last standing at the door, she raised her child up and dashed it on the pavement! It was taken up by a colored woman, and after some time came to, so that it began to cry; then, by

order of the rum-seller or some other individual, a drinking police officer took the party off to jail, followed by the little girl—the colored
woman carrying the infant, which was crying as it went along.

Reflecting upon this, I couldn't avoid making the comparison of the
leopardess fondling affectionately over her offspring whilst the human
being acted otherwise. What could have caused this strange difference,
so contrary to human nature, but rum? Recollect this occurred on the
Sabbath day, in direct violation of the laws of God and man.

I was there told if I went over the river to speak temperance, the rum-
sellers and rum-drinkers of Athens would throw me off the dock. I replied, *"After the scene I have just witnessed, I would go there to speak if it cost
me my life!"* I went over; there I found Mr. Fox and several other professors of religion standing ready to receive me and assist me in this glorious warfare. As I arose and commenced speaking, the rum-sellers
turned out (as I afterwards heard) 15 drunkards, whom they had prepared previously for the occasion—the intention being to throw me off
the dock. They came out hollowing and howling, endeavoring to drown
the sound of my voice with their noise. I used them like men, and soon
got their attention. They began to listen to my discourse; I talked about
an hour and a half. I saw before I finished their heads drooping, and the
tears freely flowing. When I closed my discourse 14 out of the 15 came
and signed the pledge; the next day the remaining one signed. The rum-
sellers perceived that they had given away their liquor for nothing.

THE TEMPERANCE FAMILY

> We are all Washingtonians,
> We have all Signed the Pledge!

Those who have ever listened to the simple and delightful music of the
"Hutchinson Family"* will remember the universal bursts of applause
with which numerous audiences throughout the country have greeted
the words at the head of this article, as they fell in rich melody upon the

*The Hutchinson Family, especially a quartet consisting of the four best singers,
were widely popular performers of temperance songs. —ed.

ear, from the harmonious voices of those charming vocalists. The harmony of the sentiment expressed, and not of the sound, is, however, our reason for placing them in their present position. The great temperance reformation has enlisted the sympathies and active energies of hosts of the benevolent of both sexes, and all conditions of society. Shades of difference in opinions and in modes of operation were of course to be expected. These have resulted in several distinct organizations, for the promotion and perpetuity of the one great object—the universal prevalence of the principle and practice of total abstinence from all use, as a beverage, of intoxicating liquors. We find, therefore, the great Washingtonian Fraternity dividing off into various separate Orders and Associations, and still retaining their own identity as distinctly as ever, and acting with their usual, and in some cases, with increased zeal in the Washingtonian ranks; while they are also devoted to the promotion and advancement of the respective societies to which they have attached themselves.

Here we view this singular and beautiful sight, viz: A Division of the "Sons of Temperance," and "Tent of Rechabites," a Union of the "Brothers of Temperance," a Tent of "United Daughters of Rechab," and a Union of the "Daughters of Temperance," enlisting the warmer sympathies of the female heart. While all these are distinct and separate in their respective halls, yet all have the same grand and sublime object, and in the glorious Washingtonian Hall are all one. Like Israel of old, they are of different Tribes and Families, and they marshall their hosts under different banners, but are all led by the pillar of cloud and of fire, to the land of temperance and peace.

Thus is presented a delightful picture. The vast whole of the Temperance Army, indissolubly united in the grand object of cutting short the reign of the bloody monster, Alcohol, and delivering their fellow men from his cruel despotism. And yet each one chooses his weapons of warfare, and enrols himself in such band as he finds most congenial; and "*On to the Rescue!*" is the stirring, animating cry of each benevolent heart. So mote it be. Give battle to this potent enemy of man. We, from the heart, cry, "God speed the Son, and the Daughter, and the Sister of Temperance—God speed the Son and the Daughter of the Rechab."

198

We are all Washingtonians,
We have all signed the Pledge.

Bibliography

WASHINGTONIAN TEMPERANCE NARRATIVES
AND RELATED MATERIAL

1836   [Dunlap, William.] *Thirty Years Ago; or, The Memoirs of a Water Drinker*. 2 vols. New York: Bancroft & Holley.

1840   Garrison, James Holley. *Behold Me Once More: The Confessions of James Holley Garrison, Brother of William Lloyd Garrison*. Edited by Walter McIntosh Merrill. Boston: Houghton Mifflin, 1954. [This drunkard's memoir lay unpublished for over a century.]

1841   *Letters from the Alms-House, on the Subject of Temperance*. By a Drunkard. Lowell, Mass.: Brown & Colby. [This is a pirated edition of "Letters from the Alms-house," taken from a popular periodical. The Advertisement to *Autobiography of a Reformed Drunkard* (1845) refers to a "miserably printed and spurious edition of the 'Letters,' without the 'Recollections,'" that was published "some time since without the knowledge of the author."]

1841   *The Price of a Glass of Brandy*. By a Lady of Baltimore. Baltimore: Robert Neilson. [Dedicated to William K. Mitchell, one of the Washingtonian founders.]

1842   Arthur, Timothy Shay. *Six Nights with the Washingtonians. A Series of Original Temperance Tales*. Philadelphia: L. A. Godey & Morton M'Michael. [Derived from Arthur's 1840 reports for the *Baltimore Merchant* on early Washingtonian "experience meetings," these tales were initially issued as six separate pamphlets in 1842: *The Broken Merchant, The Experience Meeting, The Tavern Keeper, The Drunkard's Wife, The Widow's Son, The Moderate Drinker*.]

1842   *Confessions of a Female Inebriate; or Intemperance in High Life*. By a Lady. Founded on Fact. Boston: William Henshaw. [Copyright issued to Isaac F. Shepard.]

1842   *The Drunkard's Orphan Son, His Life in London, His Astonishing Ad-*

ventures, and Circumstances That Accompanied His Connection with a Female, a South Sea Islander. The Highest Sentiments of Moral Virtue and Native Purity Are Here Delineated. Boston: Published for the Author.

1842   [Gale, James]. *A Long Voyage in a Leaky Ship; or A Forty Years' Cruise on the Sea of Intemperance, Being an Account of Some of the Principal Incidents in the Life of an Inebriate.* Written by Himself. Cambridgeport, Mass.: P. L. & H. S. Cox.

1842   Whitman, Walter. *Franklin Evans; or, The Inebriate. A Tale of The Times.* Supplement to the *New World.* New York, November 1842. [First separate book publication: New York: Random House, 1929. Reprinted: New Haven, Conn.: College & University Press, 1967.]

1843   Gatchell, Joseph. *The Disenthralled: Being Reminiscences in the Life of the Author; His Fall from Respectability by Intemperance—and Rescue by the Washington Society: Containing, Also, His Life as a Sailor, Shipwreck, and Residence among the Savage Tribes in New Holland; Remarks on America.* Third edition. Troy, N.Y.: N. Tuttle, 1845.

1843   Woodman, Charles T. *Narrative of Charles T. Woodman, A Reformed Inebriate.* Written by Himself. Boston: Theodore Abbot.

1844   *Confessions of a Reformed Inebriate.* "An Ower True Tale." New York: American Temperance Union.

1844   Marsh, Reverend John. *Hannah Hawkins, The Reformed Drunkard's Daughter.* New York: American Temperance Union.

1844   Root, J[ames]. *The Horrors of Delirium Tremens.* New York: Josiah Adams.

1845   *The Confession of a Rum-Seller.* By the Author of "Passing Thoughts." Boston: Lothrop & Bense.

1845   Gough, John Bartholomew. *An Autobiography by John B. Gough.* Boston: Published by and for the Author.

1845   [John Cotton Mather, pseudonym]. *Autobiography of a Reformed Drunkard; or, Letters and Recollections by an Inmate of the Alms-House.* Philadelphia: Griffith & Simon. [This is an authorized and expanded version of *Letters from the Alms-House* (1841).]

1846   *Goffiana; A Review of the Life of John B. Gough.* Boston: Ruggles & Company.

1846   *My Own Experience.* Second edition. Boston: Temperance Standard Press.

1846   Robinson, D. G. *The Life and Adventures of the Reformed Inebriate, D. G. Robinson, M.D.* Boston: Robinson & Graham.

1847 *An Account of the Marvelous Doings of Prince Alcohol, As Seen by One of His Enemies, In Dream.* N.p.

1847 Carter, Jacob. *My Drunken Life, In Fifteen Chapters, From 1825 to 1847.* Boston: Printed for the Author.

1847 Haydock, George. *Incidents in the Life of George Haydock, Ex-Professional Wood-Sawyer, of Hudson.* Fourth edition. Hudson, N.Y.: William B. Stoddard.

1848 Green, A[ndrus] V. *The Life and Experience of A. V. Green, The Celebrated Ohio Temperance Sledge Hammer, Together with His Reformation and Travels, In Connection with a Statistical Report of the State of Ohio, In Crime, Pauperism, &c., With Other Useful Matter.* Second edition. Wooster, Ohio: Printed for the Author by D. N. Sprague, 1849.

1850 Campbell, James. *The Life and Sketches of James Campbell, Paper Maker.* Philadelphia: Printed for the Author.

LATER TEMPERANCE NARRATIVES

1862 Hewlett, Samuel Mudway. *The Cup and Its Conqueror; or, The Triumphs of Temperance.* Boston: Redding.

1866 Rand, Festus G. *Autobiography of Festus G. Rand; A Tale of Intemperance.* Romeo, Vt.: J. Russell. Second edition: Montpelier, Vt.: J. & J. M. Poland, 1868. [With a prefatory recommendation by John Gough.]

1872 Dutcher, George M. *Disinthralled: A Story of My Life.* Hartford, Conn.: Columbian Book Company.

1876 Cox, W. T. *Out of the Depths; A Personal Narrative of My Fall Under the Power of Strong Drink and My Complete Reformation.* Sycamore, Ill.: Baker & Arnold.

1877 Benson, Luther. *Fifteen Years in Hell. An Autobiography.* Indianapolis: Tilford & Carlon. Second edition: Indianapolis: Carlon & Hollenbeck, 1885.

1878 Doner, Thomas. *Eleven Years a Drunkard; or, The Evils of Intemperance, as Evidenced in the Thrilling Experience of Thomas Doner. Having Lost Both Arms Through Intemperance, He Wrote This Book with His Teeth, as a Warning to Others.* Sycamore, Ill.: Arnold Brothers.

1878 Morris, F. Baldwin. *The Panorama of Life, and Experiences in Associating and Battling with Opium and Alcoholic Stimulants.* Philadelphia: George W. Ward.

1878 Stratton, G. *Hope for the Fallen! In Bondage Twenty Years*. Jefferson-ville, Ill.: Stratton.

1880 Calderwood, George. *Drunk and Sober—An Autobiography*. Colum-bus, Ohio: American Prohibitionist Press.

1886 Jones, Samuel Porter. *Living Words*. Toronto: William Briggs.

1888 Morris, Charles. *Broken Fetters*. Philadelphia.

1895 Fulkerson, B. H. *From the Gutter to the Ministry*. N.p.

1896 Williams, Robert G. *Thrilling Experiences of the Welsh Evangelist R. G. Williams, Reformed Drunkard and Gambler; or, Forty-Eight Years in the Light and Love of Jesus Christ*. Chicago: Marks & Wil-liams.

1907 Northrup, Herbert W. *The Prodigal's Return*. Greensboro, Vt.: W. R. Cox.

1909 Gunder, Claude A. *Life of Claude A. Gunder, Saved by the Blood from a Drunkard's Hell*. Marion, Ind.: Published by the Author.

1909 Roman, Charles. *A Man Remade*. Chicago: Reilly & Britton.

1910 Ranney, David James. *Dave Ranney; or, Thirty Years in the Bowery*. New York: American Tract Society.

1912 Maslin, Thomas. *From Saloon to Prison, From Prison to Pulpit*. Ash-land, Pa.: G. Kyle.

1913 London, Jack. *John Barleycorn*. New York: The Century Company.

1915 Francis, Joseph H. *My Last Drink; The Greatest Human Story Ever Written*. Chicago: Empire Book Company.

LIBRARY OF CONGRESS CATALOGING-IN-PUBLICATION DATA

Drunkard's progress : narratives of addiction, despair, and recovery /
    edited by John W. Crowley.
        p.   cm.
    Includes bibliographical references (p. 199).
    ISBN 0-8018-6008-3 (alk. paper).—ISBN 0-8018-6007-5 (pbk. : alk. paper)
    1. Temperance.   2. Alcoholism.   I. Crowley, John William, 1945–   .
HV5068.D78   1999
362.292—dc21   98-8732
                                                                  CIP